More Praise for Stephen King's *On Writing*

"*On Writing* is a generous and honest book about how hard work and creativity can transform a life. King dispenses his advice with a winning, self-deprecating wit that makes this book much more than a how-to guide. *On Writing* convinces because the author seems to get so much pleasure and satisfaction from his imagination. And his description of how essential his work ethic is to his success—he works every single day—should inspire writers at every level of accomplishment."

—Dana Spiotta, author of *Eat the Document*

"Stephen King's *On Writing* is my favorite book about the art and life of a writer. When I teach the book, its clarity, honesty, and gentleness always helps to demystify the craft for my anxious beginners; and when I am alone in my room with my own work and the doubt begins to swallow me whole, I turn to it to remember that a writer should always be humble, hard-working, and grateful to live the life of the imagination. The rest of us can only strive to live up to the example Stephen King sets in this, his finest and most beautiful book."

—Lauren Groff, author of *The Monsters of Templeton*

"King's most personal book and one of his best."

—*The Seattle Times*

"King's bare-knuckled approach to this book is refreshing. . . . He makes the reader feel as comfortable as sitting down at the kitchen table for a chat."

—*St. Louis Post-Dispatch*

"An elegant volume . . . *On Writing* opens with a mini-memoir so finely seasoned that it whets your appetite for a full-scale auto-biography."

—*Entertainment Weekly*

"Remarkable and revealing . . . Memoir, style manual, auto-biography—the inspiring *On Writing* seems almost unclassifiable."

—*The Wall Street Journal*

"Combines autobiography and admonition, inspiration and instruction. It's an enjoyable mix."

—*The Washington Post Book World*

On Writing

By

Stephen King

———— A Memoir of the Craft ————

Scribner

SCRIBNER

An Imprint of Simon & Schuster, Inc.
1230 Avenue of the Americas
New York, NY 10020

Author's Note
Unless otherwise attributed, all prose examples, both good and evil, were composed by the
author.

Permissions
There Is a Mountain words and music by Donovan Leitch. Copyright © 1967 by Donovan
(Music) Ltd. Administered by Peer International Corporation. Copyright renewed. International copyright secured. Used by permission. All rights reserved.
Granpa Was a Carpenter by John Prine © Walden Music, Inc. (ASCAP). All rights administered by WB Music Corp. All rights reserved. Used by permission. Warner Bros. Publications U.S. Inc., Miami, FL 33014.

Owen King's essay "Recording Audiobooks for My Dad, Stephen King" first appeared in the
New Yorker on June 16, 2018. The conversation between Stephen King and Joe Hill was hosted
by Porter Square Books at the Somerville Theatre in Somerville, MA, on October 20, 2019.

Honesty's the best policy.

—Miguel de Cervantes

Liars prosper.

—Anonymous

Contents

First Foreword

In the early nineties (it might have been 1992, but it's hard to remember when you're having a good time) I joined a rock-and-roll band composed mostly of writers. The Rock Bottom Remainders were the brainchild of Kathi Kamen Goldmark, a book publicist and musician from San Francisco. The group included Dave Barry on lead guitar, Ridley Pearson on bass, Barbara Kingsolver on keyboards, Robert Fulghum on mandolin, and me on rhythm guitar. There was also a trio of "chick singers," *à la* the Dixie Cups, made up (usually) of Kathi, Tad Bartimus, and Amy Tan.

The group was intended as a one-shot deal—we would play two shows at the American Booksellers Convention, get a few laughs, recapture our misspent youth for three or four hours, then go our separate ways.

It didn't happen that way, because the group never quite broke up. We found that we liked playing together too much to quit, and with a couple of "ringer" musicians on sax and drums (plus, in the early days, our musical guru, Al Kooper, at the heart of the group), we sounded pretty good. You'd pay to hear us. Not a lot, not U2 or E Street Band prices, but maybe what the oldtimers call "roadhouse money." We took the group on tour, wrote a book about it (my wife took the photos and danced whenever the spirit took her, which was quite often), and continue to play now and then, sometimes as The Remainders, sometimes as Raymond Burr's Legs. The personnel comes and goes—columnist Mitch Albom has replaced Barbara on keyboards, and Al doesn't play with the group anymore 'cause he and Kathi don't get along—but the core has remained Kathi, Amy, Ridley, Dave, Mitch Albom, and me . . . plus Josh Kelly on drums and Erasmo Paolo on sax.

We do it for the music, but we also do it for the companionship. We like each other, and we like having a chance to talk sometimes about the real job, the day job people are always telling us not to quit. We are writers, and we never ask one another where we get our ideas; we know we don't know.

One night while we were eating Chinese before a gig in Miami Beach, I asked Amy if there was any one question she was *never* asked during the Q-and-A that follows almost every writer's talk—that question you never get to answer when you're standing in front of a group of author-struck fans and pretending you don't put your pants on one leg at a time like everyone else. Amy paused, thinking it over very carefully, and then said: "No one ever asks about the language."

I owe an immense debt of gratitude to her for saying that. I had been playing with the idea of writing a little book about writing for a year or more at that time, but had held back because I didn't trust my own motivations—*why* did I want to write about writing? What made me think I had anything worth saying?

The easy answer is that someone who has sold as many books of fiction as I have must have *something* worthwhile to say about writing it, but the easy answer isn't always the truth. Colonel Sanders sold a hell of a lot of fried chicken, but I'm not sure anyone wants to know how he made it. If I was going to be presumptuous enough to tell people how to write, I felt there had to be a better reason than my popular success. Put another way, I didn't want to write a book, even a short one like this, that would leave me feeling like either a literary gasbag or a transcendental asshole. There are enough of those books—and those writers—on the market already, thanks.

But Amy was right: nobody ever asks about the language. They ask the DeLillos and the Updikes and the Styrons, but they don't ask popular novelists. Yet many of us proles also care about the language, in our humble way, and care passionately about the art and craft of telling stories on paper. What follows is an attempt to put down, briefly and simply, how I came to the craft, what I know about it now, and how it's done. It's about the day job; it's about the language.

This book is dedicated to Amy Tan, who told me in a very simple and direct way that it was okay to write it.

↳ Motivation to start writing

* No one asks about the language, this is what books should be

Second Foreword

This is a short book because most books about writing are filled with bullshit. Fiction writers, present company included, don't understand very much about what they do—not why it works when it's good, not why it doesn't when it's bad. I figured the shorter the book, the less the bullshit.

One notable exception to the bullshit rule is *The Elements of Style,* by William Strunk Jr. and E. B. White. There is little or no detectable bullshit in that book. (Of course it's short; at eighty-five pages it's much shorter than this one.) I'll tell you right now that every aspiring writer should read *The Elements of Style.* Rule 17 in the chapter titled "Principles of Composition" is "Omit needless words." I will try to do that here.

use of colloquial language

* Trying to make book straight to the point.

Third Foreword

One rule of the road not directly stated elsewhere in this book: "The editor is always right." The corollary is that no writer will take all of his or her editor's advice; for all have sinned and fallen short of editorial perfection. Put another way, to write is human, to edit is divine. Chuck Verrill edited this book, as he has so many of my novels. And as usual, Chuck, you were divine.

—Steve

C.V.

I was stunned by Mary Karr's memoir, *The Liars' Club*. Not just by its ferocity, its beauty, and by her delightful grasp of the vernacular, but by its *totality*—she is a woman who remembers *everything* about her early years.

I'm not that way. I lived an odd, herky-jerky childhood, raised by a single parent who moved around a lot in my earliest years and who—I am not completely sure of this—may have farmed my brother and me out to one of her sisters for awhile because she was economically or emotionally unable to cope with us for a time. Perhaps she was only chasing our father, who piled up all sorts of bills and then did a runout when I was two and my brother David was four. If so, she never succeeded in finding him. My mom, Nellie Ruth Pillsbury King, was one of America's early liberated women, but not by choice.

Mary Karr presents her childhood in an almost unbroken panorama. Mine is a fogged-out landscape from which occasional memories appear like isolated trees . . . the kind that look as if they might like to grab and eat you.

What follows are some of those memories, plus assorted snapshots from the somewhat more coherent days of my adolescence and young manhood. This is not an autobiography. It

[handwritten: writers cannot be made, writers are formed]

is, rather, a kind of *curriculum vitae*—my attempt to show how one writer was formed. Not how one writer was *made;* I don't believe writers *can* be made, either by circumstances or by self-will (although I did believe those things once). The equipment comes with the original package. Yet it is by no means unusual equipment; I believe large numbers of people have at least some talent as writers and storytellers, and that those talents can be strengthened and sharpened. If I didn't believe that, writing a book like this would be a waste of time.

This is how it was for me, that's all—a disjointed growth process in which ambition, desire, luck, and a little talent all played a part. Don't bother trying to read between the lines, and don't look for a through-line. There are *no* lines—only snapshots, most out of focus.

[handwritten: Everyone has a talent of writing, it just needs to be unlocked.]

– 1 –

My earliest memory is of imagining I was someone else—imagining that I was, in fact, the Ringling Brothers Circus Strongboy. This was at my Aunt Ethelyn and Uncle Oren's house in Durham, Maine. My aunt remembers this quite clearly, and says I was two and a half or maybe three years old.

I had found a cement cinderblock in a corner of the garage and had managed to pick it up. I carried it slowly across the garage's smooth cement floor, except in my mind I was dressed in an animal skin singlet (probably a leopard skin) and carrying the cinderblock across the center ring. The vast crowd was silent. A brilliant blue-white spotlight marked my remarkable progress. Their wondering faces told the story: never had they seen such an incredibly strong kid. "And he's only *two!*" someone muttered in disbelief.

Unknown to me, wasps had constructed a small nest in the lower half of the cinderblock. One of them, perhaps pissed off at being relocated, flew out and stung me on the ear. The pain was brilliant, like a poisonous inspiration. It was the worst pain I had ever suffered in my short life, but it only held the top spot for a few seconds. When I dropped the cinderblock on one bare foot, mashing all five toes, I forgot all about the wasp. I can't remember if I was taken to the doctor, and neither can my Aunt Ethelyn (Uncle Oren, to whom the Evil Cinderblock surely belonged, is almost twenty years dead), but she remembers the sting, the mashed toes, and my reaction. "How you howled, Stephen!" she said. "You were certainly in fine voice that day."

– 2 –

A year or so later, my mother, my brother, and I were in West De Pere, Wisconsin. I don't know why. Another of my mother's sisters, Cal (a WAAC beauty queen during World War II), lived in Wisconsin with her convivial beer-drinking husband, and maybe Mom had moved to be near them. If so, I don't remember seeing much of the Weimers. *Any* of them, actually. My mother was working, but I can't remember what her job was, either. I want to say it was a bakery she worked in, but I think that came later, when we moved to Connecticut to live near her sister Lois and *her* husband (no beer for Fred, and not much in the way of conviviality, either; he was a crewcut daddy who was proud of driving his convertible with the top *up,* God knows why).

There was a stream of babysitters during our Wisconsin period. I don't know if they left because David and I were a handful, or because they found better-paying jobs, or because my mother insisted on higher standards than they were willing to rise to; all I know is that there were a lot of them. The only one I remember with any clarity is Eula, or maybe she was Beulah. She was a teenager, she was as big as a house, and she laughed a lot. Eula-Beulah had a wonderful sense of humor, even at four I could recognize that, but it was a *dangerous* sense of humor—there seemed to be a potential thunderclap hidden inside each hand-patting, butt-rocking, head-tossing outburst of glee. When I see those hidden-camera sequences where real-life babysitters and nannies just all of a sudden wind up and clout the kids, it's my days with Eula-Beulah I always think of.

Was she as hard on my brother David as she was on me? I don't know. He's not in any of these pictures. Besides, he would have been less at risk from Hurricane Eula-Beulah's dangerous winds; at six, he would have been in the first grade and off the gunnery range for most of the day.

Eula-Beulah would be on the phone, laughing with someone, and beckon me over. She would hug me, tickle me, get me laughing, and then, still laughing, go upside my head hard enough to knock me down. Then she would tickle me with her bare feet until we were both laughing again.

Eula-Beulah was prone to farts—the kind that are both loud and smelly. Sometimes when she was so afflicted, she would throw me on the couch, drop her wool-skirted butt on my face, and let loose. "Pow!" she'd cry in high glee. It was like being buried in marshgas fireworks. I remember the dark, the sense that I was suffocating, and I remember laughing. Because, while what was happening was sort of horrible, it was also sort of funny. In many ways, Eula-Beulah prepared me for literary criticism. After having a two-hundred-pound babysitter fart on your face and yell *Pow!*, *The Village Voice* holds few terrors.

I don't know what happened to the other sitters, but Eula-Beulah was fired. It was because of the eggs. One morning Eula-Beulah fried me an egg for breakfast. I ate it and asked for another one. Eula-Beulah fried me a second egg, then asked if I wanted another one. She had a look in her eye that said, "You don't *dare* eat another one, Stevie." So I asked for another one. And another one. And so on. I stopped after seven, I think—seven is the number that sticks in my mind, and quite clearly. Maybe we ran out of eggs. Maybe I cried off. Or maybe Eula-Beulah got scared. I don't know, but probably it was good that the game ended at seven. Seven eggs is quite a few for a four-year-old.

I felt all right for awhile, and then I yarked all over the floor. Eula-Beulah laughed, then went upside my head, then shoved me into the closet and locked the door. Pow. If she'd locked me in the bathroom, she might have saved her job, but she didn't. As for me, I didn't really mind being in the closet. It was dark, but it smelled of my mother's Coty perfume, and there was a comforting line of light under the door.

I crawled to the back of the closet, Mom's coats and dresses brushing along my back. I began to belch—long loud belches that burned like fire. I don't remember being sick to my stomach but I must have been, because when I opened my mouth to let out another burning belch, I yarked again instead. All over my mother's shoes. That was the end for Eula-Beulah. When my mother came home from work that day, the babysitter was fast asleep on the couch and little Stevie was locked in the closet, fast asleep with half-digested fried eggs drying in his hair.

– 3 –

Our stay in West De Pere was neither long nor successful. We were evicted from our third-floor apartment when a neighbor spotted my six-year-old brother crawling around on the roof and called the police. I don't know where my mother was when this happened. I don't know where the babysitter of the week was, either. I only know that I was in the bathroom, standing with my bare feet on the heater, watching to see if my brother would fall off the roof or make it back into the bathroom okay. He made it back. He is now fifty-five and living in New Hampshire.

– 4 –

When I was five or six, I asked my mother if she had ever seen anyone die. Yes, she said, she had seen one person die and had heard another one. I asked how you could hear a person die and she told me that it was a girl who had drowned off Prout's Neck in the 1920s. She said the girl swam out past the rip, couldn't get back in, and began screaming for help. Several men tried to reach her, but that day's rip had developed a vicious undertow, and they were all forced back. In the end they could only stand around, tourists and townies, the teenager who became my mother among them, waiting for a rescue boat that never came and listening to that girl scream until her strength gave out and she went under. Her body washed up in New Hampshire, my mother said. I asked how old the girl was. Mom said she was fourteen, then read me a comic book and packed me off to bed. On some other day she told me about the one she saw—a sailor who jumped off the roof of the Graymore Hotel in Portland, Maine, and landed in the street.

"He splattered," my mother said in her most matter-of-fact tone. She paused, then added, "The stuff that came out of him was green. I have never forgotten it."

That makes two of us, Mom.

– 5 –

Most of the nine months I should have spent in the first grade I spent in bed. My problems started with the measles—a perfectly ordinary case—and then got steadily worse. I had bout after bout of what I mistakenly thought was called "stripe throat"; I lay in bed drinking cold water and imagining my throat in alternating stripes of red and white (this was probably not so far wrong).

At some point my ears became involved, and one day my mother called a taxi (she did not drive) and took me to a doctor too important to make house calls—an ear specialist. (For some reason I got the idea that this sort of doctor was called an otiologist.) I didn't care whether he specialized in ears or assholes. I had a fever of a hundred and four degrees, and each time I swallowed, pain lit up the sides of my face like a jukebox.

The doctor looked in my ears, spending most of his time (I think) on the left one. Then he laid me down on his examining table. "Lift up a minute, Stevie," his nurse said, and put a large absorbent cloth—it might have been a diaper—under my head, so that my cheek rested on it when I lay back

23

down. I should have guessed that something was rotten in Denmark. Who knows, maybe I did.

There was a sharp smell of alcohol. A clank as the ear doctor opened his sterilizer. I saw the needle in his hand—it looked as long as the ruler in my school pencil-box—and tensed. The ear doctor smiled reassuringly and spoke the lie for which doctors should be immediately jailed (time of incarceration to be doubled when the lie is told to a child): "Relax, Stevie, this won't hurt." I believed him.

He slid the needle into my ear and punctured my eardrum with it. The pain was beyond anything I have ever felt since—the only thing close was the first month of recovery after being struck by a van in the summer of 1999. That pain was longer in duration but not so intense. The puncturing of my eardrum was pain beyond the world. I screamed. There was a sound inside my head—a loud kissing sound. Hot fluid ran out of my ear—it was as if I had started to cry out of the wrong hole. God knows I was crying enough out of the right ones by then. I raised my streaming face and looked unbelieving at the ear doctor and the ear doctor's nurse. Then I looked at the cloth the nurse had spread over the top third of the exam table. It had a big wet patch on it. There were fine tendrils of yellow pus on it as well.

"There," the ear doctor said, patting my shoulder. "You were very brave, Stevie, and it's all over."

The next week my mother called another taxi, we went back to the ear doctor's, and I found myself once more lying on my side with the absorbent square of cloth under my head. The ear doctor once again produced the smell of alcohol—a smell I still associate, as I suppose many people do, with pain and sickness and terror—and with it, the long needle. He once more assured me that it wouldn't hurt, and I once more believed him. Not completely, but enough to be quiet while the needle slid into my ear.

It *did* hurt. Almost as much as the first time, in fact. The smooching sound in my head was louder, too; this time it was giants kissing ("suckin' face and rotatin' tongues," as we used to say). "There," the ear doctor's nurse said when it was over and I lay there crying in a puddle of watery pus. "It only hurts a little, and you don't want to be deaf, do you? Besides, it's all over."

I believed that for about five days, and then another taxi came. We went back to the ear doctor's. I remember the cab driver telling my mother that he was going to pull over and let us out if she couldn't shut that kid up.

Once again it was me on the exam table with the diaper under my head and my mom out in the waiting room with a magazine she was probably incapable of reading (or so I like to imagine). Once again the pungent smell of alcohol and the doctor turning to me with a needle that looked as long as my school ruler. Once more the smile, the approach, the assurance that *this* time it wouldn't hurt.

Since the repeated eardrum-lancings when I was six, one of my life's firmest principles has been this: Fool me once, shame on you. Fool me twice, shame on me. Fool me three times, shame on both of us. The third time on the ear doctor's table I struggled and screamed and thrashed and fought. Each time the needle came near the side of my face, I knocked it away. Finally the nurse called my mother in from the waiting room, and the two of them managed to hold me long enough for the doctor to get his needle in. I screamed so long and so loud that I can still hear it. In fact, I think that in some deep valley of my head that last scream is still echoing.

– 6 –

In a dull cold month not too long after that—it would have been January or February of 1954, if I've got the sequence right—the taxi came again. This time the specialist wasn't the ear doctor but a throat doctor. Once again my mother sat in the waiting room, once again I sat on the examining table with a nurse hovering nearby, and once again there was that sharp smell of alcohol, an aroma that still has the power to double my heartbeat in the space of five seconds.

All that appeared this time, however, was some sort of throat swab. It stung, and it tasted awful, but after the ear doctor's long needle it was a walk in the park. The throat doctor donned an interesting gadget that went around his head on a strap. It had a mirror in the middle, and a bright fierce light that shone out of it like a third eye. He looked down my gullet for a long time, urging me to open wider until my jaws creaked, but he did not put needles into me and so I loved him. After awhile he allowed me to close my mouth and summoned my mother.

"The problem is his tonsils," the doctor said. "They look like a cat clawed them. They'll have to come out."

At some point after that, I remember being wheeled under bright lights. A man in a white mask bent over me. He was standing at the head of the table I was lying on (1953 and 1954 were my years for lying on tables), and to me he looked upside down.

"Stephen," he said. "Can you hear me?"

I said I could.

"I want you to breathe deep," he said. "When you wake up, you can have all the ice cream you want."

He lowered a gadget over my face. In the eye of my memory, it looks like an outboard motor. I took a deep breath, and everything went black. When I woke up I was indeed allowed all the ice cream I wanted, which was a fine joke on me because I didn't want any. My throat felt swollen and fat. But it was better than the old needle-in-the-ear trick. Oh yes. *Anything* would have been better than the old needle-in-the-ear trick. Take my tonsils if you have to, put a steel birdcage on my leg if you must, but God save me from the otiologist.

– 7 –

That year my brother David jumped ahead to the fourth grade and I was pulled out of school entirely. I had missed too much of the first grade, my mother and the school agreed; I could start it fresh in the fall of the year, if my health was good.

Most of that year I spent either in bed or housebound. I read my way through approximately six tons of comic books, progressed to Tom Swift and Dave Dawson (a heroic World War II pilot whose various planes were always "prop-clawing for altitude"), then moved on to Jack London's bloodcurdling animal tales. At some point I began to write my own stories. Imitation preceded creation; I would copy *Combat Casey* comics word for word in my Blue Horse tablet, sometimes adding my own descriptions where they seemed appropriate. "They were camped in a big dratty farmhouse room," I might write; it was another year or two before I discovered that *drat* and *draft* were

Stephen King

different words. During that same period I remember believing that *details* were *dentals* and that a bitch was an extremely tall woman. A son of a bitch was apt to be a basketball player. When you're six, most of your Bingo balls are still floating around in the draw-tank.

Eventually I showed one of these copycat hybrids to my mother, and she was charmed—I remember her slightly amazed smile, as if she was unable to believe a kid of hers could be so smart—practically a damned prodigy, for God's sake. I had never seen that look on her face before—not on my account, anyway—and I absolutely loved it.

She asked me if I had made the story up myself, and I was forced to admit that I had copied most of it out of a funny-book. She seemed disappointed, and that drained away much of my pleasure. At last she handed back my tablet. "Write one of your own, Stevie," she said. "Those *Combat Casey* funny-books are just junk—he's always knocking someone's teeth out. I bet you could do better. Write one of your own."

– 8 –

I remember an immense feeling of *possibility* at the idea, as if I had been ushered into a vast building filled with closed doors and had been given leave to open any I liked. There were more doors than one person could ever open in a lifetime, I thought (and still think).

I eventually wrote a story about four magic animals who rode around in an old car, helping out little kids. Their leader was a large white bunny named Mr. Rabbit Trick. He got to drive the car. The story was four pages long, laboriously printed in pencil. No one in it, so far as I can remember,

jumped from the roof of the Graymore Hotel. When I finished, I gave it to my mother, who sat down in the living
room, put her pocketbook on the floor beside her, and read it
all at once. I could tell she liked it—she laughed in all the
right places—but I couldn't tell if that was because she liked
me and wanted me to feel good or because it really *was* good.

"You didn't copy this one?" she asked when she had finished. I said no, I hadn't. She said it was good enough to be in
a book. Nothing anyone has said to me since has made me
feel any happier. I wrote four more stories about Mr. Rabbit
Trick and his friends. She gave me a quarter apiece for them
and sent them around to her four sisters, who pitied her a little, I think. *They* were all still married, after all; their men had
stuck. It was true that Uncle Fred didn't have much sense of
humor and was stubborn about keeping the top of his convertible up, it was also true that Uncle Oren drank quite a bit
and had dark theories about how the Jews were running the
world, but they were *there*. Ruth, on the other hand, had
been left holding the baby when Don ran out. She wanted
them to see that he was a talented baby, at least.

Four stories. A quarter apiece. That was the first buck I
made in this business.

- 9 -

We moved to Stratford, Connecticut. By then I was in the
second grade and stone in love with the pretty teenage girl
who lived next door. She never looked twice at me in the daytime, but at night, as I lay in bed and drifted toward sleep,
we ran away from the cruel world of reality again and again.
My new teacher was Mrs. Taylor, a kind lady with gray Elsa

Lanchester–*Bride of Frankenstein* hair and protruding eyes. "When we're talking I always want to cup my hands under Mrs. Taylor's peepers in case they fall out," my mom said.

Our new third-floor apartment was on West Broad Street. A block down the hill, not far from Teddy's Market and across from Burrets Building Materials, was a huge tangled wilderness area with a junkyard on the far side and a train track running through the middle. This is one of the places I keep returning to in my imagination; it turns up in my books and stories again and again, under a variety of names. The kids in *It* called it the Barrens; we called it the jungle. Dave and I explored it for the first time not long after we had moved into our new place. It was summer. It was hot. It was great. We were deep into the green mysteries of this cool new playground when I was struck by an urgent need to move my bowels.

"Dave," I said. "Take me home! I have to push!" (This was the word we were given for this particular function.)

David didn't want to hear it. "Go do it in the woods," he said. It would take at least half an hour to walk me home, and he had no intention of giving up such a shining stretch of time just because his little brother had to take a dump.

"I can't!" I said, shocked by the idea. "I won't be able to wipe!"

"Sure you will," Dave said. "Wipe yourself with some leaves. That's how the cowboys and Indians did it."

By then it was probably too late to get home, anyway; I have an idea I was out of options. Besides, I was enchanted by the idea of shitting like a cowboy. I pretended I was Hopalong Cassidy, squatting in the underbrush with my gun drawn, not to be caught unawares even at such a personal moment. I did my business, and took care of the cleanup as my older brother had suggested, carefully wiping my ass with big handfuls of shiny green leaves. These turned out to be poison ivy.

Two days later I was bright red from the backs of my knees to my shoulderblades. My penis was spared, but my testicles turned into stoplights. My ass itched all the way up to my ribcage, it seemed. Yet worst of all was the hand I had wiped with; it swelled to the size of Mickey Mouse's after Donald Duck has bopped it with a hammer, and gigantic blisters formed at the places where the fingers rubbed together. When they burst they left deep divots of raw pink flesh. For six weeks I sat in lukewarm starch baths, feeling miserable and humiliated and stupid, listening through the open door as my mother and brother laughed and listened to Peter Tripp's countdown on the radio and played Crazy Eights.

– 10 –

Dave was a great brother, but too smart for a ten-year-old. His brains were always getting him in trouble, and he learned at some point (probably after I had wiped my ass with poison ivy) that it was usually possible to get Brother Stevie to join him in the point position when trouble was in the wind. Dave never asked me to shoulder *all* the blame for his often brilliant fuck-ups—he was neither a sneak nor a coward—but on several occasions I was asked to share it. Which was, I think, why we both got in trouble when Dave dammed up the stream running through the jungle and flooded much of lower West Broad Street. Sharing the blame was also the reason we both ran the risk of getting killed while implementing his potentially lethal school science project.

This was probably 1958. I was at Center Grammar School; Dave was at Stratford Junior High. Mom was working at the Stratford Laundry, where she was the only white lady on the mangle crew. That's what she was doing—feeding sheets into the mangle—while Dave constructed his Science Fair project. My big brother wasn't the sort of boy to content himself drawing frog-diagrams on construction paper or making The House of the Future out of plastic Tyco bricks and painted toilet-tissue rolls; Dave aimed for the stars. His project that year was Dave's Super Duper Electromagnet. My brother had great affection for things which were super duper and things which began with his own name; this latter habit culminated with *Dave's Rag,* which we will come to shortly.

His first stab at the Super Duper Electromagnet wasn't very super duper; in fact, it may not have worked at all—I don't remember for sure. It *did* come out of an actual book, rather than Dave's head, however. The idea was this: you magnetized a spike nail by rubbing it against a regular magnet. The magnetic charge imparted to the spike would be weak, the book said, but enough to pick up a few iron filings. After trying this, you were supposed to wrap a length of copper wire around the barrel of the spike, and attach the ends of the wire to the terminals of a dry-cell battery. According to the book, the electricity would strengthen the magnetism, and you could pick up a lot more iron filings.

Dave didn't just want to pick up a stupid pile of metal flakes, though; Dave wanted to pick up Buicks, railroad boxcars, possibly Army transport planes. Dave wanted to turn on the juice and move the world in its orbit.

Pow! Super!

We each had our part to play in creating the Super Duper Electromagnet. Dave's part was to build it. My part would be to test it. Little Stevie King, Stratford's answer to Chuck Yeager.

Dave's new version of the experiment bypassed the pokey old dry cell (which was probably flat anyway when we bought it at the hardware store, he reasoned) in favor of actual wall-current. Dave cut the electrical cord off an old lamp someone had put out on the curb with the trash, stripped the coating all the way down to the plug, then wrapped his magnetized spike in spirals of bare wire. Then, sitting on the floor in the kitchen of our West Broad Street apartment, he offered me the Super Duper Electromagnet and bade me do my part and plug it in.

I hesitated—give me at least that much credit—but in the end, Dave's manic enthusiasm was too much to withstand. I plugged it in. There was no noticeable magnetism, but the gadget *did* blow out every light and electrical appliance in our apartment, every light and electrical appliance in the building, and every light and electrical appliance in the building next door (where my dream-girl lived in the ground-floor apartment). Something popped in the electrical transformer out front, and some cops came. Dave and I spent a horrible hour watching from our mother's bedroom window, the only one that looked out on the street (all the others had a good view of the grassless, turd-studded yard behind us, where the only living thing was a mangy canine named Roop-Roop). When the cops left, a power truck arrived. A man in spiked shoes climbed the pole between the two apartment houses to examine the transformer. Under other circumstances, this would have absorbed us completely, but not that day. That day we could only wonder if our mother would come and see us in reform school. Eventually, the lights came back on and the power truck went away. We were not caught and lived to fight another day. Dave decided he might build a Super Duper Glider instead of a Super Duper Electromagnet for his science project. I, he told me, would get to take the first ride. Wouldn't that be great?

– 11 –

I was born in 1947 and we didn't get our first television until 1958. The first thing I remember watching on it was *Robot Monster,* a film in which a guy dressed in an ape-suit with a goldfish bowl on his head—Ro-Man, he was called—ran around trying to kill the last survivors of a nuclear war. I felt this was art of quite a high nature.

I also watched *Highway Patrol* with Broderick Crawford as the fearless Dan Matthews, and *One Step Beyond,* hosted by John Newland, the man with the world's spookiest eyes. There was *Cheyenne* and *Sea Hunt, Your Hit Parade* and *Annie Oakley;* there was Tommy Rettig as the first of Lassie's many friends, Jock Mahoney as *The Range Rider,* and Andy Devine yowling, "Hey, Wild Bill, wait for me!" in his odd, high voice. There was a whole world of vicarious adventure which came packaged in black-and-white, fourteen inches across and sponsored by brand names which still sound like poetry to me. I loved it all.

But TV came relatively late to the King household, and I'm glad. I am, when you stop to think of it, a member of a fairly select group: the final handful of American novelists who learned to read and write before they learned to eat a daily helping of video bullshit. This might not be important. On the other hand, if you're just starting out as a writer, you could do worse than strip your television's electric plug-wire, wrap a spike around it, and then stick it back into the wall. See what blows, and how far.

Just an idea.

– 12 –

In the late 1950s, a literary agent and compulsive science fiction memorabilia collector named Forrest J. Ackerman changed the lives of thousands of kids—I was one—when he began editing a magazine called *Famous Monsters of Filmland.* Ask anyone who has been associated with the fantasy–horror–science fiction genres in the last thirty years about this magazine, and you'll get a laugh, a flash of the eyes, and a stream of bright memories—I practically guarantee it.

Around 1960, Forry (who sometimes referred to himself as "the Ackermonster") spun off the short-lived but interesting *Spacemen,* a magazine which covered science fiction films. In 1960, I sent a story to *Spacemen.* It was, as well as I can remember, the first story I ever submitted for publication. I don't recall the title, but I was still in the Ro-Man phase of my development, and this particular tale undoubtedly owed a great deal to the killer ape with the goldfish bowl on his head.

My story was rejected, but Forry kept it. (Forry keeps *everything,* which anyone who has ever toured his house—the Ackermansion—will tell you.) About twenty years later, while I was signing autographs at a Los Angeles bookstore, Forry turned up in line . . . with my story, single-spaced and typed with the long-vanished Royal typewriter my mom gave me for Christmas the year I was eleven. He wanted me to sign it to him, and I guess I did, although the whole encounter was so surreal I can't be completely sure. Talk about your ghosts. Man oh man.

– 13 –

The first story I did actually publish was in a horror fanzine issued by Mike Garrett of Birmingham, Alabama (Mike is still around, and still in the biz). He published this novella under the title "In a Half-World of Terror," but I still like my title much better. Mine was "I Was a Teen-Age Grave-robber." Super Duper! Pow!

– 14 –

My first really original story idea—you always know the first one, I think—came near the end of Ike's eight-year reign of benignity. I was sitting at the kitchen table of our house in Durham, Maine, and watching my mother stick sheets of S&H Green Stamps into a book. (For more colorful stories about Green Stamps, see *The Liars' Club*.) Our little family troika had moved back to Maine so our mom could take care of her parents in their declining years. Mama was about eighty at that time, obese and hypertensive and mostly blind; Daddy Guy was eighty-two, scrawny, morose, and prone to the occasional Donald Duck outburst which only my mother could understand. Mom called Daddy Guy "Fazza."

My mother's sisters had gotten my mom this job, perhaps thinking they could kill two birds with one stone—the aged Ps would be taken care of in a homey environment by a loving daughter, and The Nagging Problem of Ruth would be solved. She would no longer be adrift, trying to take care of two boys while she floated almost aimlessly from Indiana to Wisconsin to Connecticut, baking cookies at five in the morning or pressing sheets in a laundry where the temperatures often soared to a hundred and ten in the summer and the foreman gave out salt pills at one and three every afternoon from July to the end of September.

She hated her new job, I think—in their effort to take care of her, her sisters turned our self-sufficient, funny, slightly nutty mother into a sharecropper living a largely cashless existence. The money the sisters sent her each month covered the groceries but little else. They sent boxes of clothes for us. Toward the end of each summer, Uncle Clayt and Aunt Ella (who were not, I think, real relatives at all) would bring cartons of canned vegetables and preserves. The house we lived in belonged to Aunt Ethelyn and Uncle Oren. And once she was there, Mom was caught. She got another actual job after the old folks died, but she lived in that house until the cancer got her. When she left Durham for the last time—David and his wife Linda cared for her during the final weeks of her final illness—I have an idea she was probably more than ready to go.

– 15 –

Let's get one thing clear right now, shall we? There is no Idea Dump, no Story Central, no Island of the Buried Bestsellers; good story ideas seem to come quite literally from nowhere, sailing at you right out of the empty sky: two previously unrelated ideas come together and make something new under the sun. Your job isn't to find these ideas but to recognize them when they show up.

On the day this particular idea—the first really good one—came sailing at me, my mother remarked that she needed six more books of stamps to get a lamp she wanted to give her sister Molly for Christmas, and she didn't think she would make it in time. "I guess it will have to be for her birthday, instead," she said. "These cussed things always look like a lot until you stick them in a book." Then she crossed her eyes and ran her tongue out at me. When she did, I saw her tongue was S&H green. I thought how nice it would be if you could make those damned stamps in your basement, and in that instant a story called "Happy Stamps" was born. The concept of counterfeiting Green Stamps and the sight of my mother's green tongue created it in an instant.

The hero of my story was your classic Poor Schmuck, a guy named Roger who had done jail time twice for counterfeiting money—one more bust would make him a three-time loser. Instead of money, he began to counterfeit Happy Stamps . . . except, he discovered, the design of Happy Stamps was so moronically simple that he wasn't really counterfeiting at all; he was creating reams of the actual article. In a funny scene—probably the first really competent scene I ever wrote—Roger sits in the living room with his old mom, the two of them mooning over the Happy Stamps catalogue while the printing press runs downstairs, ejecting bale after bale of those same trading stamps.

"Great Scott!" Mom says. "According to the fine print, you can get *anything* with Happy Stamps, Roger—you tell them what you want, and they figure out how many books you need to get it. Why, for six or seven million books, we could probably get a Happy Stamps house in the suburbs!"

Roger discovers, however, that although the *stamps* are perfect, the *glue* is defective. If you lap the stamps and stick them in the book they're fine, but if you send them through a mechanical licker, the pink Happy Stamps turn blue. At the end of the story, Roger is in the basement, standing in front of a mirror. Behind him, on the table, are roughly ninety books of Happy Stamps, each book filled with individually licked sheets of stamps. Our hero's lips are pink. He runs out his tongue; that's even pinker. Even his teeth are turning pink. Mom calls cheerily down the stairs, saying she has just gotten off the phone with the Happy Stamps National Redemption Center in Terre Haute, and the lady said they could probably get a nice Tudor home in Weston for only eleven million, six hundred thousand books of Happy Stamps.

"That's nice, Mom," Roger says. He looks at himself a moment longer in the mirror, lips pink and eyes bleak, then slowly returns to the table. Behind him, billions of Happy Stamps are stuffed into basement storage bins. Slowly, our hero opens a fresh stamp-book, then begins to lick sheets and stick them in. Only eleven million, five hundred and ninety thousand books to go, he thinks as the story ends, and Mom can have her Tudor.

There were things wrong with this story (the biggest hole was probably Roger's failure simply to start over with a different glue), but it was cute, it was fairly original, and I knew I had done some pretty good writing. After a long time spent studying the markets in my beat-up *Writer's Digest,* I sent "Happy Stamps" off to *Alfred Hitchcock's Mystery Magazine.* It came back three weeks later with a form rejection slip attached. This slip bore Alfred Hitchcock's unmistakable profile in red ink and wished me good luck with my story. At the bottom was an unsigned jotted message, the only personal response I got from *AHMM* over eight years of periodic submissions. "Don't staple manuscripts," the postscript read.

"Loose pages plus paperclip equal correct way to submit copy." This was pretty cold advice, I thought, but useful in its way. I have never stapled a manuscript since.

– 16 –

My room in our Durham house was upstairs, under the eaves. At night I could lie in bed beneath one of these eaves—if I sat up suddenly, I was apt to whack my head a good one—and read by the light of a gooseneck lamp that put an amusing boa constrictor of shadow on the ceiling. Sometimes the house was quiet except for the whoosh of the furnace and the patter of rats in the attic; sometimes my grandmother would spend an hour or so around midnight yelling for someone to check Dick—she was afraid he hadn't been fed. Dick, a horse she'd had in her days as a schoolteacher, was at least forty years dead. I had a desk beneath the room's other eave, my old Royal typewriter, and a hundred or so paperback books, mostly science fiction, which I lined up along the baseboard. On my bureau was a Bible won for memorizing verses in Methodist Youth Fellowship and a Webcor phonograph with an automatic changer and a turntable covered in soft green velvet. On it I played my records, mostly 45s by Elvis, Chuck Berry, Freddy Cannon, and Fats Domino. I liked Fats; he knew how to rock, and you could tell he was having fun.

When I got the rejection slip from *AHMM*, I pounded a nail into the wall above the Webcor, wrote "Happy Stamps" on the rejection slip, and poked it onto the nail. Then I sat on my bed and listened to Fats sing "I'm Ready." I felt pretty good, actually. When you're still too young to shave, optimism is a perfectly legitimate response to failure.

On Writing

By the time I was fourteen (and shaving twice a week whether I needed to or not) the nail in my wall would no longer support the weight of the rejection slips impaled upon it. I replaced the nail with a spike and went on writing. By the time I was sixteen I'd begun to get rejection slips with handwritten notes a little more encouraging than the advice to stop using staples and start using paperclips. The first of these hopeful notes was from Algis Budrys, then the editor of *Fantasy and Science Fiction,* who read a story of mine called "The Night of the Tiger" (the inspiration was, I think, an episode of *The Fugitive* in which Dr. Richard Kimble worked as an attendant cleaning out cages in a zoo or a circus) and wrote: "This is good. Not for us, but good. You have talent. Submit again."

Those four brief sentences, scribbled by a fountain pen that left big ragged blotches in its wake, brightened the dismal winter of my sixteenth year. Ten years or so later, after I'd sold a couple of novels, I discovered "The Night of the Tiger" in a box of old manuscripts and thought it was still a perfectly respectable tale, albeit one obviously written by a guy who had only begun to learn his chops. I rewrote it and on a whim resubmitted it to *F&SF.* This time they bought it.●One thing I've noticed is that when you've had a little success, magazines are a lot less apt to use that phrase, "Not for us."

Although he was a year younger than his classmates, my big brother was bored with high school. Some of this had to do with his intellect—Dave's IQ tested in the 150s or 160s—but I think it was mostly his restless nature. For Dave, high school just wasn't super duper enough—there was no pow, no wham, no *fun*. He solved the problem, at least temporarily, by creating a newspaper which he called *Dave's Rag*.

The *Rag's* office was a table located in the dirt-floored, rock-walled, spider-infested confines of our basement, somewhere north of the furnace and east of the root-cellar, where Clayt and Ella's endless cartons of preserves and canned vegetables were kept. The *Rag* was an odd combination of family newsletter and small-town bi-weekly. Sometimes it was a monthly, if Dave got sidetracked by other interests (maple-sugaring, cider-making, rocket-building, and car-customizing, just to name a few), and then there would be jokes I didn't understand about how Dave's *Rag* was a little late this month or how we shouldn't bother Dave, because he was down in the basement, on the *Rag*.

Jokes or no jokes, circulation rose slowly from about five copies per issue (sold to nearby family members) to something like fifty or sixty, with our relatives and the relatives of neighbors in our small town (Durham's population in 1962 was about nine hundred) eagerly awaiting each new edition. A typical number would let people know how Charley Harrington's broken leg was mending, what guest speakers might be coming to the West Durham Methodist Church, how much water the King boys were hauling from the town pump to keep from draining the well behind the house (of course it went dry every fucking summer no matter how much water we hauled), who was visiting the Browns or the Halls on the other side of Methodist Corners, and whose relatives were due to hit town each summer. Dave also included sports, word-games, weather reports ("It's been pretty dry, but local farmer Harold Davis says if we don't have at least one good rain in August he will smile and kiss a pig"), recipes, a continuing story (I wrote that), and Dave's Jokes and Humor, which included nuggets like these:

Stan: "What did the beaver say to the oak tree?"
Jan: "It was nice gnawing you!"

1st Beatnik: "How do you get to Carnegie Hall?"
2nd Beatnik: "Practice man practice!"

During the *Rag*'s first year, the print was purple—those issues were produced on a flat plate of jelly called a hectograph. My brother quickly decided the hectograph was a pain in the butt. It was just too slow for him. Even as a kid in short pants, Dave hated to be halted. Whenever Milt, our mom's boyfriend ("Sweeter than smart," Mom said to me one day a few months after she dropped him), got stuck in traffic or at a stoplight, Dave would lean over from the back seat of Milt's Buick and yell, "Drive over em, Uncle Milt! Drive over em!"

As a teenager, waiting for the hectograph to "freshen" between pages printed (while "freshening," the print would melt into a vague purple membrane which hung in the jelly like a manatee's shadow) drove David all but insane with impatience. Also, he badly wanted to add photographs to the newspaper. He took good ones, and by age sixteen he was developing them, as well. He rigged a darkroom in a closet and from its tiny, chemical-stinking confines produced pictures which were often startling in their clarity and composition (the photo on the back of *The Regulators,* showing me with a copy of the magazine containing my first published story, was taken by Dave with an old Kodak and developed in his closet darkroom).

In addition to these frustrations, the flats of hectograph jelly had a tendency to incubate and support colonies of strange, sporelike growths in the unsavory atmosphere of our basement, no matter how meticulous we were about covering the damned old slowcoach thing once the day's printing chores were done. What looked fairly ordinary on Monday sometimes looked like something out of an H. P. Lovecraft horror tale by the weekend.

In Brunswick, where he went to high school, Dave found a shop with a small drum printing press for sale. It worked—barely. You typed up your copy on stencils which could be purchased in a local office-supply store for nineteen cents apiece—my brother called this chore "cutting stencil," and it was usually my job, as I was less prone to make typing errors. The stencils were attached to the drum of the press, lathered up with the world's stinkiest, oogiest ink, and then you were off to the races—crank 'til your arm falls off, son. We were able to put together in two nights what had previously taken a week with the hectograph, and while the drum-press was messy, it did not look infected with a potentially fatal disease. *Dave's Rag* entered its brief golden age.

– 18 –

I wasn't much interested in the printing process, and I wasn't interested at all in the arcana of first developing and then reproducing photographs. I didn't care about putting Hearst shifters in cars, making cider, or seeing if a certain formula would send a plastic rocket into the stratosphere (usually they didn't even make it over the house). What I cared about most between 1958 and 1966 was movies.

On Writing

As the fifties gave way to the sixties, there were only two movie theaters in the area, both in Lewiston. The Empire was the first-run house, showing Disney pictures, Bible epics, and musicals in which widescreen ensembles of well-scrubbed folks danced and sang. I went to these if I had a ride—a movie was a movie, after all—but I didn't like them very much. They were boringly wholesome. They were predictable. During *The Parent Trap*, I kept hoping Hayley Mills would run into Vic Morrow from *The Blackboard Jungle*. That would have livened things up a little, by God. I felt that one look at Vic's switchblade knife and gimlet gaze would have put Hayley's piddling domestic problems in some kind of reasonable perspective. And when I lay in bed at night under my eave, listening to the wind in the trees or the rats in the attic, it was not Debbie Reynolds as Tammy or Sandra Dee as Gidget that I dreamed of, but Yvette Vickers from *Attack of the Giant Leeches* or Luana Anders from *Dementia 13*. Never mind sweet; never mind uplifting; never mind Snow White and the Seven Goddam Dwarfs. At thirteen I wanted monsters that ate whole cities, radioactive corpses that came out of the ocean and ate surfers, and girls in black bras who looked like trailer trash.

Horror movies, science fiction movies, movies about teenage gangs on the prowl, movies about losers on motorcycles—this was the stuff that turned my dials up to ten. The place to get all of this was not at the Empire, on the upper end of Lisbon Street, but at the Ritz, down at the lower end, amid the pawnshops and not far from Louie's Clothing, where in 1964 I bought my first pair of Beatle boots. The distance from my house to the Ritz was fourteen miles, and I hitchhiked there almost every weekend during the eight years between 1958 and 1966, when I finally got my driver's license. Sometimes I went with my friend Chris Chesley, sometimes I went alone, but unless I was sick or something, I always went. It was at the Ritz that I saw *I Married a Monster from Outer Space*, with Tom Tryon; *The Haunting*, with Claire Bloom and Julie Harris; *The Wild Angels*, with Peter Fonda and Nancy Sinatra. I saw Olivia de Havilland put out James Caan's eyes with makeshift knives in *Lady in a Cage*, saw Joseph Cotten come back from the dead in *Hush . . . Hush, Sweet Charlotte*, and watched with held breath (and not a little prurient interest) to see if Allison Hayes would grow all the way out of her clothes in *Attack of the 50 Ft. Woman*. At the Ritz, all the finer things in life were available . . . or *might be* available, if you only sat in the third row, paid close attention, and did not blink at the wrong moment.

Chris and I liked just about any horror movie, but our faves were the string of American-International films, most directed by Roger Corman, with titles cribbed from Edgar Allan Poe. I wouldn't say *based upon* the works of Edgar Allan Poe, because there is little in any of them which has anything to do with Poe's actual stories and poems (*The Raven* was filmed as a comedy—no kidding). And yet the best of them—*The Haunted Palace, The Conqueror Worm, The Masque of the Red Death*—achieved a hallucinatory eeriness that made them special. Chris and I had our own name for these films, one that made them into a separate genre. There were westerns, there were love stories, there were war stories . . . and there were Poepictures.

"Wanna hitch to the show Saturday afternoon?" Chris would ask. "Go to the Ritz?"

"What's on?" I'd ask.

"A motorcycle picture and a Poepicture," he'd say. I, of course, was on that combo like white on rice. Bruce Dern going batshit on a Harley and Vincent Price going batshit in a haunted castle overlooking a restless ocean: who could ask for more? You might even get Hazel Court wandering around in a lacy low-cut nightgown, if you were lucky.

Of all the Poepictures, the one that affected Chris and me the most deeply was *The Pit and the Pendulum*. Written by Richard Matheson and filmed in both widescreen and Technicolor (color horror pictures were still a rarity in 1961, when this one came out), *Pit* took a bunch of standard gothic ingredients and turned them into something special. It might have been the last really great studio horror picture before George Romero's ferocious indie *The Night of the Living Dead* came along and changed everything forever (in some few cases for the better, in most for the worse). The best scene—the one which froze Chris and me into our seats—depicted John Kerr digging into a castle wall and discovering the corpse of his sister, who was obviously buried alive. I have never forgotten the corpse's close-up, shot through a red filter and a distorting lens which elongated the face into a huge silent scream.

On the long hitch home that night (if rides were slow in coming, you might end up walking four or five miles and not get home until well after dark) I had a wonderful idea: I would turn *The Pit and the Pendulum* into a book! Would novelize it, as Monarch Books had novelized such undying film classics as *Jack the Ripper, Gorgo,* and *Konga*. But I wouldn't just write this masterpiece; I would also print it, using the drum-press in our basement, and sell copies at school! Zap! Ka-pow!

As it was conceived, so was it done. Working with the care and deliberation for which I would later be critically acclaimed, I turned out my "novel version" of *The Pit and the Pendulum* in two days, composing directly onto the stencils from which I'd print. Although no copies of that particular masterpiece survive (at least to my knowledge), I believe it was eight pages long, each page single-spaced and paragraph breaks kept to an absolute minimum (each stencil cost nineteen cents, remember). I printed sheets on both sides, just as in a standard book, and added a title page on which I drew a rudimentary pendulum dripping small black blotches which I hoped would look like blood. At the last moment I realized I had forgotten to identify the publishing house. After a half-hour or so of pleasant mulling, I typed the words **A V.I.B. BOOK** in the upper right corner of my title page. V.I.B. stood for Very Important Book.

I ran off about forty copies of *The Pit and the Pendulum,* blissfully unaware that I was in violation of every plagiarism and copyright statute in the history of the world; my thoughts were focused almost entirely on how much money I might make if my story was a hit at school. The stencils had cost me $1.71 (having to use up one whole stencil for the title page seemed a hideous waste of money, but you had to look good, I'd reluctantly decided; you had to go out there with a bit of the old attitude), the paper had cost another two bits or so, the staples were free, cribbed from my brother (you might have to paperclip stories you were sending out to magazines, but this was a *book,* this was the bigtime). After some further thought, I priced V.I.B. #1, *The Pit and the Pendulum* by Steve King, at a quarter a copy. I thought I might be able to sell ten (my mother would buy one to get me started; she could always be counted on), and that would add up to $2.50. I'd make about forty cents, which would be enough to finance another educational trip to the Ritz. If I sold two more, I could get a big sack of popcorn and a Coke, as well.

The Pit and the Pendulum turned out to be my first bestseller. I took the entire print-run to school in my book-bag (in 1961 I would have been an eighth-grader at Durham's newly built four-room elementary school), and by noon that day I had sold two dozen. By the end of lunch hour, when word had gotten around about the lady buried in the wall ("They stared with horror at the bones sticking out from the ends of her fingers, realizing she had died scratcheing madley for escape"), I had sold three dozen. I had nine dollars in change weighing down the bottom of my book-bag (upon which Durham's answer to Daddy Cool had carefully printed most of the lyrics to "The Lion Sleeps Tonight") and was walking around in a kind of dream, unable to believe my sudden ascension to previously unsuspected realms of wealth. It all seemed too good to be true.

It was. When the school day ended at two o'clock, I was summoned to the principal's office, where I was told I couldn't turn the school into a marketplace, especially not, Miss Hisler said, to sell such trash as *The Pit and the Pendulum*. Her attitude didn't much surprise me. Miss Hisler had been the teacher at my previous school, the one-roomer at Methodist Corners, where I went to the fifth and sixth grades. During that time she had spied me reading a rather sensational "teenage rumble" novel (*The Amboy Dukes,* by Irving Shulman), and had taken it away. This was just more of the same, and I was disgusted with myself for not seeing the outcome in advance. In those days we called someone who did an idiotic thing a dubber (pronounced *dubba* if you were from Maine). I had just dubbed up bigtime.

"What I don't understand, Stevie," she said, "is why you'd write junk like this in the first place. You're talented. Why do you want to waste your abilities?" She had rolled up a copy of V.I.B. #1 and was brandishing it at me the way a person might brandish a rolled-up newspaper at a dog that has piddled on the rug. She waited for me to answer—to her credit, the question was not entirely rhetorical—but I had no answer to give. I was ashamed. I have spent a good many years since—too many, I think—being ashamed about what I write. I think I was forty before I realized that almost every writer of fiction and poetry who has ever published a line has been accused by someone of wasting his or her God-given talent. If you write (or paint or dance or sculpt or sing, I suppose), someone will try to make you feel lousy about it, that's all. I'm not editorializing, just trying to give you the facts as I see them.

Miss Hisler told me I would have to give everyone's money back. I did so with no argument, even to those kids (and there were quite a few, I'm happy to say) who insisted on keeping their copies of V.I.B. #1. I ended up losing money on the deal after all, but when summer vacation came I printed four dozen copies of a new story, an original called *The Invasion of the Star-Creatures,* and sold all but four or five. I guess that means I won in the end, at least in a financial sense. But in my heart I stayed ashamed. I kept hearing Miss Hisler asking why I wanted to waste my talent, why I wanted to waste my time, why I wanted to write junk.

– 19 –

Doing a serial story for *Dave's Rag* was fun, but my other journalistic duties bored me. Still, I had worked for a newspaper of sorts, word got around, and during my sophomore year at Lisbon High I became editor of our school newspaper, *The Drum.* I don't recall being given any choice in this matter; I think I was simply appointed. My second-in-command, Danny Emond, had even less interest in the paper than I did. Danny just liked the idea that Room 4, where we did our work, was near the girls' bathroom. "Someday I'll just go crazy and hack my way in there, Steve," he told me on more than one occasion. "Hack, hack, hack." Once he added, perhaps in an effort to justify himself: "The prettiest girls in school pull up their skirts in there." This struck me as so fundamentally stupid it might actually be wise, like a Zen koan or an early story by John Updike.

The Drum did not prosper under my editorship. Then as now, I tend to go through periods of idleness followed by periods of workaholic frenzy. In the schoolyear 1963–1964, *The Drum* published just one issue, but that one was a monster thicker than the Lisbon Falls telephone book. One night— sick to death of Class Reports, Cheerleading Updates, and some lamebrain's efforts to write a school poem—I created a satiric high school newspaper of my own when I should have been captioning photographs for *The Drum.* What resulted was a four-sheet which I called *The Village Vomit.* The boxed motto in the upper lefthand corner was not "All the News That's Fit to Print" but "All the Shit That Will Stick." That piece of dimwit humor got me into the only real trouble of my high school career. It also led me to the most useful writing lesson I ever got.

In typical *Mad* magazine style ("What, me worry?"), I filled the *Vomit* with fictional tidbits about the LHS faculty, using teacher nicknames the student body would immediately recognize. Thus Miss Raypach, the study-hall monitor, became Miss Rat Pack; Mr. Ricker, the college-track English teacher (and the school's most urbane faculty member—he looked quite a bit like Craig Stevens in *Peter Gunn*), became

51

Cow Man because his family owned Ricker Dairy; Mr. Diehl, the earth-science teacher, became Old Raw Diehl.

As all sophomoric humorists must be, I was totally blown away by my own wit. What a funny fellow I was! A regular mill-town H. L. Mencken! I simply must take the *Vomit* to school and show all my friends! They would bust a collective gut!

As a matter of fact, they *did* bust a collective gut; I had some good ideas about what tickled the funnybones of high school kids, and most of them were showcased in *The Village Vomit*. In one article, Cow Man's prize Jersey won a livestock farting contest at Topsham Fair; in another, Old Raw Diehl was fired for sticking the eyeballs of specimen fetal pigs up his nostrils. Humor in the grand Swiftian manner, you see. Pretty sophisticated, eh?

During period four, three of my friends were laughing so hard in the back of study-hall that Miss Raypach (Rat Pack to you, chum) crept up on them to see what was so funny. She confiscated *The Village Vomit,* on which I had, either out of over-weening pride or almost unbelievable naiveté, put my name as Editor in Chief & Grand High Poobah, and at the close of school I was for the second time in my student career sum-moned to the office on account of something I had written.

This time the trouble was a good deal more serious. Most of the teachers were inclined to be good sports about my teasing—even Old Raw Diehl was willing to let bygones be bygones concerning the pigs' eyeballs—but one was not. This was Miss Margitan, who taught shorthand and typing to the girls in the business courses. She commanded both respect and fear; in the tradition of teachers from an earlier era, Miss Margitan did not want to be your pal, your psychologist, or your inspiration. She was there to teach business skills, and she wanted all learning to be done by the rules. *Her* rules. Girls in Miss Margitan's classes were sometimes asked to kneel on the floor, and if the hems of their skirts didn't touch the linoleum, they were sent home to change. No amount of tearful begging could soften her, no reasoning could modify her view of the world. Her detention lists were the longest of any teacher in the school, but her girls were routinely selected as valedictorians or salutatorians and usually went on to good jobs. Many came to love her. Others loathed her then and likely still do now, all these years later. These latter girls called her "Maggot" Margitan, as their mothers had no doubt before them. And in *The Village Vomit* I had an item which began, "Miss Margitan, known affectionately to Lisbonians everywhere as Maggot . . ."

Mr. Higgins, our bald principal (breezily referred to in the *Vomit* as Old Cue-Ball), told me that Miss Margitan had been very hurt and very upset by what I had written. She was apparently not too hurt to remember that old scriptural admonition which goes "Vengeance is mine, saith the shorthand teacher," however; Mr. Higgins said she wanted me suspended from school.

In my character, a kind of wildness and a deep conservatism are wound together like hair in a braid. It was the crazy part of me that had first written *The Village Vomit* and then carried it to school; now that troublesome Mr. Hyde had dubbed up and slunk out the back door. Dr. Jekyll was left to consider how my mom would look at me if she found out I had been suspended—her hurt eyes. I had to put thoughts of her out of my mind, and fast. I was a sophomore, I was a year older than most others in my class, and at six feet two I was one of the bigger boys in school. I desperately didn't want to cry in Mr. Higgins's office—not with kids surging through the halls and looking curiously in the window at us: Mr. Higgins behind his desk, me in the Bad Boy Seat.

In the end, Miss Margitan settled for a formal apology and two weeks of detention for the bad boy who had dared call her Maggot in print. It was bad, but what in high school is not? At the time we're stuck in it, like hostages locked in a Turkish bath, high school seems the most serious business in the world to just about all of us. It's not until the second or third class reunion that we start realizing how absurd the whole thing was.

A day or two later I was ushered into Mr. Higgins's office and made to stand in front of her. Miss Margitan sat ramrod-straight with her arthritic hands folded in her lap and her gray eyes fixed unflinchingly on my face, and I realized that something about her was different from any other adult I had ever met. I didn't pinpoint that difference at once, but I knew that there would be no charming this lady, no winning her over. Later, while I was flying paper planes with the other bad boys and bad girls in detention hall (detention turned out to be not so bad), I decided that it was pretty simple: Miss Margitan didn't like boys. She was the first woman I ever met in my life who didn't like boys, not even one little bit.

If it makes any difference, my apology was heartfelt. Miss Margitan really had been hurt by what I wrote, and that much I could understand. I doubt that she hated me—she was probably too busy—but she was the National Honor Society advisor at LHS, and when my name showed up on the candidate list two years later, she vetoed me. The Honor Society did not need boys "of his type," she said. I have come to believe she was right. A boy who once wiped his ass with poison ivy probably doesn't belong in a smart people's club.

I haven't trucked much with satire since then.

– 20 –

Hardly a week after being sprung from detention hall, I was once more invited to step down to the principal's office. I went with a sinking heart, wondering what new shit I'd stepped in.

It wasn't Mr. Higgins who wanted to see me, at least; this time the school guidance counsellor had issued the summons. There had been discussions about me, he said, and how to turn my "restless pen" into more constructive channels. He had enquired of John Gould, editor of Lisbon's weekly newspaper, and had discovered Gould had an opening for a sports reporter. While the school couldn't *insist* that I take this job, everyone in the front office felt it would be a good idea. *Do it or die,* the G.C.'s eyes suggested. Maybe that was just paranoia, but even now, almost forty years later, I don't think so.

I groaned inside. I was shut of *Dave's Rag,* almost shut of *The Drum,* and now here was the Lisbon *Weekly Enterprise.* Instead of being haunted by waters, like Norman Maclean in *A River Runs Through It,* I was as a teenager haunted by newspapers. Still, what could I do? I rechecked the look in the guidance counsellor's eyes and said I would be delighted to interview for the job.

Gould—not the well-known New England humorist or the novelist who wrote *The Greenleaf Fires* but a relation of both, I think—greeted me warily but with some interest. We would try each other out, he said, if that suited me.

Now that I was away from the administrative offices of Lisbon High, I felt able to muster a little honesty. I told Mr.

Gould that I didn't know much about sports. Gould said, "These are games people understand when they're watching them drunk in bars. You'll learn if you try."

He gave me a huge roll of yellow paper on which to type my copy—I think I still have it somewhere—and promised me a wage of half a cent a word. It was the first time someone had promised me wages for writing.

The first two pieces I turned in had to do with a basketball game in which an LHS player broke the school scoring record. One was a straight piece of reporting. The other was a sidebar about Robert Ransom's record-breaking performance. I brought both to Gould the day after the game so he'd have them for Friday, which was when the paper came out. He read the game piece, made two minor corrections, and spiked it. Then he started in on the feature piece with a large black pen.

I took my fair share of English Lit classes in my two remaining years at Lisbon, and my fair share of composition, fiction, and poetry classes in college, but John Gould taught me more than any of them, and in no more than ten minutes. I wish I still had the piece—it deserves to be framed, editorial corrections and all—but I can remember pretty well how it went and how it looked after Gould had combed through it with that black pen of his. Here's an example:

> Last night, in the ~~well-loved~~ gymnasium of Lisbon High School, partisans and Jay Hills fans alike were stunned by an athletic performance unequalled in school history. Bob Ransom, ~~known as "Bullet" Bob for both his size and accuracy,~~ scored thirty-seven points. Yes, you heard me right. ~~Plus~~ he did it with grace, speed . . . and with an odd courtesy as well,

committing only two personal fouls in his ~~knight-like~~
quest for a record which has eluded Lisbon ~~thinclads~~ *players*
since ~~the years of Korea~~. . . *1953.*

Gould stopped at "the years of Korea" and looked up at
me. "What year was the last record made?" he asked.

Luckily, I had my notes. "1953," I said. Gould grunted and
went back to work. When he finished marking my copy in
the manner indicated above, he looked up and saw something
on my face. I think he must have mistaken it for horror. It
wasn't; it was pure revelation. Why, I wondered, didn't
English teachers ever do this? It was like the Visible Man Old
Raw Diehl had on his desk in the biology room.

"I only took out the bad parts, you know," Gould said.
"Most of it's pretty good."

"I know," I said, meaning both things: yes, most of it was
good—okay anyway, serviceable—and yes, he had only
taken out the bad parts. "I won't do it again."

He laughed. "If that's true, you'll never have to work for a
living. You can do *this* instead. Do I have to explain any of
these marks?"

"No," I said.

"When you write a story, you're telling yourself the story,"
he said. "When you rewrite, your main job is taking out all
the things that are *not* the story."

Gould said something else that was interesting on the day
I turned in my first two pieces: write with the door closed,
rewrite with the door open. Your stuff starts out being just
for you, in other words, but then it goes out. Once you know
what the story is and get it right—as right as you can, anyway—it belongs to anyone who wants to read it. Or criticize
it. If you're very lucky (this is my idea, not John Gould's, but

I believe he would have subscribed to the notion), more will want to do the former than the latter.

– 21 –

Just after the senior class trip to Washington, D.C., I got a job at Worumbo Mills and Weaving, in Lisbon Falls. I didn't want it—the work was hard and boring, the mill itself a dingy fuckhole overhanging the polluted Androscoggin River like a workhouse in a Charles Dickens novel—but I needed the paycheck. My mother was making lousy wages as a housekeeper at a facility for the mentally ill in New Gloucester, but she was determined I was going to college like my brother David (University of Maine, class of '66, *cum laude*). In her mind, the education had become almost secondary. Durham and Lisbon Falls and the University of Maine at Orono were part of a small world where folks neighbored and still minded each other's business on the four- and six-party lines which then served the Sticksville townships. In the big world, boys who didn't go to college were being sent overseas to fight in Mr. Johnson's undeclared war, and many of them were coming home in boxes. My mother liked Lyndon's War on Poverty ("That's the war *I'm* in," she sometimes said), but not what he was up to in Southeast Asia. Once I told her that enlisting and going over there might be good for me—surely there would be a book in it, I said.

"Don't be an idiot, Stephen," she said. "With your eyes, you'd be the first one to get shot. You can't write if you're dead."

She meant it; her head was set and so was her heart. Consequently, I applied for scholarships, I applied for loans, and I went to work in the mill. I certainly wouldn't get far on the five and six dollars a week I could make writing about bowling tournaments and Soap Box Derby races for the *Enterprise.*

During my final weeks at Lisbon High, my schedule looked like this: up at seven, off to school at seven-thirty, last bell at two o'clock, punch in on the third floor of Worumbo at 2:58, bag loose fabric for eight hours, punch out at 11:02, get home around quarter of twelve, eat a bowl of cereal, fall into bed, get up the next morning, do it all again. On a few occasions I worked double shifts, slept in my '60 Ford Galaxie (Dave's old car) for an hour or so before school, then slept through periods five and six in the nurse's cubicle after lunch.

Once summer vacation came, things got easier. I was moved down to the dyehouse in the basement, for one thing, where it was thirty degrees cooler. My job was dyeing swatches of melton cloth purple or navy blue. I imagine there are still folks in New England with jackets in their closets dyed by yours truly. It wasn't the best summer I ever spent, but I managed to avoid being sucked into the machinery or stitching my fingers together with one of the heavy-duty sewing machines we used to belt the undyed cloth.

During Fourth of July week, the mill closed. Employees with five years or more at Worumbo got the week off with pay. Those with fewer than five years were offered work on a crew that was going to clean the mill from top to bottom, including the basement, which hadn't been touched in forty or fifty years. I probably would have agreed to work on this crew—it was time and a half—but all the positions were filled long before the foreman got down to the high school kids, who'd be gone in September. When I got back to work the following week, one of the dyehouse guys told me I should have been there, it was wild. "The rats down in that basement were big as cats," he said. "Some of them, goddam if they weren't as big as *dogs*."

Rats as big as dogs! Yow!

One day late in my final semester at college, finals over and at loose ends, I recalled the dyehouse guy's story about the rats under the mill—big as cats, goddam, some as big as *dogs*—and started writing a story called "Graveyard Shift." I was only passing the time on a late spring afternoon, but two months later *Cavalier* magazine bought the story for two hundred dollars. I had sold two other stories previous to this, but they had brought in a total of just sixty-five dollars. This was three times that, and at a single stroke. It took my breath away, it did. I was rich.

– 22 –

During the summer of 1969 I got a work-study job in the University of Maine library. That was a season both fair and foul. In Vietnam, Nixon was executing his plan to end the war, which seemed to consist of bombing most of Southeast Asia into Kibbles 'n Bits. "Meet the new boss," The Who sang, "same as the old boss." Eugene McCarthy was concentrating on his poetry, and happy hippies wore bell-bottom pants and tee-shirts that said things like KILLING FOR PEACE IS LIKE FUCKING FOR CHASTITY. I had a great set of muttonchop sideburns. Creedence Clearwater Revival was singing "Green River"—barefoot girls, dancing in the moonlight—and Kenny Rogers was still with The First Edition. Martin Luther King and Robert Kennedy were dead, but Janis Joplin, Jim Morrison, Bob "The Bear" Hite, Jimi Hendrix, Cass Elliot, John Lennon, and Elvis Presley were still alive and making music. I was staying just off campus in Ed Price's Rooms (seven bucks a week, one change of sheets included). Men had landed on the moon, and I had landed on the Dean's List. Miracles and wonders abounded.

One day in late June of that summer, a bunch of us library guys had lunch on the grass behind the university bookstore. Sitting between Paolo Silva and Eddie Marsh was a trim girl with a raucous laugh, red-tinted hair, and the prettiest legs I had ever seen, well-displayed beneath a short yellow skirt. She was carrying a copy of *Soul on Ice,* by Eldridge Cleaver. I hadn't run across her in the library, and I didn't believe a college student could utter such a wonderful, unafraid laugh. Also, heavy reading or no heavy reading, she swore like a millworker instead of a coed. (Having been a millworker, I was qualified to judge.) Her name was Tabitha Spruce. We got married a year and a half later. We're still married, and she has never let me forget that the first time I met her I thought she was Eddie Marsh's townie girlfriend. Maybe a book-reading waitress from the local pizza joint on her afternoon off.

– 23 –

It's worked. Our marriage has outlasted all of the world's leaders except for Castro, and if we keep talking, arguing, making love, and dancing to the Ramones—gabba-gabba-hey—it'll probably keep working. We came from different religions, but as a feminist Tabby has never been crazy about the Catholics, where the men make the rules (including the God-given directive to always go in bareback) and the women wash the underwear. And while I believe in God I have no use for organized religion. We came from similar working-class backgrounds, we both ate meat, we were both political Democrats with typical Yankee suspicions of life outside New England. We were sexually compatible and monogamous by nature. Yet what ties us most strongly are the words, the language, and the work of our lives.

We met when we were working in a library, and I fell in love with her during a poetry workshop in the fall of 1969, when I was a senior and Tabby was a junior. I fell in love with her partly because I understood what she was doing with her work. I fell because *she* understood what she was doing with it. I also fell because she was wearing a sexy black dress and silk stockings, the kind that hook with garters.

I don't want to speak too disparagingly of my generation (actually I do, we had a chance to change the world and opted for the Home Shopping Network instead), but there was a view among the student writers I knew at that time that good writing came spontaneously, in an uprush of feeling that had to be caught at once; when you were building that all-important stairway to heaven, you couldn't just stand around with your hammer in your hand. *Ars poetica* in 1969 was perhaps best expressed by a Donovan Leitch song that went, "First there is a mountain / Then there is no mountain / Then there is." Would-be poets were living in a dewy Tolkien-tinged world, catching poems out of the ether. It was pretty much unanimous: serious art came from . . . *out there!* Writers were blessed stenographers taking divine dictation. I don't want to embarrass any of my old mates from that period, so here is a fictionalized version of what I'm talking about, created from bits of many actual poems:

> *i close my eyes*
> *in th dark i see*

On Writing

Rodan   Rimbaud
in th dark
i swallow th cloth
of loneliness
crow i am here
raven i am here

If you were to ask the poet what this poem *meant,* you'd likely get a look of contempt. A slightly uncomfortable silence was apt to emanate from the rest. Certainly the fact that the poet would likely have been unable to tell you anything about the mechanics of creation would not have been considered important. If pressed, he or she might have said that there *were* no mechanics, only that seminal spurt of feeling: first there is a mountain, then there is no mountain, then there is. And if the resulting poem is sloppy, based on the assumption that such general words as "loneliness" mean the same thing to all of us—hey man, so what, let go of that outdated bullshit and just dig the heaviness. I didn't cop to much of this attitude (although I didn't dare say so out loud, at least not in so many words), and was overjoyed to find that the pretty girl in the black dress and the silk stockings didn't cop to much of it, either. She didn't come right out and say so, but she didn't need to. Her work spoke for her.

The workshop group met once or twice a week in the living room of instructor Jim Bishop's house, perhaps a dozen undergrads and three or four faculty members working in a marvellous atmosphere of equality. Poems were typed up and mimeographed in the English Department office on the day of each workshop. Poets read while the rest of us followed along on our copies. Here is one of Tabby's poems from that fall:

Stephen King

A Gradual Canticle for Augustine

The thinnest bear is awakened in the winter
by the sleep-laughter of locusts,
by the dream-blustering of bees,
by the honeyed scent of desert sands
that the wind carries in her womb
into the distant hills, into the houses of Cedar.

The bear has heard a sure promise.
Certain words are edible; they nourish
more than snow heaped upon silver plates
or ice overflowing golden bowls. Chips of ice
from the mouth of a lover are not always better,
Nor a desert dreaming always a mirage.
The rising bear sings a gradual canticle
woven of sand that conquers cities
by a slow cycle. His praise seduces
a passing wind, traveling to the sea
wherein a fish, caught in a careful net,
hears a bear's song in the cool-scented snow.

There was silence when Tabby finished reading. No one knew exactly how to react. Cables seemed to run through the poem, tightening the lines until they almost hummed. I found the combination of crafty diction and delirious imagery exciting and illuminating. Her poem also made me feel that I wasn't alone in my belief that good writing can be simultaneously intoxicating and idea-driven. If stone-sober people can fuck like they're out of their minds—can actually be out of their minds while caught in that throe—why shouldn't writers be able to go bonkers and still stay sane?

There was also a work-ethic in the poem that I liked, something that suggested writing poems (or stories, or essays) had as much in common with sweeping the floor as with mythy moments of revelation. There's a place in *A Raisin in the Sun* where a character cries out: "I want to fly! I want to touch the sun!" to which his wife replies, "First eat your eggs."

In the discussion that followed Tab's reading, it became clear to me that she understood her own poem. She knew exactly what she had meant to say, and had said most of it. Saint Augustine (A.D. 354–430) she knew both as a Catholic and as a history major. Augustine's mother (a saint herself) was a Christian, his father a pagan. Before his conversion, Augustine pursued both money and women. Following it he continued to struggle with his sexual impulses, and is known for the Libertine's Prayer, which goes: "O Lord, make me chaste . . . but not yet." In his writing he focused on man's struggle to give up belief in self in favor of belief in God. And he sometimes likened himself to a bear. Tabby has a way of tilting her chin down when she smiles—it makes her look both wise and severely cute. She did that then, I remember, and said, "Besides, I like bears."

The canticle is gradual perhaps because the bear's awakening is gradual. The bear is powerful and sensual, although thin because he is out of his time. In a way, Tabby said when called upon to explicate, the bear can be seen as a symbol of mankind's troubling and wonderful habit of dreaming the right dreams at the wrong time. Such dreams are difficult because they're inappropriate, but also wonderful in their promise. The poem also suggests that dreams are powerful—the bear's is strong enough to seduce the wind into bringing his song to a fish caught in a net.

I won't try to argue that "A Gradual Canticle" is a great poem (although I think it's a pretty good one). The point is that it was a reasonable poem in a hysterical time, one sprung from a writing ethic that resonated all through my heart and soul.

Tabby was in one of Jim Bishop's rocking chairs that night. I was sitting on the floor beside her. I put my hand on her calf as she spoke, cupping the curve of warm flesh through her stocking. She smiled at me. I smiled back. Sometimes these things are not accidents. I'm almost sure of it.

– 24 –

We had two kids by the time we'd been married three years. They were neither planned nor unplanned; they came when they came, and we were glad to have them. Naomi was prone to ear infections. Joe was healthy enough but never seemed to sleep. When Tabby went into labor with him, I was at a drive-in movie in Brewer with a friend—it was a Memorial Day triple feature, three horror films. We were on the third movie *(The Corpse Grinders)* and the second sixpack when the guy in the office broke in with an announcement. There were still pole-speakers in those days; when you parked your car you lifted one off and hung it over your window. The manager's announcement thus rang across the entire parking lot: *"STEVE KING, PLEASE GO HOME! YOUR WIFE IS IN LABOR! STEVE KING, PLEASE GO HOME! YOUR WIFE IS GOING TO HAVE THE BABY!"*

As I drove our old Plymouth toward the exit, a couple of hundred horns blared a satiric salute. Many people flicked their headlights on and off, bathing me in a stuttery glow. My friend Jimmy Smith laughed so hard he slid into the footwell on the passenger side of the front seat. There he remained for most of the trip back to Bangor, chortling among the beer-cans. When I got home, Tabby was calm and packed. She gave birth to Joe less than three hours later. He entered the world easily. For the next five years or so, nothing else about Joe was easy. But he was a treat. Both of them were, really. Even when Naomi was tearing off the wallpaper above her crib (maybe she thought she was housekeeping) and Joe was shitting in the wicker seat of the rocker we kept on the porch of our apartment on Sanford Street, they were a treat.

– 25 –

My mother knew I wanted to be a writer (with all those rejection slips hanging from the spike on my bedroom wall, how could she not?), but she encouraged me to get a teacher's credential "so you'll have something to fall back on."

"You may want to get married, Stephen, and a garret by the Seine is only romantic if you're a bachelor," she'd said once. "It's no place to raise a family."

I did as she suggested, entering the College of Education at UMO and emerging four years later with a teacher's certificate . . . sort of like a golden retriever emerging from a pond with a dead duck in its jaws. It was dead, all right. I couldn't find a teaching job and so went to work at New Franklin Laundry for wages not much higher than those I had been making at Worumbo Mills and Weaving four years before. I was keeping my family in a series of garrets which overlooked not the Seine but some of Bangor's less appetizing streets, the ones where the police cruisers always seemed to show up at two o'clock on Saturday morning.

I never saw personal laundry at New Franklin unless it was a "fire order" being paid for by an insurance company (most fire orders consisted of clothes that *looked* okay but smelled like barbecued monkeymeat). The greater part of what I loaded and pulled were motel sheets from Maine's coastal towns and table linen from Maine's coastal restaurants. The table linen was desperately nasty. When tourists go out to dinner in Maine, they usually want clams and lobster. Mostly lobster. By the time the tablecloths upon which these delicacies had been served reached me, they stank to high heaven and were often boiling with maggots. The maggots would try to crawl up your arms as you loaded the washers; it was as if the little fuckers knew you were planning to cook them. I thought I'd get used to them in time but I never did. The maggots were bad; the smell of decomposing clams and lobster-meat was even worse. *Why are people such slobs?* I would wonder, loading feverish linens from Testa's of Bar Harbor into my machines. *Why are people such fucking slobs?*

Hospital sheets and linens were even worse. These also crawled with maggots in the summertime, but it was blood they were feeding on instead of lobster-meat and clam-jelly. Clothes, sheets, and pillowslips deemed to be infected were stuffed inside what we called "plague-bags" which dissolved when the hot water hit them, but blood was not, in those times, considered to be especially dangerous. There were often little extras in the hospital laundry; those loads were like nasty boxes of Cracker Jacks with weird prizes in them. I found a steel bedpan in one load and a pair of surgical shears in another (the bedpan was of no practical use, but the shears were a damned handy kitchen implement). Ernest "Rocky" Rockwell, the guy I worked with, found twenty dollars in a load from Eastern Maine Medical Center and punched out at noon to start drinking. (Rocky referred to quitting time as "Slitz o'clock.")

On one occasion I heard a strange clicking from inside one of the Washex three-pockets which were my responsibility. I hit the Emergency Stop button, thinking the goddam thing was stripping its gears or something. I opened the doors and hauled out a huge wad of dripping surgical tunics and green caps, soaking myself in the process. Below them, lying scattered across the colander-like inner sleeve of the middle pocket, was what looked like a complete set of human teeth. It crossed my mind that they would make an interesting necklace, then I scooped them out and tossed them in the trash. My wife has put up with a lot from me over the years, but her sense of humor stretches only so far.

– 26 –

From a financial point of view, two kids were probably two too many for college grads working in a laundry and the second shift at Dunkin' Donuts. The only edge we had came courtesy of magazines like *Dude, Cavalier, Adam,* and *Swank*—what my Uncle Oren used to call "the titty books." By 1972 they were showing quite a lot more than bare breasts and fiction was on its way out, but I was lucky enough to ride the last wave. I wrote after work; when we lived on Grove Street, which was close to the New Franklin, I would sometimes write a little on my lunch hour, too. I suppose that sounds almost impossibly Abe Lincoln, but it was no big deal—I was having fun. Those stories, grim as some of them were, served as brief escapes from the boss, Mr. Brooks, and Harry the floor-man.

Harry had hooks instead of hands as a result of a tumble into the sheet-mangler during World War II (he was dusting the beams above the machine and fell off). A comedian at heart, he would sometimes duck into the bathroom and run water from the cold tap over one hook and water from the hot tap over the other. Then he'd sneak up behind you while you were loading laundry and lay the steel hooks on the back of your neck. Rocky and I spent a fair amount of time speculating on how Harry accomplished certain bathroom cleanup activities. "Well," Rocky said one day while we were drinking our lunch in his car, "at least he don't need to wash his hands."

There were times—especially in summer, while swallowing my afternoon salt-pill—when it occurred to me that I was simply repeating my mother's life. Usually this thought struck me as funny. But if I happened to be tired, or if there were extra bills to pay and no money to pay them with, it seemed awful. I'd think *This isn't the way our lives are supposed to be going.* Then I'd think *Half the world has the same idea.*

The stories I sold to the men's magazines between August of 1970, when I got my two-hundred-dollar check for "Graveyard Shift," and the winter of 1973–1974 were just enough to create a rough sliding margin between us and the welfare office (my mother, a Republican all her life, had communicated her deep horror of "going on the county" to me; Tabby had some of that same horror).

My clearest memory of those days is of our coming back to the Grove Street apartment one Sunday afternoon after spending the weekend at my mother's house in Durham— this would have been right around the time the symptoms of the cancer which killed her started to show themselves. I have a picture from that day—Mom, looking both tired and amused, is sitting in a chair in her dooryard, holding Joe in her lap while Naomi stands sturdily beside her. Naomi wasn't so sturdy by Sunday afternoon, however; she had come down with an ear infection, and was burning with fever.

Trudging from the car to our apartment building on that summer afternoon was a low point. I was carrying Naomi and a tote-bag full of baby survival equipment (bottles, lotions, diapers, sleep suits, undershirts, socks) while Tabby carried Joe, who had spit up on her. She was dragging a sack of dirty diapers behind her. We both knew Naomi needed THE PINK STUFF, which was what we called liquid amoxicillin. THE PINK STUFF was expensive, and we were broke. I mean stony.

I managed to get the downstairs door open without dropping my daughter and was easing her inside (she was so feverish she glowed against my chest like a banked coal) when I saw there was an envelope sticking out of our mailbox—a rare Saturday delivery. Young marrieds don't get much mail; everyone but the gas and electric companies seems to forget they are alive. I snagged it, praying it wouldn't turn out to be another bill. It wasn't. My friends at the Dugent Publishing Corporation, purveyors of *Cavalier* and many other fine adult publications, had sent me a check for "Sometimes They Come Back," a long story I hadn't believed would sell anywhere. The check was for five hundred dollars, easily the largest sum I'd ever received. Suddenly we were able to afford not only a doctor's visit and a bottle of THE PINK STUFF, but also a nice Sunday-night meal. And I imagine that once the kids were asleep, Tabby and I got friendly.

I think we had a lot of happiness in those days, but we were scared a lot, too. We weren't much more than kids ourselves (as the saying goes), and being friendly helped keep the mean reds away. We took care of ourselves and the kids and each other as best we could. Tabby wore her pink uniform out to Dunkin' Donuts and called the cops when the drunks who came in for coffee got obstreperous. I washed motel sheets and kept writing one-reel horror movies.

– 27 –

By the time I started *Carrie,* I had landed a job teaching English in the nearby town of Hampden. I would be paid sixty-four hundred dollars a year, which seemed an unthinkable sum after earning a dollar-sixty an hour at the laundry. If I'd done the math, being careful to add in all the time spent in after-school conferences and correcting papers at home, I might have seen it was a very thinkable sum indeed, and that our situation was worse than ever. By the late winter of 1973 we were living in a doublewide trailer in Hermon, a little town west of Bangor. (Much later, when asked to do the *Playboy* Interview, I called Hermon "The asshole of the world." Hermonites were infuriated by that, and I hereby apologize. Hermon is really no more than the armpit of the world.) I was driving a Buick with transmission problems we couldn't afford to fix, Tabby was still working at Dunkin' Donuts, and we had no telephone. We simply couldn't afford the monthly charge. Tabby tried her hand at confession stories during that period ("Too Pretty to Be a Virgin"—stuff like that), and got personal responses of the this-isn't-quite-right-for-us-but-try-again type immediately. She would have broken through if given an extra hour or two in every day, but she was stuck with the usual twenty-four. Besides, any amusement value the confession-mag formula (it's called the Three R's—Rebellion, Ruin, and Redemption) might have had for her at the start wore off in a hurry.

I wasn't having much success with my own writing, either. Horror, science fiction, and crime stories in the men's magazines were being replaced by increasingly graphic tales of sex. That was part of the trouble, but not all of it. The bigger deal was that, for the first time in my life, writing was *hard*. The problem was the teaching. I liked my coworkers and loved the kids—even the Beavis and Butt-Head types in Living with English could be interesting—but by most Friday afternoons I felt as if I'd spent the week with jumper cables clamped to my brain. If I ever came close to despairing about my future as a writer, it was then. I could see myself thirty years on, wearing the same shabby tweed coats with patches on the elbows, potbelly rolling over my Gap khakis from too much beer. I'd have a cigarette cough from too many packs of Pall Malls, thicker glasses, more dandruff, and in my desk drawer, six or seven unfinished manuscripts which I would take out and tinker with from time to time, usually when drunk. If asked what I did in my spare time, I'd tell people I was writing a book—what else does *any* self-respecting creative-writing teacher do with his or her spare time? And of course I'd lie to myself, telling myself there was still time, it wasn't too late, there were novelists who didn't get started until they were fifty, hell, even sixty. Probably plenty of them.

My wife made a crucial difference during those two years I spent teaching at Hampden (and washing sheets at New Franklin Laundry during the summer vacation). If she had suggested that the time I spent writing stories on the front porch of our rented house on Pond Street or in the laundry room of our rented trailer on Klatt Road in Hermon was wasted time, I think a lot of the heart would have gone out of me. Tabby never voiced a single doubt, however. Her support was a constant, one of the few good things I could take as a given. And whenever I see a first novel dedicated to a wife (or a husband), I smile and think, *There's someone who knows.* Writing is a lonely job. Having someone who believes in you makes a lot of difference. They don't have to make speeches. Just believing is usually enough.

– 28 –

While he was going to college my brother Dave worked summers as a janitor at Brunswick High, his old alma mater. For part of one summer I worked there, too. I can't remember which year, only that it was before I met Tabby but after I started to smoke. That would have made me nineteen or twenty, I suppose. I got paired with a guy named Harry, who wore green fatigues, a big keychain, and walked with a limp. (He *did* have hands instead of hooks, however.) One lunch hour Harry told me what it had been like to face a Japanese *banzai* charge on the island of Tarawa, all the Japanese officers waving swords made out of Maxwell House coffee cans, all the screaming enlisted men behind them stoned out of their gourds and smelling of burned poppies. Quite a raconteur was my pal Harry.

One day he and I were supposed to scrub the rust-stains off the walls in the girls' shower. I looked around the locker room with the interest of a Muslim youth who for some reason finds himself deep within the women's quarters. It was the same as the boys' locker room, and yet completely different. There were no urinals, of course, and there were two extra

74

metal boxes on the tile walls—unmarked, and the wrong size for paper towels. I asked what was in them. "Pussy-plugs," Harry said. "For them certain days of the month."

I also noticed that the showers, unlike those in the boys' locker room, had chrome U-rings with pink plastic curtains attached. You could actually shower in privacy. I mentioned this to Harry, and he shrugged. "I guess young girls are a bit more shy about being undressed."

This memory came back to me one day while I was working at the laundry, and I started seeing the opening scene of a story: girls showering in a locker room where there were no U-rings, pink plastic curtains, or privacy. And this one girl starts to have her period. Only she doesn't know what it is, and the other girls—grossed out, horrified, amused—start pelting her with sanitary napkins. Or with tampons, which Harry had called pussy-plugs. The girl begins to scream. All that blood! She thinks she's dying, that the other girls are making fun of her even while she's bleeding to death . . . she reacts . . . fights back . . . but how?

I'd read an article in *Life* magazine some years before, suggesting that at least some reported poltergeist activity might actually be telekinetic phenomena—telekinesis being the ability to move objects just by thinking about them. There was some evidence to suggest that young people might have such powers, the article said, especially girls in early adolescence, right around the time of their first—

Pow! Two unrelated ideas, adolescent cruelty and telekinesis, came together, and I had an idea. I didn't leave my post at Washex #2, didn't go running around the laundry waving my arms and shouting "Eureka!," however. I'd had many other ideas as good and some that were better. Still, I thought I might have the basis for a good *Cavalier* yarn, with the possibility of *Playboy* lurking in the back of my mind. *Playboy* paid up to two thousand dollars for short fiction. Two thousand bucks would buy a new transmission for the Buick with plenty left over for groceries. The story remained on the back burner for awhile, simmering away in that place that's not quite the conscious but not quite the subconscious, either. I had started my teaching career before I sat down one night to give it a shot. I did three single-spaced pages of a first draft, then crumpled them up in disgust and threw them away.

I had four problems with what I'd written. First and least important was the fact that the story didn't move me emotionally. Second and slightly more important was the fact that I didn't much like the lead character. Carrie White seemed thick and passive, a ready-made victim. The other girls were chucking tampons and sanitary napkins at her, chanting "Plug it up! Plug it up!" and I just didn't care. Third and more important still was not feeling at home with either the surroundings or my all-girl cast of supporting characters. I had landed on Planet Female, and one sortie into the girls' locker room at Brunswick High School years before wasn't much help in navigating there. For me writing has always been best when it's intimate, as sexy as skin on skin. With *Carrie* I felt as if I were wearing a rubber wet-suit I couldn't pull off. Fourth and most important of all was the realization that the story wouldn't pay off unless it was pretty long, probably even longer than "Sometimes They Come Back," which had been at the absolute outer limit of what the men's magazine market could accept in terms of word-count. You had to save plenty of room for those pictures of cheerleaders who had somehow forgotten to put on their underpants—they were what guys really bought the magazines for. I couldn't see wasting two weeks, maybe even a month, creating a novella I didn't like and wouldn't be able to sell. So I threw it away.

The next night, when I came home from school, Tabby had the pages. She'd spied them while emptying my wastebasket, had shaken the cigarette ashes off the crumpled balls of paper, smoothed them out, and sat down to read them. She wanted me to go on with it, she said. She wanted to know the rest of the story. I told her I didn't know jackshit about high school girls. She said she'd help me with that part. She had her chin tilted down and was smiling in that severely cute way of hers. "You've got something here," she said. "I really think you do."

– 29 –

I never got to like Carrie White and I never trusted Sue Snell's motives in sending her boyfriend to the prom with her, but I *did* have something there. Like a whole career. Tabby somehow knew it, and by the time I had piled up fifty single-spaced pages, I knew it, too. For one thing, I didn't think any of the characters who went to Carrie White's prom would ever forget it. Those few who lived through it, that was.

I had written three other novels before *Carrie*—*Rage, The Long Walk,* and *The Running Man* were later published. *Rage* is the most troubling of them. *The Long Walk* may be the best of them. But none of them taught me the things I learned from Carrie White. The most important is that the writer's original perception of a character or characters may be as erroneous as the reader's. Running a close second was the realization that stopping a piece of work just because it's hard, either emotionally or imaginatively, is a bad idea. Sometimes you have to go on when you don't feel like it, and sometimes you're doing good work when it feels like all you're managing is to shovel shit from a sitting position.

Tabby helped me, beginning with the information that the sanitary-napkin dispensers in high schools were usually not coin-op—faculty and administration didn't like the idea of girls' walking around with blood all over their skirts just because they happened to come to school short a quarter, my wife said. And I also helped myself, digging back to my memories of high school (my job teaching English didn't help; I was twenty-six by then, and on the wrong side of the desk), remembering what I knew about the two loneliest, most reviled girls in my class—how they looked, how they acted, how they were treated. Very rarely in my career have I explored more distasteful territory.

I'll call one of these girls Sondra. She and her mother lived in a trailer home not too far from me, with their dog, Cheddar Cheese. Sondra had a burbly, uneven voice, as if she were always speaking through a throatful of tightly packed phlegm. She wasn't fat, but her flesh had a loose, pale look, like the undersides of some mushrooms. Her hair clung to her pimply cheeks in tight Little Orphan Annie curls. She had no friends (except for Cheddar Cheese, I guess). One day her mother hired me to move some furniture. Dominating the trailer's living room was a nearly life-sized crucified Jesus, eyes turned up, mouth turned down, blood dribbling from beneath the crown of thorns on his head. He was naked except for a rag twisted around his hips and loins. Above this bit of breechclout were the hollowed belly and the jutting ribs of a concentration-camp inmate. It occurred to me that Sondra had grown up beneath the agonal gaze of this dying god, and doing so had undoubtedly played a part in making her what she was when I knew her: a timid and homely outcast who went scuttling through the halls of Lisbon High like a frightened mouse.

"That's Jesus Christ, my Lord and Savior," Sondra's mother said, following my gaze. "Have *you* been saved, Steve?"

I hastened to tell her I was saved as saved could be, although I didn't think you could ever be good enough to have *that* version of Jesus intervene on your behalf. The pain had driven him out of his mind. You could see it on his face. If *that* guy came back, he probably wouldn't be in a saving mood.

The other girl I'll call Dodie Franklin, only the other girls called her Dodo or Doodoo. Her parents were interested in only one thing, and that was entering contests. They were good at them, too; they had won all sorts of odd stuff, including a year's supply of Three Diamonds Brand Fancy Tuna and Jack Benny's Maxwell automobile. The Maxwell sat off to the left of their house in that part of Durham known as Southwest Bend, gradually sinking into the landscape. Every year or two, one of the local papers—the Portland *Press-Herald,* the Lewiston *Sun,* the Lisbon *Weekly Enterprise*—would do a piece on all the weird shit Dodie's folks had won in raffles and sweepstakes and giant prize drawings. Usually there would be a photo of the Maxwell, or Jack Benny with his violin, or both.

Whatever the Franklins might have won, a supply of clothes for growing teenagers wasn't part of the haul. Dodie and her brother Bill wore the same stuff every day for the first year and a half of high school: black pants and a short-sleeved checked sport shirt for him, a long black skirt, gray knee-socks, and a sleeveless white blouse for her. Some of my readers may not believe I am being literal when I say *every day,* but those who grew up in country towns during the fifties and sixties will know that I am. In the Durham of my childhood, life wore little or any makeup. I went to school with kids who wore the same neckdirt for months, kids whose skin festered with sores and rashes, kids with the eerie dried-apple-doll faces that result from untreated burns, kids who were sent to school with stones in their dinnerbuckets and nothing but air in their Thermoses. It wasn't Arcadia; for the most part it was Dogpatch with no sense of humor.

Dodie and Bill Franklin got on all right at Durham Elementary, but high school meant a much bigger town, and for children like Dodie and Bill, Lisbon Falls meant ridicule and ruin. We watched in amusement and horror as Bill's sport shirt faded and began to unravel from the short sleeves up. He replaced a missing button with a paperclip. Tape, carefully colored black with a crayon to match his pants, appeared over a rip behind one knee. Dodie's sleeveless white blouse began to grow yellow with wear, age, and accumulated sweat-stains. As it grew thinner, the straps of her bra showed through more and more clearly. The other girls made fun of her, at first behind her back and then to her face. Teasing became taunting. The boys weren't a part of it; we had Bill to take care of (yes, I helped—not a whole lot, but I was there). Dodie had it worse, I think. The girls didn't just laugh at Dodie; they hated her, too. Dodie was everything they were afraid of.

After Christmas vacation of our sophomore year, Dodie came back to school resplendent. The dowdy old black skirt had been replaced by a cranberry-colored one that stopped at her knees instead of halfway down her shins. The tatty kneesocks had been replaced by nylon stockings, which looked pretty good because she had finally shaved the luxuriant mat of black hair off her legs. The ancient sleeveless blouse had given way to a soft wool sweater. She'd even had a permanent. Dodie was a girl transformed, and you could see by her face that she knew it. I have no idea if she saved for those new clothes, if they were given to her for Christmas by her parents, or if she went through a hell of begging that finally bore dividends. It doesn't matter, because mere clothes changed nothing. The teasing that day was worse than ever. Her peers had no intention of letting her out of the box they'd put her in; she was punished for even trying to break free. I had several classes with her, and was able to observe Dodie's ruination at first hand. I saw her smile fade, saw the light in her eyes first dim and then go out. By the end of the day she was the girl she'd been before Christmas vacation—a dough-faced and freckle-cheeked wraith, scurrying through the halls with her eyes down and her books clasped to her chest.

She wore the new skirt and sweater the next day. And the next. And the next. When the school year ended she was still wearing them, although by then the weather was much too hot for wool and there were always beads of sweat at her temples and on her upper lip. The home permanent wasn't repeated and the new clothes took on a matted, dispirited look, but the teasing had dropped back to its pre-Christmas levels and the taunting stopped entirely. Someone made a break for the fence and had to be knocked down, that was all. Once the escape was foiled and the entire company of prisoners was once more accounted for, life could go back to normal.

Both Sondra and Dodie were dead by the time I started writing *Carrie*. Sondra moved out of the trailer in Durham, out from beneath the agonal gaze of the dying savior, and into an apartment in Lisbon Falls. She must have worked somewhere close by, probably in one of the mills or shoe factories. She was epileptic and died during a seizure. She lived alone, so there was no one to help her when she went down with her head bent the wrong way. Dodie married a TV weatherman who gained something of a reputation in New England for his drawling downeast delivery. Following the birth of a child— I think it was their second—Dodie went into the cellar and put a .22 bullet in her abdomen. It was a lucky shot (or unlucky, depending on your point of view, I guess), hitting the portal vein and killing her. In town they said it was postpartum depression, how sad. Myself, I suspected high school hangover might have had something to do with it.

I never liked Carrie, that female version of Eric Harris and Dylan Klebold, but through Sondra and Dodie I came at last to understand her a little. I pitied her and I pitied her classmates as well, because I had been one of them once upon a time.

– 30 –

The manuscript of *Carrie* went off to Doubleday, where I had made a friend named William Thompson. I pretty much forgot about it and moved on with my life, which at that time consisted of teaching school, raising kids, loving my wife, getting drunk on Friday afternoons, and writing stories.

My free period that semester was five, right after lunch. I usually spent it in the teachers' room, grading papers and wishing I could stretch out on the couch and take a nap—in the early afternoon I have all the energy of a boa constrictor that's just swallowed a goat. The intercom came on and Colleen Sites in the office asked if I was there. I said I was, and she asked me to come to the office. I had a phone call. My wife.

The walk from the teachers' room in the lower wing to the main office seemed long even with classes in session and the halls mostly empty. I hurried, not quite running, my heart beating hard. Tabby would have had to dress the kids in their boots and jackets to use the neighbors' phone, and I could think of only two reasons she might have done so. Either Joe or Naomi had fallen off the stoop and broken a leg, or I had sold *Carrie*.

My wife, sounding out of breath but deliriously happy, read me a telegram. Bill Thompson (who would later go on to discover a Mississippi scribbler named John Grisham) had sent it after trying to call and discovering the Kings no longer had a phone. CONGRATULATIONS, it read. CARRIE OFFICIALLY A DOUBLEDAY BOOK. IS $2500 ADVANCE OKAY? THE FUTURE LIES AHEAD. LOVE, BILL.

Twenty-five hundred dollars was a very small advance, even for the early seventies, but I didn't know that and had no literary agent to know it for me. Before it occurred to me that I might actually need an agent, I had generated well over three million dollars' worth of income, a good deal of it for the publisher. (The standard Doubleday contract in those days was better than indentured servitude, but not much.) And my little high school horror novel marched toward publication with excruciating slowness. Although it was accepted in late March or early April of 1973, publication wasn't slated until the spring of 1974. This wasn't unusual. In those days Doubleday was an enormous fiction-mill churning out mysteries, romances, science fiction yarns, and Double D westerns at a rate of fifty or more a month, all of this in addition to a robust frontlist including books by heavy hitters like Leon Uris and Allen Drury. I was only one small fish in a very busy river.

Tabby asked if I could quit teaching. I told her no, not based on a twenty-five-hundred-dollar advance and only nebulous possibilities beyond that. If I'd been on my own, maybe (hell, *probably*). But with a wife and two kids? Not happening. I remember the two of us lying in bed that night, eating toast and talking until the small hours of the morning. Tabby asked me how much we'd make if Doubleday was able to sell paperback reprint rights to *Carrie,* and I said I didn't know. I'd read that Mario Puzo had just scored a huge advance for paperback rights to *The Godfather*—four hundred thousand dollars according to the newspaper—but I didn't believe *Carrie* would fetch anything near that, assuming it sold to paperback at all.

Tabby asked—rather timidly for my normally outspoken wife—if *I* thought the book would find a paperback publisher. I told her I thought the chances were pretty good, maybe seven or eight in ten. She asked how much it might bring. I said my best guess would be somewhere between ten and sixty thousand dollars.

"Sixty thousand dollars?" She sounded almost shocked. "Is that much even possible?"

I said it was—not *likely,* perhaps, but *possible.* I also reminded her that my contract specified a fifty-fifty paperback split, which meant that if Ballantine or Dell *did* pay sixty grand, we'd only get thirty. Tabby didn't dignify this with a reply—she didn't have to. Thirty thousand dollars was what I could expect to make in four years of teaching, even with annual salary increases thrown in. It was a lot of money. Probably just pie in the sky, but it was a night for dreaming.

– 31 –

Carrie inched along toward publication. We spent the advance on a new car (a standard shift which Tabby hated and reviled in her most colorful millworker's language) and I signed a teaching contract for the 1973–1974 academic year. I was writing a new novel, a peculiar combination of *Peyton Place* and *Dracula* which I called *Second Coming*. We had moved to a ground-floor apartment back in Bangor, a real pit, but we were in town again, we had a car covered by an actual warranty, and we had a telephone.

To tell you the truth, *Carrie* had fallen off my radar screen almost completely. The kids were a handful, both the ones at school and the ones at home, and I had begun to worry about my mother. She was sixty-one, still working at Pineland Training Center and as funny as ever, but Dave said she didn't feel very well a lot of the time. Her bedside table was covered with prescription painkillers, and he was afraid there might be something seriously wrong with her. "She's always smoked like a chimney, you know," Dave said. He was a great one to talk, since he smoked like a chimney himself (so did I, and how my wife hated the expense and the constant ashy dirt of it), but I knew what he meant. And although I didn't live as close to her as Dave and didn't see her as often, the last time I *had* seen her I could tell she had lost weight.

"What can we do?" I asked. Behind the question was all we knew of our mother, who "kept herself to herself," as she liked to say. The result of that philosophy was a vast gray space where other families have histories; Dave and I knew almost nothing about our father or his family, and little enough about our own mother's past, which included an incredible (to me, at least) eight dead brothers and sisters and her own failed ambition to become a concert pianist (she did play the organ on some of the NBC radio soaps and Sunday church shows during the war, she claimed).

"We can't do anything," Dave replied, "until she asks."

One Sunday not long after that call, I got another one from Bill Thompson at Doubleday. I was alone in the apartment; Tabby had packed the kids off to her mother's for a visit, and I was working on the new book, which I thought of as *Vampires in* Our Town.

"Are you sitting down?" Bill asked.

"No," I said. Our phone hung on the kitchen wall, and I was standing in the doorway between the kitchen and the living room. "Do I need to?"

"You might," he said. "The paperback rights to *Carrie* went to Signet Books for four hundred thousand dollars."

When I was a little kid, Daddy Guy had once said to my mother: "Why don't you shut that kid up, Ruth? When Stephen opens his mouth, all his guts fall out." It was true then, has been true all my life, but on that Mother's Day in May of 1973 I was completely speechless. I stood there in the doorway, casting the same shadow as always, but I couldn't talk. Bill asked if I was still there, kind of laughing as he said it. He knew I was.

I hadn't heard him right. Couldn't have. The idea allowed me to find my voice again, at least. "Did you say it went for forty thousand dollars?"

"Four *hundred thousand* dollars," he said. "Under the rules of the road"—meaning the contract I'd signed—"two hundred K of it's yours. Congratulations, Steve."

I was still standing in the doorway, looking across the living room toward our bedroom and the crib where Joe slept. Our place on Sanford Street rented for ninety dollars a month and this man I'd only met once face-to-face was telling me I'd just won the lottery. The strength ran out of my legs. I didn't fall, exactly, but I kind of whooshed down to a sitting position there in the doorway.

"Are you sure?" I asked Bill.

He said he was. I asked him to say the number again, very slowly and very clearly, so I could be sure I hadn't misunderstood. He said the number was a four followed by five zeros. "After that a decimal point and two more zeros," he added.

We talked for another half an hour, but I don't remember a single word of what we said. When the conversation was over, I tried to call Tabby at her mother's. Her youngest sister, Marcella, said Tab had already left. I walked back and forth through the apartment in my stocking feet, exploding with good news and without an ear to hear it. I was shaking all over. At last I pulled on my shoes and walked downtown. The only store that was open on Bangor's Main Street was LaVerdiere's Drug. I suddenly felt that I had to buy Tabby a Mother's Day present, something wild and extravagant. I tried, but here's one of life's true facts: there's nothing really wild and extravagant for sale at LaVerdiere's. I did the best I could. I got her a hair-dryer.

When I got back home she was in the kitchen, unpacking the baby bags and singing along with the radio. I gave her the hair-dryer. She looked at it as if she'd never seen one before. "What's this for?" she asked.

I took her by the shoulders. I told her about the paperback sale. She didn't appear to understand. I told her again. Tabby looked over my shoulder at our shitty little four-room apartment, just as I had, and began to cry.

– 32 –

I got drunk for the first time in 1966. This was on the senior class trip to Washington. We went on a bus, about forty kids and three chaperones (one of them was Old Cue-Ball, as a matter of fact), and spent the first night in New York, where the drinking age was then eighteen. Thanks to my bad ears and shitty tonsils, I was almost nineteen. Room to spare.

A bunch of us more adventurous boys found a package store around the corner from the hotel. I cast an eye over the shelves, aware that my spending money was far from a fortune. There was too much—too many bottles, too many brands, too many prices over ten dollars. Finally I gave up and asked the guy behind the counter (the same bald, bored-looking, gray-coated guy who has, I'm convinced, sold alcohol virgins their first bottle since the dawn of commerce) what was cheap. Without a word, he put a pint of Old Log Cabin whiskey down on the Winston mat beside the cash register. The sticker on the label said $1.95. The price was right.

I have a memory of being led onto the elevator later that night—or maybe it was early the next morning—by Peter Higgins (Old Cue-Ball's son), Butch Michaud, Lenny Partridge, and John Chizmar. This memory is more like a scene from a TV show than a real memory. I seem to be outside of myself, watching the whole thing. There's just enough of me left inside to know that I am globally, perhaps even galactically, fucked up.

The camera watches as we go up to the girls' floor. The camera watches as I am propelled up and down the hall, a kind of rolling exhibit. An amusing one, it seems. The girls are in nighties, robes, curlers, cold cream. They are all laughing at me, but their laughter seems good-natured enough. The sound is muted, as if I am hearing them through cotton. I am trying to tell Carole Lemke that I love the way she wears her hair, and that she has the most beautiful blue eyes in the world. What comes out is something like "Uggin-wuggin-blue eyes, wuggin-ruggin-whole world." Carole laughs and nods as if she understands completely. I am very happy. The world is seeing an asshole, no doubt, but he is a *happy* asshole, and everyone loves him. I spend several minutes trying to tell Gloria Moore that I've discovered The Secret Life of Dean Martin.

At some point after that I am in my bed. The bed holds still but the room starts to spin around it, faster and faster. It occurs to me that it's spinning like the turntable of my Webcor phonograph, on which I used to play Fats Domino and now play Dylan and the Dave Clark Five. The room is the turntable, I am the spindle, and pretty soon the spindle is going to start tossing its platters.

I go away for a little bit. When I wake up, I'm on my knees in the bathroom of the double room I'm sharing with my friend Louis Purington. I have no idea how I got in there, but it's good that I did because the toilet is full of bright yellow puke. *Looks like Niblets,* I think, and that's all it takes to get me going again. Nothing comes up but whiskey-flavored strings of spit, but my head feels like it's going to explode. I can't walk. I crawl back to bed with my sweaty hair hanging in my eyes. *I'll feel better tomorrow,* I think, and then I go away again.

In the morning my stomach has settled a little but my diaphragm is sore from vomiting and my head is throbbing like a mouthful of infected teeth. My eyes have turned into magnifying glasses; the hideously bright morning light coming in through the hotel windows is being concentrated by them and will soon set my brains on fire.

Participating in that day's scheduled activities—a walk to Times Square, a boat ride to the Statue of Liberty, a climb to the top of the Empire State Building—is out of the question. Walking? Urk. Boats? Double urk. Elevators? Urk to the fourth power. Christ, I can hardly move. I make some sort of feeble excuse and spend most of the day in bed. By late afternoon I'm feeling a little better. I dress, creep down the hall to the elevator, and descend to the first floor. Eating is still impossible, but I believe I'm ready for a ginger ale, a cigarette, and a magazine. And who should I see in the lobby, sitting in a chair and reading a newspaper, but Mr. Earl Higgins, alias Old Cue-Ball. I pass him as silently as I can, but it's no good. When I come back from the gift shop he's sitting with his newspaper in his lap, looking at me. I feel my stomach drop. Here is more trouble with the principal, probably even worse than the trouble I got into over *The Village Vomit*. He calls me over and I discover something interesting: Mr. Higgins is actually an okay guy. He bounced me pretty hard over my joke newspaper, but perhaps Miss Margitan had insisted on that. And I'd just been sixteen, after all. On the day of my first hangover I'm going on nineteen, I've been accepted at the state university, and I have a mill job waiting for me when the class trip is over.

"I understand you were too sick to tour New York with the rest of the boys and girls," Old Cue-Ball says. He eyes me up and down.

I say that's right, I'd been sick.

"A shame for you to miss the fun," Old Cue-Ball says. "Feeling better now?"

Yes, I was feeling better. Probably stomach flu, one of those twenty-four-hour bugs.

"I hope you won't get that bug again," he says. "At least not on this trip." He looks at me for a moment longer, his eyes asking if we understand each other.

"I'm sure I won't," I say, meaning it. I know what drunk is like, now—a vague sense of roaring goodwill, a clearer sense that most of your consciousness is out of your body, hovering like a camera in a science fiction movie and filming everything, and then the sickness, the puking, the aching head. No, I won't get that bug again, I tell myself, not on this trip, not ever. Once is enough, just to find out what it's like. Only an idiot would make a second experiment, and only a lunatic—a *masochistic* lunatic—would make booze a regular part of his life.

The next day we go on to Washington, making one stop in Amish country on the way. There's a liquor store near where the bus parks. I go in and look around. Although the drinking age in Pennsylvania is twenty-one, I must look easily that in my one good suit and Fazza's old black overcoat—in fact, I probably look like a freshly released young convict, tall and hungry and very likely not bolted together right. The clerk sells me a fifth of Four Roses without asking to see any ID, and by the time we stop for the night I'm drunk again.

Ten years or so later I'm in an Irish saloon with Bill Thompson. We have lots to celebrate, not the least of which is the completion of my third book, *The Shining*. That's the one which just happens to be about an alcoholic writer and ex-schoolteacher. It's July, the night of the All-Star baseball game. Our plan is to eat a good old-fashioned meal from the dishes set out on the steam table, then get shitfaced. We begin with a couple at the bar, and I start reading all the signs. HAVE A MANHATTAN IN MANHATTAN, says one. TUESDAYS ARE TWOFORS, says another. WORK IS THE CURSE OF THE DRINKING CLASS, says a third. And there, right in front of me, is one which reads: EARLY BIRD SPECIAL! SCREWDRIVERS A BUCK MONDAY–FRIDAY 8–10 A.M.

I motion to the bartender. He comes over. He's bald, he's wearing a gray jacket, he could be the guy who sold me my first pint back in 1966. Probably he is. I point to the sign and ask, "Who comes in at eight-fifteen in the morning and orders a screwdriver?"

I'm smiling but he doesn't smile back. "College boys," he replies. "Just like you."

– 33 –

In 1971 or '72, Mom's sister Carolyn Weimer died of breast cancer. My mother and my Aunt Ethelyn (Carolyn's twin) flew out to Aunt Cal's funeral in Minnesota. It was the first time my mother had flown in twenty years. On the plane trip back, she began to bleed profusely from what she would have called "her privates." Although long past her change of life by that point, she told herself it was simply one final menstrual period. Locked in the tiny bathroom of a bouncing TWA jet, she stanched the bleeding with tampons (*plug it up, plug it up,* as Sue Snell and her friends might have cried), then returned to her seat. She said nothing to Ethelyn and nothing to David and me. She didn't go to see Joe Mendes in Lisbon Falls, her physician since time out of mind. Instead of any of those things, she did what she always did in times of trouble: kept herself to herself. For awhile, things seemed to be all right. She enjoyed her job, she enjoyed her friends, and she enjoyed her four grandchildren, two from Dave's family and two from mine. Then things stopped being all right. In August of 1973, during a checkup following an operation to "strip" some of her outrageously varicose veins, my mother was diagnosed with uterine cancer. I think Nellie Ruth Pillsbury King, who once dumped a bowl of Jell-O on the floor and then danced in it while her two boys lay collapsed in the corner, screaming with laughter, actually died of embarrassment.

The end came in February of 1974. By then a little of the money from *Carrie* had begun to flow and I was able to help with some of the medical expenses—there was that much to be glad about. And I was there for the last of it, staying in the back bedroom of Dave and Linda's place. I'd been drunk the night before but was only moderately hungover, which was good. One wouldn't want to be too hungover at the deathbed of one's mother.

Dave woke me at 6:15 in the morning, calling softly through the door that he thought she was going. When I got into the master bedroom he was sitting beside her on the bed and holding a Kool for her to smoke. This she did between harsh gasps for breath. She was only semiconscious, her eyes going from Dave to me and then back to Dave again. I sat next to Dave, took the cigarette, and held it to her mouth. Her lips stretched out to clamp on the filter. Beside her bed, reflected over and over again in a cluster of glasses, was an early bound galley of *Carrie*. Aunt Ethelyn had read it to her aloud a month or so before she died.

Mom's eyes went from Dave to me, Dave to me, Dave to me. She had gone from one hundred and sixty pounds to about ninety. Her skin was yellow and so tightly stretched that she looked like one of those mummies they parade through the streets of Mexico on the Day of the Dead. We took turns holding the cigarette for her, and when it was down to the filter, I put it out.

"My boys," she said, then lapsed into what might have been sleep or unconsciousness. My head ached. I took a couple of aspirin from one of the many bottles of medicine on her table. Dave held one of her hands and I held the other. Under the sheet was not the body of our mother but that of a starved and deformed child. Dave and I smoked and talked a little. I don't remember what we said. It had rained the night before, then the temperature had dropped and the morning streets were filled with ice. We could hear the pause after each rasping breath she drew growing longer and longer. Finally there were no more breaths and it was all pause.

– 34 –

My mother was buried out of the Congregational Church at Southwest Bend; the church she'd attended in Methodist Corners, where my brother and I grew up, was closed because of the cold. I gave the eulogy. I think I did a pretty good job, considering how drunk I was.

– 35 –

Alcoholics build defenses like the Dutch build dikes. I spent the first twelve years or so of my married life assuring myself that I "just liked to drink." I also employed the world-famous Hemingway Defense. Although never clearly articulated (it would not be manly to do so), the Hemingway Defense goes something like this: as a writer, I am a very sensitive fellow, but I am also a man, and real men don't give in to their sensitivities. Only *sissy*-men do that. Therefore I drink. How else can I face the existential horror of it all and continue to work? Besides, come on, I can handle it. A real man always can.

Then, in the early eighties, Maine's legislature enacted a returnable-bottle and -can law. Instead of going into the trash, my sixteen-ounce cans of Miller Lite started going into a plastic container in the garage. One Thursday night I went out there to toss in a few dead soldiers and saw that this container, which had been empty on Monday night, was now almost full. And since I was the only one in the house who drank Miller Lite—

Holy shit, I'm an alcoholic, I thought, and there was no dissenting opinion from inside my head—I was, after all, the guy who had written *The Shining* without even realizing (at least until that night) that I was writing about myself. My reaction to this idea wasn't denial or disagreement; it was what I'd call frightened determination. *You have to be careful, then,* I clearly remember thinking. *Because if you fuck up—*

If I fucked up, rolled my car over on a back road some night or blew an interview on live TV, someone would tell me I ought to get control of my drinking, and telling an alcoholic to control his drinking is like telling a guy suffering the world's most cataclysmic case of diarrhea to control his shitting. A friend of mine who has been through this tells an amusing story about his first tentative effort to get a grip on his increasingly slippery life. He went to a counsellor and said his wife was worried that he was drinking too much.

"How much do you drink?" the counsellor asked.

My friend looked at the counsellor with disbelief. "All of it," he said, as if that should have been self-evident.

I know how he felt. It's been almost twelve years since I took a drink, and I'm still struck by disbelief when I see someone in a restaurant with a half-finished glass of wine near at hand. I want to get up, go over, and yell "Finish that! Why don't you finish that?" into his or her face. I found the idea of social drinking ludicrous—if you didn't want to get drunk, why not just have a Coke?

My nights during the last five years of my drinking always ended with the same ritual: I'd pour any beers left in the refrigerator down the sink. If I didn't, they'd talk to me as I lay in bed until I got up and had another. And another. And one more.

– 36 –

By 1985 I had added drug addiction to my alcohol problem, yet I continued to function, as a good many substance abusers do, on a marginally competent level. I was terrified not to; by then I had no idea of how to live any other life. I hid the drugs I was taking as well as I could, both out of terror—what would happen to me without dope? I had forgotten the trick of being straight—and out of shame. I was wiping my ass with poison ivy again, this time on a daily basis, but I couldn't ask for help. That's not the way you did things in my family. In my family what you did was smoke your cigarettes and dance in the Jell-O and keep yourself to yourself.

Yet the part of me that writes the stories, the deep part that knew I was an alcoholic as early as 1975, when I wrote *The Shining,* wouldn't accept that. Silence isn't what that part is about. It began to scream for help in the only way it knew how, through my fiction and through my monsters. In late 1985 and early 1986 I wrote *Misery* (the title quite aptly described my state of mind), in which a writer is held prisoner and tortured by a psychotic nurse. In the spring and summer of 1986 I wrote *The Tommyknockers,* often working until midnight with my heart running at a hundred and thirty beats a minute and cotton swabs stuck up my nose to stem the coke-induced bleeding.

Tommyknockers is a forties-style science fiction tale in which the writer-heroine discovers an alien spacecraft buried in the

ground. The crew is still on board, not dead but only hiber-
nating. These alien creatures got into your head and just
started . . . well, tommyknocking around in there. What
you got was energy and a kind of superficial intelligence (the
writer, Bobbi Anderson, creates a telepathic typewriter and an
atomic hot-water heater, among other things). What you
gave up in exchange was your soul. It was the best metaphor
for drugs and alcohol my tired, overstressed mind could come
up with.

Not long after that my wife, finally convinced that I
wasn't going to pull out of this ugly downward spiral on my
own, stepped in. It couldn't have been easy—by then I was no
longer within shouting distance of my right mind—but she
did it. She organized an intervention group formed of family
and friends, and I was treated to a kind of *This Is Your Life* in
hell. Tabby began by dumping a trashbag full of stuff from
my office out on the rug: beercans, cigarette butts, cocaine in
gram bottles and cocaine in plastic Baggies, coke spoons
caked with snot and blood, Valium, Xanax, bottles of Robi-
tussin cough syrup and NyQuil cold medicine, even bottles of
mouthwash. A year or so before, observing the rapidity with
which huge bottles of Listerine were disappearing from the
bathroom, Tabby asked me if I drank the stuff. I responded
with self-righteous hauteur that I most certainly did not.
Nor did I. I drank the Scope instead. It was tastier, had that
hint of mint.

The point of this intervention, which was certainly as
unpleasant for my wife and kids and friends as it was for me,
was that I was dying in front of them. Tabby said I had my
choice: I could get help at a rehab or I could get the hell out
of the house. She said that she and the kids loved me, and for
that very reason none of them wanted to witness my suicide.

I bargained, because that's what addicts do. I was charming, because that's what addicts are. In the end I got two weeks to think about it. In retrospect, this seems to summarize all the insanity of that time. Guy is standing on top of a burning building. Helicopter arrives, hovers, drops a rope ladder. *Climb up!* the man leaning out of the helicopter's door shouts. Guy on top of the burning building responds, *Give me two weeks to think about it.*

I did think, though—as well as I could in my addled state—and what finally decided me was Annie Wilkes, the psycho nurse in *Misery.* Annie was coke, Annie was booze, and I decided I was tired of being Annie's pet writer. I was afraid that I wouldn't be able to work anymore if I quit drinking and drugging, but I decided (again, so far as I was able to decide anything in my distraught and depressed state of mind) that I would trade writing for staying married and watching the kids grow up. If it came to that.

It didn't, of course. The idea that creative endeavor and mind-altering substances are entwined is one of the great pop-intellectual myths of our time. The four twentieth-century writers whose work is most responsible for it are probably Hemingway, Fitzgerald, Sherwood Anderson, and the poet Dylan Thomas. They are the writers who largely formed our vision of an existential English-speaking wasteland where people have been cut off from one another and live in an atmosphere of emotional strangulation and despair. These concepts are very familiar to most alcoholics; the common reaction to them is amusement. Substance-abusing writers are just substance abusers—common garden-variety drunks and druggies, in other words. Any claims that the drugs and alcohol are necessary to dull a finer sensibility are just the usual self-serving bullshit. I've heard alcoholic snowplow drivers make the same claim, that they drink to still the demons. It doesn't matter if you're James Jones, John Cheever, or a stewbum snoozing in Penn Station; for an addict, the right to the drink or drug of choice must be preserved at all costs. Hemingway and Fitzgerald didn't drink because they were creative, alienated, or morally weak. They drank because it's what alkies are wired up to do. Creative people probably *do* run a greater risk of alcoholism and addiction than those in some other jobs, but so what? We all look pretty much the same when we're puking in the gutter.

– 37 –

At the end of my adventures I was drinking a case of sixteen-ounce tallboys a night, and there's one novel, *Cujo,* that I barely remember writing at all. I don't say that with pride or shame, only with a vague sense of sorrow and loss. I like that book. I wish I could remember enjoying the good parts as I put them down on the page.

At the worst of it I no longer wanted to drink and no longer wanted to be sober, either. I felt evicted from life. At the start of the road back I just tried to believe the people who said that things would get better if I gave them time to do so. And I never stopped writing. Some of the stuff that came out was tentative and flat, but at least it was there. I buried those unhappy, lackluster pages in the bottom drawer of my desk and got on to the next project. Little by little I found the beat again, and after that I found the joy again. I came back to my family with gratitude, and back to my work with relief—I came back to it the way folks come back to a summer cottage after a long winter, checking first to make sure nothing has been stolen or broken during the cold season. Nothing had been. It was still all there, still all whole. Once the pipes were thawed out and the electricity was turned back on, everything worked fine.

– 38 –

The last thing I want to tell you in this part is about my desk. For years I dreamed of having the sort of massive oak slab that would dominate a room—no more child's desk in a trailer laundry-closet, no more cramped kneehole in a rented house. In 1981 I got the one I wanted and placed it in the middle of a spacious, skylighted study (it's a converted stable loft at the rear of the house). For six years I sat behind that desk either drunk or wrecked out of my mind, like a ship's captain in charge of a voyage to nowhere.

A year or two after I sobered up, I got rid of that monstrosity and put in a living-room suite where it had been, picking out the pieces and a nice Turkish rug with my wife's help. In the early nineties, before they moved on to their own lives, my kids sometimes came up in the evening to watch a basketball game or a movie and eat pizza. They usually left a boxful of crusts behind when they moved on, but I didn't care. They came, they seemed to enjoy being with me, and I know I enjoyed being with them. I got another desk—it's handmade, beautiful, and half the size of the *T. rex* desk. I put it at the far west end of the office, in a corner under the eave. That eave is very like the one I slept under in Durham, but there are no rats in the walls and no senile grandmother downstairs yelling for someone to feed Dick the horse. I'm sitting under it now, a fifty-three-year-old man with bad eyes, a gimp leg, and no hangover. I'm doing what I know how to do, and as well as I know how to do it. I came through all the stuff I told you about (and plenty more that I didn't), and now I'm going to tell you as much as I can about the job. As promised, it won't take long.

It starts with this: put your desk in the corner, and every time you sit down there to write, remind yourself why it isn't in the middle of the room. Life isn't a support-system for art. It's the other way around.

What Writing Is

Telepathy, of course. It's amusing when you stop to think about it—for years people have argued about whether or not such a thing exists, folks like J. B. Rhine have busted their brains trying to create a valid testing process to isolate it, and all the time it's been right there, lying out in the open like Mr. Poe's Purloined Letter. All the arts depend upon telepathy to some degree, but I believe that writing offers the purest distillation. Perhaps I'm prejudiced, but even if I am we may as well stick with writing, since it's what we came here to think and talk about.

My name is Stephen King. I'm writing the first draft of this part at my desk (the one under the eave) on a snowy morning in December of 1997. There are things on my mind. Some are worries (bad eyes, Christmas shopping not even started, wife under the weather with a virus), some are good things (our younger son made a surprise visit home from college, I got to play Vince Taylor's "Brand New Cadillac" with The Wallflowers at a concert), but right now all that stuff is up top. I'm in another place, a basement place where there are lots of bright lights and clear images. This is a place I've built for myself over the years. It's a far-seeing place. I know it's a little strange, a little bit of a contradiction, that a far-seeing place should also be a basement place, but that's how it is with me. If you construct your own far-seeing place, you might put it in a treetop or on the roof of the World Trade Center or on the edge of the Grand Canyon. That's your little red wagon, as Robert McCammon says in one of his novels.

This book is scheduled to be published in the late summer or early fall of 2000. If that's how things work out, then you are somewhere downstream on the timeline from me . . . but you're quite likely in your own far-seeing place, the one where you go to receive telepathic messages. Not that you *have* to be there; books are a uniquely portable magic. I usually listen to one in the car (always unabridged; I think abridged audiobooks are the pits), and carry another wherever I go. You just never know when you'll want an escape hatch: mile-long lines at tollbooth plazas, the fifteen minutes you have to spend in the hall of some boring college building waiting for your advisor (who's got some yank-off in there threatening to commit suicide because he/she is flunking Custom Kurm-furling 101) to come out so you can get his signature on a drop-card, airport boarding lounges, laundromats on rainy afternoons, and the absolute worst, which is the doctor's office when the guy is running late and you have to wait half an hour in order to have something sensitive mauled. At such times I find a book vital. If I have to spend time in purgatory before going to one place or the other, I guess I'll be all right as long as there's a lending library (if there is it's probably stocked with nothing but novels by Danielle Steel and *Chicken Soup* books, ha-ha, joke's on you, Steve).

So I read where I can, but I have a favorite place and probably you do, too—a place where the light is good and the vibe is usually strong. For me it's the blue chair in my study. For you it might be the couch on the sunporch, the rocker in the kitchen, or maybe it's propped up in your bed—reading in bed can be heaven, assuming you can get just the right amount of light on the page and aren't prone to spilling your coffee or cognac on the sheets.

So let's assume that you're in your favorite receiving place just as I am in the place where I do my best transmitting. We'll have to perform our mentalist routine not just over distance but over time as well, yet that presents no real problem; if we can still read Dickens, Shakespeare, and (with the help of a footnote or two) Herodotus, I think we can manage the gap between 1997 and 2000. And here we go—actual telepathy in action. You'll notice I have nothing up my sleeves and that my lips never move. Neither, most likely, do yours.

Look—here's a table covered with a red cloth. On it is a cage the size of a small fish aquarium. In the cage is a white rabbit with a pink nose and pink-rimmed eyes. In its front paws is a carrot-stub upon which it is contentedly munching. On its back, clearly marked in blue ink, is the numeral 8.

Do we see the same thing? We'd have to get together and compare notes to make absolutely sure, but I think we do. There will be necessary variations, of course: some receivers will see a cloth which is turkey red, some will see one that's scarlet, while others may see still other shades. (To color-blind receivers, the red tablecloth is the dark gray of cigar ashes.) Some may see scalloped edges, some may see straight ones. Decorative souls may add a little lace, and welcome— my tablecloth is your tablecloth, knock yourself out.

Likewise, the matter of the cage leaves quite a lot of room for individual interpretation. For one thing, it is described in terms of *rough comparison,* which is useful only if you and I see the world and measure the things in it with similar eyes. It's easy to become careless when making rough comparisons, but the alternative is a prissy attention to detail that takes all the fun out of writing. What am I going to say, "on the table is a cage three feet, six inches in length, two feet in width, and fourteen inches high"? That's not prose, that's an instruction manual. The paragraph also doesn't tell us what sort of material the cage is made of—wire mesh? steel rods? glass?—but does it really matter? We all understand the cage is a see-through medium; beyond that, we don't care. The most interesting thing here isn't even the carrot-munching rabbit in the cage, but the number on its back. Not a six, not a four, not nineteen-point-five. It's an eight. This is what we're looking at, and we all see it. I didn't tell you. You didn't ask me. I never opened my mouth and you never opened yours. We're not even in the same *year* together, let alone the same room . . . except we *are* together. We're close.

We're having a meeting of the minds.

I sent you a table with a red cloth on it, a cage, a rabbit, and the number eight in blue ink. You got them all, especially that blue eight. We've engaged in an act of telepathy. No mythy-mountain shit; real telepathy. I'm not going to belabor the point, but before we go any further you have to understand that I'm not trying to be cute; there *is* a point to be made.

You can approach the act of writing with nervousness, excitement, hopefulness, or even despair—the sense that you can never completely put on the page what's in your mind and heart. You can come to the act with your fists clenched and your eyes narrowed, ready to kick ass and take down names. You can come to it because you want a girl to marry you or because you want to change the world. Come to it any way but lightly. Let me say it again: *you must not come lightly to the blank page.*

I'm not asking you to come reverently or unquestioningly; I'm not asking you to be politically correct or cast aside your sense of humor (please God you have one). This isn't a popularity contest, it's not the moral Olympics, and it's not church. But it's *writing,* damn it, not washing the car or putting on eyeliner. If you can take it seriously, we can do business. If you can't or won't, it's time for you to close the book and do something else.

Wash the car, maybe.

TOOLBOX

Grandpa was a carpenter,
he built houses, stores and banks,
he chain-smoked Camel cigarettes
and hammered nails in planks.
He was level-on-the-level,
shaved even every door,
and voted for Eisenhower
'cause Lincoln won the war.

That's one of my favorite John Prine lyrics, probably because my grandpa was also a carpenter. I don't know about stores and banks, but Guy Pillsbury built his share of houses and spent a good many years making sure the Atlantic Ocean and the harsh seacoast winters didn't wash away the Winslow Homer estate in Prout's Neck. Fazza smoked cigars, though, not Camels. It was my Uncle Oren, also a carpenter, who smoked the Camels. And when Fazza retired, it was Uncle Oren who inherited the old fellow's toolbox. I don't remember its being there in the garage on the day I dropped the cinderblock on my foot, but it probably was sitting in its accustomed place just outside the nook where my cousin Donald kept his hockey sticks, ice skates, and baseball glove.

The toolbox was what we called a big 'un. It had three levels, the top two removable, all three containing little drawers as cunning as Chinese boxes. It was handmade, of course. Dark wooden slats were bound together by tiny nails and strips of brass. The lid was held down by big latches; to my child's eye they looked like the latches on a giant's lunchbox. Inside the top was a silk lining, rather odd in such a context and made more striking still by the pattern, which was pinkish-red cabbage roses fading into a smog of grease and dirt. On the sides were great big grabhandles. You never saw a toolbox like this one for sale at Wal-Mart or Western Auto, believe me. When my uncle first got it, he found a brass etching of a famous Homer painting—I believe it was *The Undertow*—lying in the bottom. Some years later Uncle Oren had it authenticated by a Homer expert in New York, and a few years after that I believe he sold it for a good piece of money. Exactly how or why Fazza came by the engraving in the first place is a mystery, but there was no mystery about the origins of the toolbox—he made it himself.

One summer day I helped Uncle Oren replace a broken screen on the far side of the house. I might have been eight or nine at the time. I remember following him with the replacement screen balanced on my head, like a native bearer in a Tarzan movie. He had the toolbox by the grabhandles, horsing it along at thigh level. As always, Uncle Oren was wearing khaki pants and a clean white tee-shirt. Sweat gleamed in his graying Army crewcut. A Camel hung from his lower lip. (When I came in years later with a pack of Chesterfields in my breast pocket, Uncle Oren sneered at them and called them "stockade cigarettes.")

We finally reached the window with the broken screen and he set the toolbox down with an audible sigh of relief.

When Dave and I tried to lift it from its place on the garage floor, each of us holding one of the handles, we could barely budge it. Of course we were just little kids back then, but even so I'd guess that Fazza's fully loaded toolbox weighed between eighty and a hundred and twenty pounds.

Uncle Oren let me undo the big latches. The common tools were all on the top layer of the box. There was a hammer, a saw, the pliers, a couple of sized wrenches and an adjustable; there was a level with that mystic yellow window in the middle, a drill (the various bits were neatly drawered farther down in the depths), and two screwdrivers. Uncle Oren asked me for a screwdriver.

"Which one?" I asked.

"Either-or," he replied.

The broken screen was held on by loophead screws, and it really didn't matter whether he used a regular screwdriver or the Phillips on them; with loopheads you just stuck the screwdriver's barrel through the hole at the top of the screw and then spun it the way you spin a tire iron once you've got the lugnuts loose.

Uncle Oren took the screws out—there were eight, which he handed to me for safekeeping—and then removed the old screen. He set it against the house and held up the new one. The holes in the screen's frame mated up neatly with the holes in the window-frame. Uncle Oren grunted with approval when he saw this. He took the loophead screws back from me, one after the other, got them started with his fingers, then tightened them down just as he'd loosened them, by inserting the screwdriver's barrel through the loops and turning them.

When the screen was secure, Uncle Oren gave me the screwdriver and told me to put it back in the toolbox and "latch her up." I did, but I was puzzled. I asked him why he'd lugged Fazza's toolbox all the way around the house, if all he'd needed was that one screwdriver. He could have carried a screwdriver in the back pocket of his khakis.

"Yeah, but Stevie," he said, bending to grasp the handles, "I didn't know what else I might find to do once I got out here, did I? It's best to have your tools with you. If you don't, you're apt to find something you didn't expect and get discouraged."

I want to suggest that to write to your best abilities, it behooves you to construct your own toolbox and then build up enough muscle so you can carry it with you. Then, instead of looking at a hard job and getting discouraged, you will perhaps seize the correct tool and get immediately to work.

Fazza's toolbox had three levels. I think that yours should have at least four. You could have five or six, I suppose, but there comes a point where a toolbox becomes too large to be portable and thus loses its chief virtue. You'll also want all those little drawers for your screws and nuts and bolts, but where you put those drawers and what you put in them . . . well, that's your little red wagon, isn't it? You'll find you have most of the tools you need already, but I advise you to look at each one again as you load it into your box. Try to see each one new, remind yourself of its function, and if some are rusty (as they may be if you haven't done this seriously in awhile), clean them off.

Common tools go on top. The commonest of all, the bread of writing, is vocabulary. In this case, you can happily pack what you have without the slightest bit of guilt and inferiority. As the whore said to the bashful sailor, "It ain't how much you've got, honey, it's how you use it."

Some writers have enormous vocabularies; these are folks

who'd know if there really *is* such a thing as an insalubrious dithyramb or a cozening raconteur, people who haven't missed a multiple-choice answer in Wilfred Funk's *It Pays to Increase Your Word Power* in oh, thirty years or so. For example:

> The leathery, undeteriorative, and almost indestructible quality was an inherent attribute of the thing's form of organization, and pertained to some paleogean cycle of invertebrate evolution utterly beyond our powers of speculation.
>
> —H. P. Lovecraft, *At the Mountains of Madness*

Like it? Here's another:

> In some [of the cups] there was no evidence whatever that anything had been planted; in others, wilted brown stalks gave testimony to some inscrutable depredation.
>
> —T. Coraghessan Boyle, *Budding Prospects*

And yet a third—this is a good one, you'll like it:

> Someone snatched the old woman's blindfold from her and she and the juggler were clouted away and when the company turned in to sleep and the low fire was roaring in the blast like a thing alive these four yet crouched at the edge of the firelight among their strange chattels and watched how the ragged flames fled down the wind as if sucked by some maelstrom out there in the void, some vortex in that waste apposite to which man's transit and his reckonings alike lay abrogate.
>
> —Cormac McCarthy, *Blood Meridian*

Other writers use smaller, simpler vocabularies. Examples of this hardly seem necessary, but I'll offer a couple of my favorites, just the same:

He came to the river. The river was there.
—Ernest Hemingway, "Big Two-Hearted River"

They caught the kid doing something nasty under the bleachers.
—Theodore Sturgeon, *Some of Your Blood*

This is what happened.
—Douglas Fairbairn, *Shoot*

Some of the owner men were kind because they hated what they had to do, and some of them were angry because they hated to be cruel, and some of them were cold because they had long ago found that one could not be an owner unless one were cold.
—John Steinbeck, *The Grapes of Wrath*

The Steinbeck sentence is especially interesting. It's fifty words long. Of those fifty words, thirty-nine have but one syllable. That leaves eleven, but even that number is deceptive; Steinbeck uses **because** three times, **owner** twice, and **hated** twice. There is no word longer than two syllables in the entire sentence. The structure is complex; the vocabulary is not far removed from the old Dick and Jane primers. *The Grapes of Wrath* is, of course, a fine novel. I believe that *Blood Meridian* is another, although there are great whacks of it that I don't fully understand. What of that? I can't decipher the words to many of the popular songs I love, either.

There's also stuff you'll never find in the dictionary, but it's still vocabulary. Check out the following:

> "Egggh, whaddaya? Whaddaya want from me?"
> "Here come Hymie!"
> "Unnh! Unnnh! Unnnhh!"
> "Chew my willie, Yo' Honor."
> "Yeggghhh, fuck you, too, man!"
> —Tom Wolfe, *Bonfire of the Vanities*

This last is phonetically rendered street vocabulary. Few writers have Wolfe's ability to translate such stuff to the page. (Elmore Leonard is another writer who can do it.) Some street-rap gets into the dictionary eventually, but not until it's safely dead. And I don't think you'll ever find **Yeggghhh** in Webster's Unabridged.

Put your vocabulary on the top shelf of your toolbox, and don't make any conscious effort to improve it. (You'll be doing that as you read, of course . . . but that comes later.) One of the really bad things you can do to your writing is to dress up the vocabulary, looking for long words because you're maybe a little bit ashamed of your short ones. This is like dressing up a household pet in evening clothes. The pet is embarrassed and the person who committed this act of premeditated cuteness should be even more embarrassed. Make yourself a solemn promise right now that you'll never use "emolument" when you mean "tip" and you'll never say **John stopped long enough to perform an act of excretion** when you mean **John stopped long enough to take a shit.** If you believe "take a shit" would be considered offensive or inappropriate by your audience, feel free to say **John stopped long enough to move his bowels** (or perhaps **John stopped** long enough to "push"). I'm not trying to get you to talk dirty, only plain and direct. Remember that the basic rule of vocabulary is *use the first word that comes to your mind, if it is appropriate and colorful.* If you hesitate and cogitate, you will come up with another word—of course you will, there's always another word—but it probably won't be as good as your first one, or as close to what you really mean.

This business of meaning is a very big deal. If you doubt it, think of all the times you've heard someone say "I just can't describe it" or "That isn't what I mean." Think of all the times you've said those things yourself, usually in a tone of mild or serious frustration. The word is only a representation of the meaning; even at its best, writing almost always falls short of full meaning. Given that, why in God's name would you want to make things worse by choosing a word which is only cousin to the one you really wanted to use?

And *do* feel free to take appropriateness into account; as George Carlin once observed, in some company it's perfectly all right to prick your finger, but very bad form to finger your prick.

– 2 –

You'll also want grammar on the top shelf of your toolbox, and don't annoy me with your moans of exasperation or your cries that you *don't understand* grammar, you *never did understand* grammar, you flunked that *whole semester* in Sophomore English, writing is fun but grammar sucks the big one.

Relax. Chill. We won't spend much time here because we don't need to. One either absorbs the grammatical principles of one's native language in conversation and in reading or one does not. What Sophomore English does (or tries to do) is little more than the naming of parts.

And this isn't high school. Now that you're not worried that (a) your skirt is too short or too long and the other kids will laugh at you, (b) you're not going to make the varsity swimming team, (c) you're still going to be a pimple-studded virgin when you graduate (probably when you die, for that matter), (d) the physics teacher won't grade the final on a curve, or (e) nobody really likes you anyway AND THEY NEVER DID . . . now that all that extraneous shit is out of the way, you can study certain academic matters with a degree of concentration you could never manage while attending the local textbook loonybin. And once you start, you'll find you know almost all of the stuff anyway—it is, as I said, mostly a matter of cleaning the rust off the drillbits and sharpening the blade of your saw.

Plus . . . oh, to hell with it. If you can remember all the accessories that go with your best outfit, the contents of your purse, the starting lineup of the New York Yankees or the Houston Oilers, or what label "Hang On Sloopy" by The McCoys was on, you are capable of remembering the difference between a gerund (verb form used as a noun) and a participle (verb form used as an adjective).

I thought long and hard about whether or not to include a detailed section on grammar in this little book. Part of me would actually like to; I taught it successfully at high school (where it hid under the name Business English), and I enjoyed it as a student. American grammar doesn't have the sturdiness of British grammar (a British advertising man with a proper education can make magazine copy for ribbed condoms sound like the Magna goddam Carta), but it has its own scruffy charm.

In the end I decided against it, probably for the same reason William Strunk decided not to recap the basics when he wrote the first edition of *The Elements of Style:* if you don't know, it's too late. And those really incapable of grasping grammar—as I am incapable of playing certain guitar riffs and progressions—will have little or no use for a book like this, anyway. In that sense I am preaching to the converted. Yet allow me to go on just a little bit further—will you indulge me?

Vocabulary used in speech or writing organizes itself in seven parts of speech (eight, if you count interjections such as **Oh!** and **Gosh!** and **Fuhgeddaboudit!**). Communication composed of these parts of speech must be organized by rules of grammar upon which we agree. When these rules break down, confusion and misunderstanding result. Bad grammar produces bad sentences. My favorite example from Strunk and White is this one: **"As a mother of five, with another one on the way, my ironing board is always up."**

Nouns and verbs are the two indispensable parts of writing. Without one of each, no group of words can be a sentence, since a sentence is, by definition, a group of words containing a subject (noun) and a predicate (verb); these strings of words begin with a capital letter, end with a period, and combine to make a complete thought which starts in the writer's head and then leaps to the reader's.

Must you write complete sentences each time, every time? Perish the thought. If your work consists only of fragments and floating clauses, the Grammar Police aren't going to come and take you away. Even William Strunk, that Mussolini of rhetoric, recognized the delicious pliability of language. "It is an old observation," he writes, "that the best writers sometimes disregard the rules of rhetoric." Yet he goes on to add this thought, which I urge you to consider:

"Unless he is certain of doing well, [the writer] will probably do best to follow the rules."

The telling clause here is *Unless he is certain of doing well*. If you don't have a rudimentary grasp of how the parts of speech translate into coherent sentences, how can you be certain that you *are* doing well? How will you know if you're doing ill, for that matter? The answer, of course, is that you can't, you won't. One who does grasp the rudiments of grammar finds a comforting simplicity at its heart, where there need be only nouns, the words that name, and verbs, the words that act.

Take any noun, put it with any verb, and you have a sentence. It never fails. **Rocks explode. Jane transmits. Mountains float.** These are all perfect sentences. Many such thoughts make little rational sense, but even the stranger ones (**Plums deify!**) have a kind of poetic weight that's nice. The simplicity of noun-verb construction is useful—at the very least it can provide a safety net for your writing. Strunk and White caution against too many simple sentences in a row, but simple sentences provide a path you can follow when you fear getting lost in the tangles of rhetoric—all those restrictive and nonrestrictive clauses, those modifying phrases, those appositives and compound-complex sentences. If you start to freak out at the sight of such unmapped territory (unmapped by you, at least), just remind yourself that rocks explode, Jane transmits, mountains float, and plums deify. Grammar is not just a pain in the ass; it's the pole you grab to get your thoughts up on their feet and walking. Besides, all those simple sentences worked for Hemingway, didn't they? Even when he was drunk on his ass, he was a fucking genius.

If you want to refurbish your grammar, go to your local used-book store and find a copy of *Warriner's English Grammar and Composition*—the same book most of us took home and dutifully covered with brown paper shopping-bags when we were sophomores and juniors in high school. You'll be relieved and delighted, I think, to find that almost all you need is summarized on the front and back endpapers of the book.

– 3 –

Despite the brevity of his style manual, William Strunk found room to discuss his own dislikes in matters of grammar and usage. He hated the phrase "student body," for instance, insisting that "studentry" was both clearer and without the ghoulish connotations he saw in the former term. He thought "personalize" a pretentious word. (Strunk suggests "Get up a letterhead" to replace "Personalize your stationery.") He hated phrases such as "the fact that" and "along these lines."

I have my own dislikes—I believe that anyone using the phrase "That's so cool" should have to stand in the corner and that those using the far more odious phrases "at this point in time" and "at the end of the day" should be sent to bed without supper (or writing-paper, for that matter). Two of my other pet peeves have to do with this most basic level of writing, and I want to get them off my chest before we move along.

Verbs come in two types, active and passive. With an active verb, the subject of the sentence is doing something. With a passive verb, something is being done *to* the subject of the sentence. The subject is just letting it happen. *You should avoid the passive tense.* I'm not the only one who says so; you can find the same advice in *The Elements of Style.*

Messrs. Strunk and White don't speculate as to why so

many writers are attracted to passive verbs, but I'm willing to; I think timid writers like them for the same reason timid lovers like passive partners. The passive voice is safe. There is no troublesome action to contend with; the subject just has to close its eyes and think of England, to paraphrase Queen Victoria. I think unsure writers also feel the passive voice somehow lends their work authority, perhaps even a quality of majesty. If you find instruction manuals and lawyers' torts majestic, I guess it does.

The timid fellow writes **The meeting will be held at seven o'clock** because that somehow says to him, "Put it this way and people will believe *you really know.*" Purge this quisling thought! Don't be a muggle! Throw back your shoulders, stick out your chin, and put that meeting in charge! Write **The meeting's at seven.** There, by God! Don't you feel better?

I won't say there's no place for the passive tense. Suppose, for instance, a fellow dies in the kitchen but ends up somewhere else. **The body was carried from the kitchen and placed on the parlor sofa** is a fair way to put this, although "was carried" and "was placed" still irk the shit out of me. I accept them but I don't embrace them. What I would embrace is **Freddy and Myra carried the body out of the kitchen and laid it on the parlor sofa.** Why does the body have to be the subject of the sentence, anyway? It's dead, for Christ's sake! Fuhgeddaboudit!

Two pages of the passive voice—just about any business document ever written, in other words, not to mention reams of bad fiction—make me want to scream. It's weak, it's circuitous, and it's frequently tortuous, as well. How about this: **My first kiss will always be recalled by me as how my romance with Shayna was begun.** Oh, man—who farted, right? A simpler way to express this idea—sweeter and more forceful, as well—might be this: **My romance with Shayna began with our first kiss. I'll never forget it.** I'm not in love with this because it uses *with* twice in four words, but at least we're out of that awful passive voice.

You might also notice how much simpler the thought is to understand when it's broken up into *two* thoughts. This makes matters easier for the reader, and the reader must always be your main concern; without Constant Reader, you are just a voice quacking in the void. And it's no walk in the park being the guy on the receiving end. "[Will Strunk] felt the reader was in serious trouble most of the time," E. B. White writes in his introduction to *The Elements of Style,* "a man floundering in a swamp, and that it was the duty of any-one trying to write English to drain this swamp quickly and get his man up on dry ground, or at least throw him a rope." And remember: **The writer threw the rope,** not **The rope was thrown by the writer.** Please oh please.

The other piece of advice I want to give you before moving on to the next level of the toolbox is this: *The adverb is not your friend.*

Adverbs, you will remember from your own version of Business English, are words that modify verbs, adjectives, or other adverbs. They're the ones that usually end in **-ly.** Adverbs, like the passive voice, seem to have been created with the timid writer in mind. With the passive voice, the writer usually expresses fear of not being taken seriously; it is the voice of little boys wearing shoepolish mustaches and lit-tle girls clumping around in Mommy's high heels. With adverbs, the writer usually tells us he or she is afraid he/she isn't expressing himself/herself clearly, that he or she is not getting the point or the picture across.

Consider the sentence **He closed the door firmly.** It's by no means a terrible sentence (at least it's got an active verb going for it), but ask yourself if **firmly** really has to be there. You can argue that it expresses a degree of difference between **He closed the door** and **He slammed the door,** and you'll get no argument from me . . . but what about context? What about all the enlightening (not to say emotionally moving) prose which came *before* **He closed the door firmly**? Shouldn't this tell us how he closed the door? And if the foregoing prose *does* tell us, isn't **firmly** an extra word? Isn't it redundant?

Someone out there is now accusing me of being tiresome and anal-retentive. I deny it. I believe the road to hell is paved with adverbs, and I will shout it from the rooftops. To put it another way, they're like dandelions. If you have one on your lawn, it looks pretty and unique. If you fail to root it out, however, you find five the next day . . . fifty the day after that . . . and then, my brothers and sisters, your lawn is **totally, completely,** and **profligately** covered with dandelions. By then you see them for the weeds they really are, but by then it's—*GASP!!*—too late.

I can be a good sport about adverbs, though. Yes I can. With one exception: dialogue attribution. I insist that you use the adverb in dialogue attribution only in the rarest and most special of occasions . . . and not even then, if you can avoid it. Just to make sure we all know what we're talking about, examine these three sentences:

> **"Put it down!"** she shouted.
> **"Give it back,"** he pleaded, **"it's mine."**
> **"Don't be such a fool, Jekyll,"** Utterson said.

In these sentences, **shouted, pleaded,** and **said** are verbs of dialogue attribution. Now look at these dubious revisions:

125

"Put it down!" she shouted menacingly.

"Give it back," he pleaded abjectly, "it's mine."

"Don't be such a fool, Jekyll," Utterson said contemptuously.

The three latter sentences are all weaker than the three former ones, and most readers will see why immediately. **"Don't be such a fool, Jekyll," Utterson said contemptuously** is the best of the lot; it is only a cliché, while the other two are actively ludicrous. Such dialogue attributions are sometimes known as "Swifties," after Tom Swift, the brave inventor-hero in a series of boys' adventure novels written by Victor Appleton II. Appleton was fond of such sentences as **"Do your worst!" Tom cried bravely** and **"My father helped with the equations," Tom said modestly.** When I was a teenager there was a party-game based on one's ability to create witty (or half-witty) Swifties. **"You got a nice butt, lady," he said cheekily** is one I remember; another is **"I'm the plumber," he said, with a flush.** (In this case the modifier is an adverbial phrase.) When debating whether or not to make some pernicious dandelion of an adverb part of your dialogue attribution, I suggest you ask yourself if you really want to write the sort of prose that might wind up in a party-game.

Some writers try to evade the no-adverb rule by shooting the attribution verb full of steroids. The result is familiar to any reader of pulp fiction or paperback originals:

"Put down the gun, Utterson!" Jekyll grated.

"Never stop kissing me!" Shayna gasped.

"You damned tease!" Bill jerked out.

Don't do these things. Please oh please.

The best form of dialogue attribution is **said,** as in **he said, she said, Bill said, Monica said.** If you want to see this put stringently into practice, I urge you to read or reread a novel by Larry McMurtry, the Shane of dialogue attribution. That looks damned snide on the page, but I'm speaking with complete sincerity. McMurtry has allowed few adverbial dandelions to grow on his lawn. He believes in he-said/she-said even in moments of emotional crisis (and in Larry McMurtry novels there are a lot of those). Go and do thou likewise.

Is this a case of "Do as I say, not as I do?" The reader has a perfect right to ask the question, and I have a duty to provide an honest answer. Yes. It is. You need only look back through some of my own fiction to know that I'm just another ordinary sinner. I've been pretty good about avoiding the passive tense, but I've spilled out my share of adverbs in my time, including some (it shames me to say it) in dialogue attribution. (I have never fallen so low as "he grated" or "Bill jerked out," though.) When I do it, it's usually for the same reason any writer does it: because I am afraid the reader won't understand me if I don't.

I'm convinced that fear is at the root of most bad writing. If one is writing for one's own pleasure, that fear may be mild—*timidity* is the word I've used here. If, however, one is working under deadline—a school paper, a newspaper article, the SAT writing sample—that fear may be intense. Dumbo got airborne with the help of a magic feather; you may feel the urge to grasp a passive verb or one of those nasty adverbs for the same reason. Just remember before you do that Dumbo didn't need the feather; the magic was in him.

You probably *do* know what you're talking about, and can

safely energize your prose with active verbs. And you probably *have* told your story well enough to believe that when you use **he said,** the reader will know how he said it—fast or slowly, happily or sadly. Your man may be floundering in a swamp, and by all means throw him a rope if he is . . . but there's no need to knock him unconscious with ninety feet of steel cable.

Good writing is often about letting go of fear and affectation. Affectation itself, beginning with the need to define some sorts of writing as "good" and other sorts as "bad," is fearful behavior. Good writing is also about making good choices when it comes to picking the tools you plan to work with.

No writer is entirely without sin in these matters. Although William Strunk got E. B. White in his clutches when White was but a naive undergraduate at Cornell (give them to me when they're young and they're mine forever, heh-heh-heh), and although White both understood and shared Strunk's prejudice against loose writing and the loose thinking which prompts it, he admits, "I suppose I have written *the fact that* a thousand times in the heat of composition, revised it out maybe five hundred times in the cool aftermath. To be batting only .500 this late in the season, to fail half the time to connect with this fat pitch, saddens me . . ." Yet E. B. White went on to write for a good many years following his initial revisions of Strunk's "little book" in 1957. I will go on writing in spite of such stupid lapses as **"You can't be serious," Bill said unbelievingly.** I expect you to do the same thing. There is a core simplicity to the English language and its American variant, but it's a slippery core. All I ask is that you do as well as you can, and remember that, while to write adverbs is human, to write **he said** or **she said** is divine.

– 4 –

Lift out the top layer of your toolbox—your vocabulary and all the grammar stuff. On the layer beneath go those elements of style upon which I've already touched. Strunk and White offer the best tools (and the best rules) you could hope for, describing them simply and clearly. (They are offered with a refreshing strictness, beginning with the rule on how to form possessives: you always add **'s,** even when the word you're modifying ends in *s*—always write **Thomas's bike** and never **Thomas' bike**—and ending with ideas about where it's best to place the most important parts of a sentence. They say at the end, and everyone's entitled to his/her opinion, but I don't believe **With a hammer he killed Frank** will ever replace **He killed Frank with a hammer.**)

Before leaving the basic elements of form and style, we ought to think for a moment about the paragraph, the form of organization which comes after the sentence. To that end, grab a novel—preferably one you haven't yet read—down from your shelf (the stuff I'm telling you applies to most prose, but since I'm a fiction writer, it's fiction I usually think about when I think about writing). Open the book in the middle and look at any two pages. Observe the pattern—the lines of type, the margins, and most particularly the blocks of white space where paragraphs begin or leave off.

You can tell *without even reading* if the book you've chosen is apt to be easy or hard, right? Easy books contain lots of short paragraphs—including dialogue paragraphs which may only be a word or two long—and lots of white space.

They're as airy as Dairy Queen ice cream cones. Hard books, ones full of ideas, narration, or description, have a stouter look. A *packed* look. Paragraphs are almost as important for how they look as for what they say; they are maps of intent.

In expository prose, paragraphs can (and should) be neat and utilitarian. The ideal expository graf contains a topic sentence followed by others which explain or amplify the first. Here are two paragraphs from the ever-popular "informal essay" which illustrate this simple but powerful form of writing:

When I was ten, I feared my sister Megan. It was impossible for her to come into my room without breaking at least one of my favorite toys, usually the favorite of favorites. Her gaze had some magical tape-destroying quality; any poster she looked at seemed to fall off the wall only seconds later. Well-loved articles of clothing disappeared from the closet. She didn't take them (at least I don't think so), only made them vanish. I'd usually find that treasured tee-shirt or my favorite Nikes deep under the bed months later, looking sad and abandoned among the dust kitties. When Megan was in my room, stereo speakers blew, window-shades flew up with a bang, and the lamp on my desk usually went dead.

She could be consciously cruel, too. On one occasion, Megan poured orange juice into my cereal. On another, she squirted toothpaste into the toes of my socks while I was taking a shower. And although she never admitted it, I am positive that whenever I fell asleep on the couch during half-time of the Sunday afternoon pro football games on TV, she rubbed boogers in my hair.

Informal essays are, by and large, silly and insubstantial things; unless you get a job as a columnist at your local newspaper, writing such fluffery is a skill you'll never use in the actual mall-and-filling-station world. Teachers assign them when they can't think of any other way to waste your time. The most notorious subject, of course, is "How I Spent My Summer Vacation." I taught writing for a year at the University of Maine in Orono and had one class loaded with athletes and cheerleaders. They liked informal essays, greeting them like the old high school friends they were. I spent one whole semester fighting the urge to ask them to write two pages of well-turned prose on the subject of "If Jesus Were My Teammate." What held me back was the sure and terrible knowledge that most of them would take to the task with enthusiasm. Some might actually weep while in the throes of composition.

Even in the informal essay, however, it's possible to see how strong the basic paragraph form can be. Topic-sentence-followed-by-support-and-description insists that the writer organize his/her thoughts, and it also provides good insurance against wandering away from the topic. Wandering isn't a big deal in an informal essay, is practically *de rigueur,* as a matter of fact—but it's a very bad habit to get into when working on more serious subjects in a more formal manner. Writing is refined thinking. If your master's thesis is no more organized than a high school essay titled "Why Shania Twain Turns Me On," you're in big trouble.

In fiction, the paragraph is less structured—it's the beat instead of the actual melody. The more fiction you read and write, the more you'll find your paragraphs forming on their own. And that's what you want. When composing it's best not to think too much about where paragraphs begin and end; the trick is to let nature take its course. If you don't like it later on, fix it then. That's what rewrite is all about. Now check out the following:

Big Tony's room wasn't what Dale had expected. The light had an odd yellowish cast that reminded him of cheap motels he'd stayed in, the ones where he always seemed to end up with a scenic view of the parking lot. The only picture was Miss May hanging askew on a push-pin. One shiny black shoe stuck out from under the bed.

"I dunno why you keep askin me about O'Leary," Big Tony said. "You think my story's gonna change?"

"Is it?" Dale asked.

"When your story's true it don't change. The truth is always the same boring shit, day in and day out."

Big Tony sat down, lit a cigarette, ran a hand through his hair.

"I ain't seen that fuckin mick since last summer. I let him hang around because he made me laugh, once showed me this thing he wrote about what it woulda been like if Jesus was on his high school football team, had a picture of Christ in a helmet and kneepads and everythin, but what a troublesome little fuck he turned out to be! I wish I'd never seen him!"

We could have a fifty-minute writing class on just this brief passage. It would encompass dialogue attribution (not necessary if we know who's speaking; Rule 17, omit needless words, in action), phonetically rendered language (**dunno, gonna**), the use of the comma (there is none in the line

When your story's true it don't change because I want you to hear it coming out all in one breath, without a pause), the decision not to use the apostrophe where the speaker has dropped a *g* . . . and all that stuff is just from the top level of the toolbox.

Let's stick with the paragraphs, though. Notice how easily they flow, with the turns and rhythms of the story dictating where each one begins and ends. The opening graf is of the classic type, beginning with a topic sentence that is supported by the sentences which follow. Others, however, exist solely to differentiate between Dale's dialogue and Big Tony's.

The most interesting paragraph is the fifth one: **Big Tony sat down, lit a cigarette, ran a hand through his hair.** It's only a single sentence long, and expository paragraphs almost never consist of a single sentence. It's not even a very *good* sentence, technically speaking; to make it perfect in the *Warriner's* sense, there should be a conjunction (**and**). Also, what exactly is the purpose of this paragraph?

First, the sentence may be flawed in a technical sense, but it's a good one in terms of the entire passage. Its brevity and telegraphic style vary the pace and keep the writing fresh. Suspense novelist Jonathan Kellerman uses this technique very successfully. In *Survival of the Fittest,* he writes: **The boat was thirty feet of sleek white fiberglass with gray trim. Tall masts, the sails tied. *Satori* painted on the hull in black script edged with gold.**

It is possible to overuse the well-turned fragment (and Kellerman sometimes does), but frags can also work beautifully to streamline narration, create clear images, and create tension as well as to vary the prose-line. A series of grammatically proper sentences can stiffen that line, make it less pliable. Purists hate to hear that and will deny it to their dying breath, but it's true. Language does not always have to wear a tie and lace-up shoes. The object of fiction isn't grammatical correctness but to make the reader welcome and then tell a story . . . to make him/her forget, whenever possible, that he/she is reading a story at all. The single-sentence paragraph more closely resembles talk than writing, and that's good. Writing is seduction. Good talk is part of seduction. If not so, why do so many couples who start the evening at dinner wind up in bed?

The other uses of this paragraph include stage direction, minor but useful enhancement of character and setting, and a vital moment of transition. From protesting that his story is true, Big Tony moves on to his memories of O'Leary. Since the source of dialogue doesn't change, Tony's sitting down and lighting up could take place in the same paragraph, with the dialogue picking up again afterward, but the writer doesn't elect to do it that way. Because Big Tony takes a new tack, the writer breaks the dialogue into two paragraphs. It's a decision made instantaneously in the course of writing, one based entirely on the beat the writer hears in his/her own head. That beat is part of the genetic hardwiring (Kellerman writes a lot of frags because he *hears* a lot of frags), but it's also the result of the thousands of hours that writer has spent composing, and the *tens* of thousands of hours he/she may have spent reading the compositions of others.

I would argue that the paragraph, not the sentence, is the basic unit of writing—the place where coherence begins and words stand a chance of becoming more than mere words. If the moment of quickening is to come, it comes at the level of the paragraph. It is a marvellous and flexible instrument that can be a single word long or run on for pages (one paragraph in Don Robertson's historical novel *Paradise Falls* is sixteen pages long; there are paragraphs in Ross Lockridge's *Raintree County* which are nearly that). You must learn to use it well if you are to write well. What this means is lots of practice; you have to learn the beat.

– 5 –

Grab that book you were looking at off the shelf again, would you? The weight of it in your hands tells you other stuff that you can take in without reading a single word. The book's length, naturally, but more: the commitment the writer shouldered in order to create the work, the commitment Constant Reader must make to digest it. Not that length and weight alone indicate excellence; many epic tales are pretty much epic crap—just ask my critics, who will moan about entire Canadian forests massacred in order to print my drivel. Conversely, short doesn't always mean sweet. In some cases (*The Bridges of Madison County,* for instance), short means far *too* sweet. But there is that matter of commitment, whether a book is good or bad, a failure or a success. Words have weight. Ask anyone who works in the shipping department of a book company warehouse, or in the storage room of a large bookstore.

Words create sentences; sentences create paragraphs; sometimes paragraphs quicken and begin to breathe. Imagine, if you like, Frankenstein's monster on its slab. Here comes lightning, not from the sky but from a humble paragraph of English words. Maybe it's the first really good paragraph you ever wrote, something so fragile and yet full of possibility that you are frightened. You feel as Victor Frankenstein must have when the dead conglomeration of sewn-together spare parts suddenly opened its watery yellow eyes. *Oh my God, it's breathing,* you realize. *Maybe it's even thinking. What in hell's name do I do next?*

You go on to the third level, of course, and begin to write real fiction. Why shouldn't you? Why should you fear? Carpenters don't build monsters, after all; they build houses, stores, and banks. They build some of wood a plank at a time and some of brick a brick at a time. You will build a paragraph at a time, constructing these of your vocabulary and your knowledge of grammar and basic style. As long as you stay level-on-the-level and shave even every door, you can build whatever you like—whole mansions, if you have the energy.

Is there any rationale for building entire mansions of words? I think there is, and that the readers of Margaret Mitchell's *Gone with the Wind* and Charles Dickens's *Bleak House* understand it: sometimes even a monster is no monster. Sometimes it's beautiful and we fall in love with all that story, more than any film or TV program could ever hope to provide. Even after a thousand pages we don't want to leave the world the writer has made for us, or the make-believe people who live there. You wouldn't leave after two thousand pages, if there were two thousand. The *Rings* trilogy of J. R. R. Tolkien is a perfect example of this. A thousand pages of hobbits hasn't been enough for three generations of post–World War II fantasy fans; even when you add in that clumsy, galumphing dirigible of an epilogue, *The Silmarillion,* it hasn't been enough. Hence Terry Brooks, Piers Anthony, Robert Jordan, the questing rabbits of *Watership Down,* and half a hundred others. The writers of these books are creating the hobbits they still love and pine for; they are trying to bring Frodo and Sam back from the Grey Havens because Tolkien is no longer around to do it for them.

On Writing

At its most basic we are only discussing a learned skill, but do we not agree that sometimes the most basic skills can create things far beyond our expectations? We are talking about tools and carpentry, about words and style . . . but as we move along, you'd do well to remember that we are also talking about magic.

ON WRITING

There are no bad dogs, according to the title of a popular training manual, but don't tell that to the parent of a child mauled by a pit bull or a rottweiler; he or she is apt to bust your beak for you. And no matter how much I want to encourage the man or woman trying for the first time to write seriously, I can't lie and say there are no bad writers. Sorry, but there are *lots* of bad writers. Some are on-staff at your local newspaper, usually reviewing little-theater productions or pontificating about the local sports teams. Some have scribbled their way to homes in the Caribbean, leaving a trail of pulsing adverbs, wooden characters, and vile passive-voice constructions behind them. Others hold forth at open-mike poetry slams, wearing black turtlenecks and wrinkled khaki pants; they spout doggerel about "my angry lesbian breasts" and "the tilted alley where I cried my mother's name."

Writers form themselves into the pyramid we see in all areas of human talent and human creativity. At the bottom are the bad ones. Above them is a group which is slightly smaller but still large and welcoming; these are the competent writers. They may also be found on the staff of your local newspaper, on the racks at your local bookstore, and at poetry readings on Open Mike Night. These are folks who somehow understand that although a lesbian may be angry, her breasts will remain breasts.

The next level is much smaller. These are the really good writers. Above them—above almost all of us—are the Shakespeares, the Faulkners, the Yeatses, Shaws, and Eudora Weltys. They are geniuses, divine accidents, gifted in a way which is beyond our ability to understand, let alone attain. Shit, most geniuses aren't able to understand themselves, and many of them lead miserable lives, realizing (at least on some level) that they are nothing but fortunate freaks, the intellectual version of runway models who just happen to be born with the right cheekbones and with breasts which fit the image of an age.

I am approaching the heart of this book with two theses, both simple. The first is that good writing consists of mastering the fundamentals (vocabulary, grammar, the elements of style) and then filling the third level of your toolbox with the right instruments. The second is that while it is impossible to make a competent writer out of a bad writer, and while it is equally impossible to make a great writer out of a good one, it *is* possible, with lots of hard work, dedication, and timely help, to make a good writer out of a merely competent one.

I'm afraid this idea is rejected by lots of critics and plenty of writing teachers, as well. Many of these are liberals in their politics but crustaceans in their chosen fields. Men and women who would take to the streets to protest the exclusion of African-Americans or Native Americans (I can imagine what Mr. Strunk would have made of these politically correct but clunky terms) from the local country club are often the same men and women who tell their classes that writing ability is fixed and immutable; once a hack, always a hack.

Even if a writer rises in the estimation of an influential critic or two, he/she always carries his/her early reputation along, like a respectable married woman who was a wild child as a teenager. Some people never forget, that's all, and a good deal of literary criticism serves only to reinforce a caste system which is as old as the intellectual snobbery which nurtured it. Raymond Chandler may be recognized now as an important figure in twentieth-century American literature, an early voice describing the anomie of urban life in the years after World War II, but there are plenty of critics who will reject such a judgment out of hand. He's a hack! they cry indignantly. A hack with pretensions! The worst kind! The kind who thinks he can pass for one of *us!*

Critics who try to rise above this intellectual hardening of the arteries usually meet with limited success. Their colleagues may accept Chandler into the company of the great, but are apt to seat him at the foot of the table. And there are always those whispers: *Came out of the pulp tradition, you know . . . carries himself well for one of those, doesn't he? . . . did you know he wrote for* Black Mask *in the thirties . . . yes, regrettable . . .*

Even Charles Dickens, the Shakespeare of the novel, has faced a constant critical attack as a result of his often sensational subject matter, his cheerful fecundity (when he wasn't creating novels, he and his wife were creating children), and, of course, his success with the book-reading groundlings of his time and ours. Critics and scholars have always been suspicious of popular success. Often their suspicions are justified. In other cases, these suspicions are used as an excuse not to think. No one can be as intellectually slothful as a really smart person; give smart people half a chance and they will ship their oars and drift . . . dozing to Byzantium, you might say.

So yes—I expect to be accused by some of promoting a brainless and happy Horatio Alger philosophy, defending my own less-than-spotless reputation while I'm at it, and of encouraging people who are "just not our sort, old chap" to apply for membership at the country club. I guess I can live with that. But before we go on, let me repeat my basic premise: if you're a bad writer, no one can help you become a good one, or even a competent one. If you're good and want to be great . . . fuhgeddaboudit.

What follows is everything I know about how to write good fiction. I'll be as brief as possible, because your time is valuable and so is mine, and we both understand that the hours we spend talking about writing is time we don't spend actually *doing* it. I'll be as encouraging as possible, because it's my nature and because I love this job. I want you to love it, too. But if you don't want to work your ass off, you have no business trying to write well—settle back into competency and be grateful you have even that much to fall back on. There is a muse,* but he's not going to come fluttering down into your writing room and scatter creative fairy-dust all over your typewriter or computer station. He lives in the ground. He's a basement guy. You have to descend to his level, and once you get down there you have to furnish an apartment for him to live in. You have to do all the grunt labor, in other words, while the muse sits and smokes cigars and admires his bowling trophies and pretends to ignore you. Do you think this is fair? *I* think it's fair. He may not be much to look at, that muse-guy, and he may not be much of a conversationalist (what I get out of mine is mostly surly

---

*Traditionally, the muses were women, but mine's a guy; I'm afraid we'll just have to live with that.

grunts, unless he's on duty), but he's got the inspiration. It's right that you should do all the work and burn all the midnight oil, because the guy with the cigar and the little wings has got a bag of magic. There's stuff in there that can change your life.

Believe me, I know.

– 1 –

If you want to be a writer, you must do two things above all others: read a lot and write a lot. There's no way around these two things that I'm aware of, no shortcut.

I'm a slow reader, but I usually get through seventy or eighty books a year, mostly fiction. I don't read in order to study the craft; I read because I like to read. It's what I do at night, kicked back in my blue chair. Similarly, I don't read fiction to study the art of fiction, but simply because I like stories. Yet there is a learning process going on. Every book you pick up has its own lesson or lessons, and quite often the bad books have more to teach than the good ones.

When I was in the eighth grade, I happened upon a paperback novel by Murray Leinster, a science fiction pulp writer who did most of his work during the forties and fifties, when magazines like *Amazing Stories* paid a penny a word. I had read other books by Mr. Leinster, enough to know that the quality of his writing was uneven. This particular tale, which was about mining in the asteroid belt, was one of his less successful efforts. Only that's too kind. It was terrible, actually, a story populated by paper-thin characters and driven by outlandish plot developments. Worst of all (or so it seemed to me at the time), Leinster had fallen in love with the word *zestful.*

Characters watched the approach of ore-bearing asteroids with *zestful smiles.* Characters sat down to supper aboard their mining ship with *zestful anticipation.* Near the end of the book, the hero swept the large-breasted, blonde heroine into a *zestful embrace.* For me, it was the literary equivalent of a smallpox vaccination: I have never, so far as I know, used the word *zestful* in a novel or a story. God willing, I never will.

Asteroid Miners (which wasn't the title, but that's close enough) was an important book in my life as a reader. Almost everyone can remember losing his or her virginity, and most writers can remember the first book he/she put down thinking: *I can do better than this. Hell, I am doing better than this!* What could be more encouraging to the struggling writer than to realize his/her work is unquestionably better than that of someone who actually got paid for his/her stuff?

One learns most clearly what not to do by reading bad prose—one novel like *Asteroid Miners* (or *Valley of the Dolls, Flowers in the Attic,* and *The Bridges of Madison County,* to name just a few) is worth a semester at a good writing school, even with the superstar guest lecturers thrown in.

Good writing, on the other hand, teaches the learning writer about style, graceful narration, plot development, the creation of believable characters, and truth-telling. A novel like *The Grapes of Wrath* may fill a new writer with feelings of despair and good old-fashioned jealousy—"I'll never be able to write anything that good, not if I live to be a thousand"— but such feelings can also serve as a spur, goading the writer to work harder and aim higher. Being swept away by a combination of great story and great writing—of being flattened, in fact—is part of every writer's necessary formation. You cannot hope to sweep someone else away by the force of your writing until it has been done to you.

So we read to experience the mediocre and the outright rotten; such experience helps us to recognize those things when they begin to creep into our own work, and to steer clear of them. We also read in order to measure ourselves against the good and the great, to get a sense of all that can be done. And we read in order to experience different styles.

You may find yourself adopting a style you find particularly exciting, and there's nothing wrong with that. When I read Ray Bradbury as a kid, I wrote like Ray Bradbury—everything green and wondrous and seen through a lens smeared with the grease of nostalgia. When I read James M. Cain, everything I wrote came out clipped and stripped and hard-boiled. When I read Lovecraft, my prose became luxurious and Byzantine. I wrote stories in my teenage years where all these styles merged, creating a kind of hilarious stew. This sort of stylistic blending is a necessary part of developing one's own style, but it doesn't occur in a vacuum. You have to read widely, constantly refining (and redefining) your own work as you do so. It's hard for me to believe that people who read very little (or not at all in some cases) should presume to write and expect people to like what they have written, but I know it's true. If I had a nickel for every person who ever told me he/she wanted to become a writer but "didn't have time to read," I could buy myself a pretty good steak dinner. Can I be blunt on this subject? If you don't have time to read, you don't have the time (or the tools) to write. Simple as that.

Reading is the creative center of a writer's life. I take a book with me everywhere I go, and find there are all sorts of opportunities to dip in. The trick is to teach yourself to read in small sips as well as in long swallows. Waiting rooms were made for books—of course! But so are theater lobbies before the show, long and boring checkout lines, and everyone's favorite, the john. You can even read while you're driving, thanks to the audiobook revolution. Of the books I read each year, anywhere from six to a dozen are on tape. As for all the wonderful radio you will be missing, come on—how many times can you listen to Deep Purple sing "Highway Star"?

Reading at meals is considered rude in polite society, but if you expect to succeed as a writer, rudeness should be the second-to-least of your concerns. The least of all should be polite society and what it expects. If you intend to write as truthfully as you can, your days as a member of polite society are numbered, anyway.

Where else can you read? There's always the treadmill, or whatever you use down at the local health club to get aerobic. I try to spend an hour doing that every day, and I think I'd go mad without a good novel to keep me company. Most exercise facilities (at home as well as outside it) are now equipped with TVs, but TV—while working out or anywhere else—really is about the last thing an aspiring writer needs. If you feel you must have the news analyst blowhards on CNN while you exercise, or the stock market blowhards on MSNBC, or the sports blowhards on ESPN, it's time for you to question how serious you really are about becoming a writer. You must be prepared to do some serious turning inward toward the life of the imagination, and that means, I'm afraid, that Geraldo, Keith Obermann, and Jay Leno must go. Reading takes time, and the glass teat takes too much of it.

Once weaned from the ephemeral craving for TV, most people will find they enjoy the time they spend reading. I'd like to suggest that turning off that endlessly quacking box is apt to improve the quality of your life as well as the quality of your writing. And how much of a sacrifice are we talking about here? How many *Frasier* and *ER* reruns does it take to make one American life complete? How many Richard Simmons infomercials? How many whiteboy/fatboy Beltway insiders on CNN? Oh man, don't get me started. Jerry-Springer-Dr.-Dre-Judge-Judy-Jerry-Falwell-Donny-and-Marie, I rest my case.

When my son Owen was seven or so, he fell in love with Bruce Springsteen's E Street Band, particularly with Clarence Clemons, the band's burly sax player. Owen decided he wanted to learn to play like Clarence. My wife and I were amused and delighted by this ambition. We were also hopeful, as any parent would be, that our kid would turn out to be talented, perhaps even some sort of prodigy. We got Owen a tenor saxophone for Christmas and lessons with Gordon Bowie, one of the local music men. Then we crossed our fingers and hoped for the best.

Seven months later I suggested to my wife that it was time to discontinue the sax lessons, if Owen concurred. Owen did, and with palpable relief—he hadn't wanted to say it himself, especially not after asking for the sax in the first place, but seven months had been long enough for him to realize that, while he might love Clarence Clemons's big sound, the saxophone was simply not for him—God had not given him that particular talent.

I knew, not because Owen stopped practicing, but because he was practicing only during the periods Mr. Bowie had set for him: half an hour after school four days a week, plus an hour on the weekends. Owen mastered the scales and the notes—nothing wrong with his memory, his lungs, or his eye-hand coordination—but we never heard him taking off, surprising himself with something new, blissing himself out. And as soon as his practice time was over, it was back into the case with the horn, and there it stayed until the next lesson or practice-time. What this suggested to me was that when it came to the sax and my son, there was never going to be any real play-time; it was all going to be rehearsal. That's no good. If there's no joy in it, it's just no good. It's best to go on to some other area, where the deposits of talent may be richer and the fun quotient higher.

Talent renders the whole idea of rehearsal meaningless; when you find something at which you are talented, you do it (whatever *it* is) until your fingers bleed or your eyes are ready to fall out of your head. Even when no one is listening (or reading, or watching), every outing is a bravura performance, because you as the creator are happy. Perhaps even ecstatic. That goes for reading and writing as well as for playing a musical instrument, hitting a baseball, or running the four-forty. The sort of strenuous reading and writing program I advocate—four to six hours a day, every day—will not seem strenuous if you really enjoy doing these things and have an aptitude for them; in fact, you may be following such a program already. If you feel you need permission to do all the reading and writing your little heart desires, however, consider it hereby granted by yours truly.

The real importance of reading is that it creates an ease and intimacy with the process of writing; one comes to the country of the writer with one's papers and identification pretty much in order. Constant reading will pull you into a place (a mind-set, if you like the phrase) where you can write eagerly and without self-consciousness. It also offers you a constantly growing knowledge of what has been done and what hasn't, what is trite and what is fresh, what works and what just lies there dying (or dead) on the page. The more you read, the less apt you are to make a fool of yourself with your pen or word processor.

– 2 –

If "read a lot, write a lot" is the Great Commandment—and I assure you that it is—how much writing constitutes a lot? That varies, of course, from writer to writer. One of my favorite stories on the subject—probably more myth than truth—concerns James Joyce.* According to the story, a friend came to visit him one day and found the great man sprawled across his writing desk in a posture of utter despair.

"James, what's wrong?" the friend asked. "Is it the work?"

Joyce indicated assent without even raising his head to look at the friend. Of course it was the work; isn't it always?

"How many words did you get today?" the friend pursued.

Joyce (still in despair, still sprawled facedown on his desk): "Seven."

"Seven? But James . . . that's *good,* at least for you!"

"Yes," Joyce said, finally looking up. "I suppose it is . . . but I don't know what *order* they go in!"

At the other end of the spectrum, there are writers like Anthony Trollope. He wrote humongous novels (*Can You Forgive Her?* is a fair enough example; for modern audiences it might be retitled *Can You Possibly Finish It?*), and he pumped them out with amazing regularity. His day job was as a clerk in the British Postal Department (the red public mailboxes all

---

*There are some great stories about Joyce. My absolute favorite is that, as his vision failed, he took to wearing a milkman's uniform while writing. Supposedly he believed it caught the sunlight and reflected it down on his page.

over Britain were Anthony Trollope's invention); he wrote for two and a half hours each morning before leaving for work. This schedule was ironclad. If he was in mid-sentence when the two and a half hours expired, he left that sentence unfinished until the next morning. And if he happened to finish one of his six-hundred-page heavyweights with fifteen minutes of the session remaining, he wrote **The End,** set the manuscript aside, and began work on the next book.

John Creasey, a British mystery novelist, wrote five hundred (yes, you read it correctly) novels under ten different names. I've written thirty-five or so—some of Trollopian length—and am considered prolific, but I look positively blocked next to Creasey. Several other contemporary novelists (they include Ruth Rendell/Barbara Vine, Evan Hunter/Ed McBain, Dean Koontz, and Joyce Carol Oates) have written easily as much as I have; some have written a good deal more.

On the other hand—the James Joyce hand—there is Harper Lee, who wrote only one book (the brilliant *To Kill a Mockingbird*). Any number of others, including James Agee, Malcolm Lowry, and Thomas Harris (so far), wrote under five. Which is okay, but I always wonder two things about these folks: how long did it take them to write the books they *did* write, and what did they do the rest of their time? Knit afghans? Organize church bazaars? Deify plums? I'm probably being snotty here, but I am also, believe me, honestly curious. If God gives you something you can do, why in God's name wouldn't you do it?

My own schedule is pretty clear-cut. Mornings belong to whatever is new—the current composition. Afternoons are for naps and letters. Evenings are for reading, family, Red Sox games on TV, and any revisions that just cannot wait. Basically, mornings are my prime writing time.

On Writing

Once I start work on a project, I don't stop and I don't slow down unless I absolutely have to. If I don't write every day, the characters begin to stale off in my mind—they begin to *seem* like characters instead of real people. The tale's narrative cutting edge starts to rust and I begin to lose my hold on the story's plot and pace. Worst of all, the excitement of spinning something new begins to fade. The work starts to *feel* like work, and for most writers that is the smooch of death. Writing is at its best—always, always, always—when it is a kind of inspired play for the writer. I can write in cold blood if I have to, but I like it best when it's fresh and almost too hot to handle.

I used to tell interviewers that I wrote every day except for Christmas, the Fourth of July, and my birthday. That was a lie. I told them that because if you agree to an interview you have to say *something,* and it plays better if it's something at least half-clever. Also, I didn't want to sound like a workaholic dweeb (just a workaholic, I guess). The truth is that when I'm writing, I write every day, workaholic dweeb or not. That *includes* Christmas, the Fourth, and my birthday (at my age you try to ignore your goddam birthday anyway). And when I'm not working, I'm not working at all, although during those periods of full stop I usually feel at loose ends with myself and have trouble sleeping. For me, not working is the real work. When I'm writing, it's all the playground, and the worst three hours I ever spent there were still pretty damned good.

I used to be faster than I am now; one of my books *(The Running Man)* was written in a single week, an accomplishment John Creasey would perhaps have appreciated (although I have read that Creasey wrote several of his mysteries in *two days).* I think it was quitting smoking that slowed me down;

nicotine is a great synapse enhancer. The problem, of course, is that it's killing you at the same time it's helping you compose. Still, I believe the first draft of a book—even a long one—should take no more than three months, the length of a season. Any longer and—for me, at least—the story begins to take on an odd foreign feel, like a dispatch from the Romanian Department of Public Affairs, or something broadcast on high-band shortwave during a period of severe sunspot activity.

I like to get ten pages a day, which amounts to 2,000 words. That's 180,000 words over a three-month span, a goodish length for a book—something in which the reader can get happily lost, if the tale is done well and stays fresh. On some days those ten pages come easily; I'm up and out and doing errands by eleven-thirty in the morning, perky as a rat in liverwurst. More frequently, as I grow older, I find myself eating lunch at my desk and finishing the day's work around one-thirty in the afternoon. Sometimes, when the words come hard, I'm still fiddling around at teatime. Either way is fine with me, but only under dire circumstances do I allow myself to shut down before I get my 2,000 words.

The biggest aid to regular (Trollopian?) production is working in a serene atmosphere. It's difficult for even the most naturally productive writer to work in an environment where alarms and excursions are the rule rather than the exception. When I'm asked for "the secret of my success" (an absurd idea, that, but impossible to get away from), I sometimes say there are two: I stayed physically healthy (at least until a van knocked me down by the side of the road in the summer of 1999), and I stayed married. It's a good answer because it makes the question go away, and because there is an element of truth in it. The combination of a healthy body and a stable relationship with a self-reliant woman who takes zero shit from me or anyone else has made the continuity of my working life possible. And I believe the converse is also true: that my writing and the pleasure I take in it has contributed to the stability of my health and my home life.

– 3 –

You can read anywhere, almost, but when it comes to writing, library carrels, park benches, and rented flats should be courts of last resort—Truman Capote said he did his best work in motel rooms, but he is an exception; most of us do our best in a place of our own. Until you get one, you'll find your new resolution to write a lot hard to take seriously.

Your writing room doesn't have to sport a Playboy Philosophy decor, and you don't need an Early American rolltop desk in which to house your writing implements. I wrote my first two published novels, *Carrie* and *'Salem's Lot,* in the laundry room of a doublewide trailer, pounding away on my wife's portable Olivetti typewriter and balancing a child's desk on my thighs; John Cheever reputedly wrote in the basement of his Park Avenue apartment building, near the furnace. The space can be humble (probably *should* be, as I think I have already suggested), and it really needs only one thing: a door which you are willing to shut. The closed door is your way of telling the world and yourself that you mean business; you have made a serious commitment to write and intend to walk the walk as well as talk the talk.

By the time you step into your new writing space and close the door, you should have settled on a daily writing goal. As with physical exercise, it would be best to set this goal low at first, to avoid discouragement. I suggest a thousand words a day, and because I'm feeling magnanimous, I'll also suggest that you can take one day a week off, at least to begin with. No more; you'll lose the urgency and immediacy of your story if you do. With that goal set, resolve to yourself that the door stays closed until that goal is met. Get busy putting those thousand words on paper or on a floppy disk. In an early interview (this was to promote *Carrie,* I think), a radio talk-show host asked me how I wrote. My reply—"One word at a time"—seemingly left him without a reply. I think he was trying to decide whether or not I was joking. I wasn't. In the end, it's always that simple. Whether it's a vignette of a single page or an epic trilogy like *The Lord of the Rings,* the work is always accomplished one word at a time. The door closes the rest of the world out; it also serves to close you in and keep you focused on the job at hand.

If possible, there should be no telephone in your writing room, certainly no TV or videogames for you to fool around with. If there's a window, draw the curtains or pull down the shades unless it looks out at a blank wall. For any writer, but for the beginning writer in particular, it's wise to eliminate every possible distraction. If you continue to write, you will begin to filter out these distractions naturally, but at the start it's best to try and take care of them before you write. I work to loud music—hard-rock stuff like AC/DC, Guns 'n Roses, and Metallica have always been particular favorites—but for me the music is just another way of shutting the door. It surrounds me, keeps the mundane world out. When you write, you want to get rid of the world, do you not? Of course you do. When you're writing, you're creating your own worlds.

I think we're actually talking about creative sleep. Like your bedroom, your writing room should be private, a place where you go to dream. Your schedule—in at about the same time every day, out when your thousand words are on paper or disk—exists in order to habituate yourself, to make yourself ready to dream just as you make yourself ready to sleep by going to bed at roughly the same time each night and following the same ritual as you go. In both writing and sleeping, we learn to be physically still at the same time we are encouraging our minds to unlock from the humdrum rational thinking of our daytime lives. And as your mind and body grow accustomed to a certain amount of sleep each night—six hours, seven, maybe the recommended eight—so can you train your waking mind to sleep creatively and work out the vividly imagined waking dreams which are successful works of fiction.

But you need the room, you need the door, and you need the determination to shut the door. You need a concrete goal, as well. The longer you keep to these basics, the easier the act of writing will become. Don't wait for the muse. As I've said, he's a hardheaded guy who's not susceptible to a lot of creative fluttering. This isn't the Ouija board or the spirit-world we're talking about here, but just another job like laying pipe or driving long-haul trucks. Your job is to make sure the muse knows where you're going to be every day from nine 'til noon or seven 'til three. If he does know, I assure you that sooner or later he'll start showing up, chomping his cigar and making his magic.

– 4 –

So okay—there you are in your room with the shade down and the door shut and the plug pulled out of the base of the telephone. You've blown up your TV and committed yourself to a thousand words a day, come hell or high water. Now comes the big question: What are you going to write about? And the equally big answer: Anything you damn well want. Anything at all . . . *as long as you tell the truth.*

The dictum in writing classes used to be "write what you know." Which sounds good, but what if you want to write about starships exploring other planets or a man who murders his wife and then tries to dispose of her body with a wood-chipper? How does the writer square either of these, or a thousand other fanciful ideas, with the "write-what-you-know" directive?

I think you begin by interpreting "write what you know" as broadly and inclusively as possible. If you're a plumber, you know plumbing, but that is far from the extent of your knowledge; the heart also knows things, and so does the imagination. Thank God. If not for heart and imagination, the world of fiction would be a pretty seedy place. It might not even exist at all.

In terms of genre, it's probably fair to assume that you will begin by writing what you love to read—certainly I have recounted my early love affair with the EC horror comics until the tale has gone stale. But I *did* love them, ditto horror movies like *I Married a Monster from Outer Space,* and the result was stories like "I Was a Teenage Graverobber." Even today I'm not above writing slightly more sophisticated versions of that tale; I was built with a love of the night and the unquiet coffin, that's all. If you disapprove, I can only shrug my shoulders. It's what I have.

If you happen to be a science fiction fan, it's natural that you should want to write science fiction (and the more sf you've read, the less likely it is that you'll simply revisit the field's well-mined conventions, such as space opera and dystopian satire). If you're a mystery fan, you'll want to write mysteries, and if you enjoy romances, it's natural for you to want to write romances of your own. There's nothing wrong with writing any of these things. What would be very wrong, I think, is to turn away from what you know and like (or love, the way I loved those old ECs and black-and-white horror flicks) in favor of things you believe will impress your friends, relatives, and writing-circle colleagues. What's equally wrong is the deliberate turning toward some genre or type of fiction in order to make money. It's morally wonky, for one thing—the job of fiction is to find the truth inside the story's web of lies, not to commit intellectual dishonesty in the hunt for the buck. Also, brothers and sisters, it doesn't work.

When I'm asked why I decided to write the sort of thing I do write, I always think the question is more revealing than any answer I could possibly give. Wrapped within it, like the chewy stuff in the center of a Tootsie Pop, is the assumption that the writer controls the material instead of the other way around.* The writer who is serious and committed is incapable of sizing up story material the way an investor might size up various stock offerings, picking out the ones which seem likely to provide a good return. If it could indeed be done that way, every novel published would be a best-seller and the huge advances paid to a dozen or so "big-name writers" would not exist (publishers would like that).

Grisham, Clancy, Crichton, and myself—among others— are paid these large sums of money because we are selling uncommonly large numbers of books to uncommonly large

---

*Kirby McCauley, my first real agent, used to quote science fiction writer Alfred Bester (*The Stars My Destination, The Demolished Man*) on this subject. "The book is the boss," Alfie used to say in tones indicating that that closed the subject.

audiences. A critical assumption is sometimes made that we have access to some mystical vulgate that other (and often better) writers either cannot find or will not deign to use. I doubt if this is true. Nor do I believe the contention of some popular novelists (although she was not the only one, I am thinking of the late Jacqueline Susann) that their success is based on literary merit—that the public understands true greatness in ways the tight-assed, consumed-by-jealousy literary establishment cannot. This idea is ridiculous, a product of vanity and insecurity.

Book-buyers aren't attracted, by and large, by the literary merits of a novel; book-buyers want a good story to take with them on the airplane, something that will first fascinate them, then pull them in and keep them turning the pages. This happens, I think, when readers recognize the people in a book, their behaviors, their surroundings, and their talk. When the reader hears strong echoes of his or her own life and beliefs, he or she is apt to become more invested in the story. I'd argue that it's impossible to make this sort of connection in a premeditated way, gauging the market like a racetrack tout with a hot tip.

Stylistic imitation is one thing, a perfectly honorable way to get started as a writer (and impossible to avoid, really; some sort of imitation marks each new stage of a writer's development), but one cannot imitate a writer's approach to a particular genre, no matter how simple what that writer is doing may seem. You can't aim a book like a cruise missile, in other words. People who decide to make a fortune writing like John Grisham or Tom Clancy produce nothing but pale imitations, by and large, because vocabulary is not the same thing as feeling and plot is light-years from the truth as it is understood by the mind and the heart. When you see a novel with "**In the tradition of** (John Grisham/Patricia Cornwell/Mary Higgins Clark/Dean Koontz)" on the cover, you know you are looking at one of these overcalculated (and likely boring) imitations.

Write what you like, then imbue it with life and make it unique by blending in your own personal knowledge of life, friendship, relationships, sex, and work. Especially work. People love to read about work. God knows why, but they do. If you're a plumber who enjoys science fiction, you might well consider a novel about a plumber aboard a starship or on an alien planet. Sound ludicrous? The late Clifford D. Simak wrote a novel called *Cosmic Engineers* which is close to just that. And it's a terrific read. What you need to remember is that there's a difference between lecturing about what you know and using it to enrich the story. The latter is good. The former is not.

Consider John Grisham's breakout novel, *The Firm.* In this story, a young lawyer discovers that his first job, which seemed too good to be true, really is—he's working for the Mafia. Suspenseful, involving, and paced at breakneck speed, *The Firm* sold roughly nine gazillion copies. What seemed to fascinate its audience was the moral dilemma in which the young lawyer finds himself: working for the mob is bad, no argument there, but the frocking pay is *great!* You can drive a Beemer, and that's just for openers!

Audiences also enjoyed the lawyer's resourceful efforts to extricate himself from his dilemma. It might not be the way most people would behave, and the *deus ex machina* clanks pretty steadily in the last fifty pages, but it *is* the way most of us would *like* to behave. And wouldn't we also like to have a *deus ex machina* in our lives?

Although I don't know for sure, I'd bet my dog and lot

that John Grisham never worked for the mob. All of that is total fabrication (and total fabrication is the fiction-writer's purest delight). He *was* once a young lawyer, though, and he has clearly forgotten none of the struggle. Nor has he forgotten the location of the various financial pitfalls and honeytraps that make the field of corporate law so difficult. Using plainspun humor as a brilliant counterpoint and never substituting cant for story, he sketches a world of Darwinian struggle where all the savages wear three-piece suits. And—here's the good part—*this is a world impossible not to believe.* Grisham has been there, spied out the land and the enemy positions, and brought back a full report. He told the truth of what he knew, and for that if nothing else, he deserves every buck *The Firm* made.

Critics who dismissed *The Firm* and Grisham's later books as poorly written and who profess themselves to be mystified by his success are either missing the point because it's so big and obvious or because they are being deliberately obtuse. Grisham's make-believe tale is solidly based in a reality he knows, has personally experienced, and which he wrote about with total (almost naive) honesty. The result is a book which is—cardboard characters or no, we could argue about that—both brave and uniquely satisfying. You as a beginning writer would do well not to imitate the lawyers-in-trouble genre Grisham seems to have created but to emulate Grisham's openness and inability to do anything other than get right to the point.

John Grisham, of course, knows lawyers. What *you* know makes you unique in some other way. Be brave. Map the enemy's positions, come back, tell us all you know. And remember that plumbers in space is not such a bad setup for a story.

– 5 –

In my view, stories and novels consist of three parts: narration, which moves the story from point A to point B and finally to point Z; description, which creates a sensory reality for the reader; and dialogue, which brings characters to life through their speech.

You may wonder where plot is in all this. The answer—my answer, anyway—is nowhere. I won't try to convince you that I've never plotted any more than I'd try to convince you that I've never told a lie, but I do both as infrequently as possible. I distrust plot for two reasons: first, because our *lives* are largely plotless, even when you add in all our reasonable precautions and careful planning; and second, because I believe plotting and the spontaneity of real creation aren't compatible. It's best that I be as clear about this as I can—I want you to understand that my basic belief about the making of stories is that they pretty much make themselves. The job of the writer is to give them a place to grow (and to transcribe them, of course). If you can see things this way (or at least try to), we can work together comfortably. If, on the other hand, you decide I'm crazy, that's fine. You won't be the first.

When, during the course of an interview for *The New Yorker,* I told the interviewer (Mark Singer) that I believed stories are found things, like fossils in the ground, he said that he didn't believe me. I replied that that was fine, as long as he believed that *I* believe it. And I do. Stories aren't souvenir tee-shirts or GameBoys. Stories are relics, part of an undiscovered pre-existing world. The writer's job is to use the tools in his or her toolbox to get as much of each one out of the ground intact as possible. Sometimes the fossil you uncover is small; a seashell. Sometimes it's enormous, a *Tyrannosaurus Rex* with all those gigantic ribs and grinning teeth. Either way, short story or thousand-page whopper of a novel, the techniques of excavation remain basically the same.

No matter how good you are, no matter how much experience you have, it's probably impossible to get the entire fossil out of the ground without a few breaks and losses. To get even *most* of it, the shovel must give way to more delicate tools: airhose, palm-pick, perhaps even a toothbrush. Plot is a far bigger tool, the writer's jackhammer. You can liberate a fossil from hard ground with a jackhammer, no argument there, but you know as well as I do that the jackhammer is going to break almost as much stuff as it liberates. It's clumsy, mechanical, anticreative. Plot is, I think, the good writer's last resort and the dullard's first choice. The story which results from it is apt to feel artificial and labored.

I lean more heavily on intuition, and have been able to do that because my books tend to be based on situation rather than story. Some of the ideas which have produced those books are more complex than others, but the majority start out with the stark simplicity of a department store window display or a waxwork tableau. I want to put a group of characters (perhaps a pair; perhaps even just one) in some sort of predicament and then watch them try to work themselves free. My job isn't to *help* them work their way free, or manipulate them to safety—those are jobs which require the noisy jackhammer of plot—but to watch what happens and then write it down.

The situation comes first. The characters—always flat and unfeatured, to begin with—come next. Once these things are fixed in my mind, I begin to narrate. I often have an idea of what the outcome may be, but I have never demanded of a set of characters that they do things my way. On the contrary, I want them to do things *their* way. In some instances, the outcome is what I visualized. In most, however, it's something I never expected. For a suspense novelist, this is a great thing. I am, after all, not just the novel's creator but its first reader. And if *I'm* not able to guess with any accuracy how the damned thing is going to turn out, even with my inside knowledge of coming events, I can be pretty sure of keeping the reader in a state of page-turning anxiety. And why worry about the ending anyway? Why be such a control freak? Sooner or later every story comes out *somewhere*.

In the early 1980s, my wife and I went to London on a combined business/pleasure trip. I fell asleep on the plane and had a dream about a popular writer (it may or may not have been me, but it sure to God wasn't James Caan) who fell into the clutches of a psychotic fan living on a farm somewhere out in the back of the beyond. The fan was a woman isolated by her growing paranoia. She kept some livestock in the barn, including her pet pig, Misery. The pig was named after the continuing main character in the writer's best-selling bodice-rippers. My clearest memory of this dream upon waking was something the woman said to the writer, who had a broken leg and was being kept prisoner in the back bedroom. I wrote it on an American Airlines cocktail napkin so I wouldn't for-get it, then put it in my pocket. I lost it somewhere, but can remember most of what I wrote down:

She speaks earnestly but never quite makes eye contact. A big woman and solid all through; she is an absence of hiatus. (What-ever *that* means; remember, I'd just woken up.) *"I wasn't try-ing to be funny in a mean way when I named my pig Misery, no sir. Please don't think that. No, I named her in the spirit of fan love, which is the purest love there is. You should be flattered."*

Tabby and I stayed at Brown's Hotel in London, and on our first night there I was unable to sleep. Some of it was what sounded like a trio of little-girl gymnasts in the room directly above ours, some of it was undoubtedly jet lag, but a lot of it was that airline cocktail napkin. Jotted on it was the seed of what I thought could be a really excellent story, one that might turn out funny and satiric as well as scary. I thought it was just too rich not to write.

I got up, went downstairs, and asked the concierge if there was a quiet place where I could work longhand for a bit. He led me to a gorgeous desk on the second-floor stair landing. It had been Rudyard Kipling's desk, he told me with perhaps justifiable pride. I was a little intimidated by this intelligence, but the spot was quiet and the desk seemed hospitable enough; it featured about an acre of cherrywood working surface, for one thing. Stoked on cup after cup of tea (I drank it by the gallon when I wrote . . . unless I was drinking beer, that is), I filled sixteen pages of a steno notebook. I like to work longhand, actually; the only problem is that, once I get jazzed, I can't keep up with the lines forming in my head and I get frazzled.

When I called it quits, I stopped in the lobby to thank the concierge again for letting me use Mr. Kipling's beautiful desk. "I'm so glad you enjoyed it," he replied. He was wearing a misty, reminiscent little smile, as if he had known the writer himself. "Kipling died there, actually. Of a stroke. While he was writing."

I went back upstairs to catch a few hours' sleep, thinking of how often we are given information we really could have done without.

The working title of my story, which I thought would be a novella of about 30,000 words, was "The Annie Wilkes Edition." When I sat down at Mr. Kipling's beautiful desk I had the basic situation—crippled writer, psycho fan—firmly fixed in my mind. The actual *story* did not as then exist (well, it did, but as a relic buried—except for sixteen handwritten pages, that is—in the earth), but knowing the story wasn't necessary for me to begin work. I had located the fossil; the rest, I knew, would consist of careful excavation.

I'd suggest that what works for me may work equally well for you. If you are enslaved to (or intimidated by) the tiresome tyranny of the outline and the notebook filled with "Character Notes," it may liberate you. At the very least, it will turn your mind to something more interesting than Developing the Plot.

(An amusing sidelight: the century's greatest supporter of Developing the Plot may have been Edgar Wallace, a bestselling potboiler novelist of the 1920s. Wallace invented—and patented—a device called the Edgar Wallace Plot Wheel. When you got stuck for the next Plot Development or needed an Amazing Turn of Events in a hurry, you simply spun the Plot Wheel and read what came up in the window: **a fortuitous arrival,** perhaps, or **Heroine declares her love.** These gadgets apparently sold like hotcakes.)

By the time I had finished that first Brown's Hotel session, in which Paul Sheldon wakes up to find himself Annie Wilkes's prisoner, I thought I knew what was going to happen. Annie would demand that Paul write another novel about his plucky continuing character, Misery Chastain, one just for her. After first demurring, Paul would of course agree (a psychotic nurse, I thought, could be very persuasive). Annie would tell him she intended to sacrifice her beloved pig, Misery, to this project. *Misery's Return* would, she'd say, consist of but one copy: a holographic manuscript bound in pigskin!

Here we'd fade out, I thought, and return to Annie's remote Colorado retreat six or eight months later for the surprise ending.

Paul is gone, his sickroom turned into a shrine to Misery Chastain, but Misery the pig is still very much in evidence, grunting serenely away in her sty beside the barn. On the walls of the "Misery Room" are book covers, stills from the Misery movies, pictures of Paul Sheldon, perhaps a newspaper headline reading FAMED ROMANCE NOVELIST STILL MISSING. In the center of the room, carefully spotlighted, is a single book on a small table (a cherrywood table, of course, in honor of Mr. Kipling). It is the Annie Wilkes Edition of *Misery's Return*. The binding is beautiful, and it should be; it is the skin of Paul Sheldon. And Paul himself? His bones might be buried behind the barn, but I thought it likely that the pig would have eaten the tasty parts.

Not bad, and it would have made a pretty good story (not such a good novel, however; no one likes to root for a guy over the course of three hundred pages only to discover that between chapters sixteen and seventeen the pig ate him), but that wasn't the way things eventually went. Paul Sheldon turned out to be a good deal more resourceful than I initially thought, and his efforts to play Scheherazade and save his life gave me a chance to say some things about the redemptive power of writing that I had long felt but never articulated. Annie also turned out to be more complex than I'd first imagined her, and she was great fun to write about—here was a woman pretty much stuck with "cockadoodie brat" when it came to profanity, but who felt absolutely no qualms about chopping off her favorite writer's foot when he tried to get away from her. In the end, I felt that Annie was almost as much to be pitied as to be feared. And none of the story's details and incidents proceeded from plot; they were organic, each arising naturally from the initial situation, each an uncovered part of the fossil. And I'm writing all this with a smile. As sick with drugs and alcohol as I was much of the time, I had such fun with that one.

Gerald's Game and *The Girl Who Loved Tom Gordon* are two other purely situational novels. If *Misery* is "two characters in a house," then *Gerald* is "one woman in a bedroom" and *The Girl Who* is "one kid lost in the woods." As I told you, I *have* written plotted novels, but the results, in books like *Insomnia* and *Rose Madder,* have not been particularly inspiring. These are (much as I hate to admit it) stiff, trying-too-hard novels. The only plot-driven novel of mine which I really like is *The Dead Zone* (and in all fairness, I must say I like that one a great deal). One book which *seems* plotted—*Bag of Bones*—is actually another situation: "widowed writer in a haunted house." The back story of *Bag of Bones* is satisfyingly gothic (at least I think so) and very complex, but none of the details were premeditated. The history of TR-90 and the story of what widowed writer Mike Noonan's wife was really up to during the last summer of her life arose spontaneously—all those details were parts of the fossil, in other words.

A strong enough situation renders the whole question of plot moot, which is fine with me. The most interesting situations can usually be expressed as a *What-if* question:

What if vampires invaded a small New England village? (*'Salem's Lot*)

What if a policeman in a remote Nevada town went berserk and started killing everyone in sight? (*Desperation*)

What if a cleaning woman suspected of a murder she got away with (her husband) fell under suspicion for a murder she did not commit (her employer)? (*Dolores Claiborne*)

What if a young mother and her son became trapped in their stalled car by a rabid dog? *(Cujo)*

These were all situations which occurred to me—while showering, while driving, while taking my daily walk—and which I eventually turned into books. In no case were they plotted, not even to the extent of a single note jotted on a single piece of scrap paper, although some of the stories (*Dolores Claiborne,* for instance) are almost as complex as those you find in murder mysteries. Please remember, however, that there is a huge difference between story and plot. Story is honorable and trustworthy; plot is shifty, and best kept under house arrest.

Each of the novels summarized above was smoothed out and detailed by the editorial process, of course, but most of the elements existed to begin with. "A movie should be there in rough cut," the film editor Paul Hirsch once told me. The same is true of books. I think it's rare that incoherence or dull storytelling can be solved by something so minor as a second draft.

This isn't a textbook, and so there aren't a lot of exercises, but I want to offer you one now, in case you feel that all this talk about situation replacing plot is so much woolly-headed bullshit. I am going to show you the location of a fossil. Your job is to write five or six pages of unplotted narration concerning this fossil. Put another way, I want you to dig for the bones and see what they look like. I think you may be quite surprised and delighted with the results. Ready? Here we go.

Everyone is familiar with the basic details of the following story; with small variations, it seems to pop up in the Police Beat section of metropolitan daily papers every other week or so. A woman—call her Jane—marries a man who is bright, witty, and pulsing with sexual magnetism. We'll call the guy

Dick; it's the world's most Freudian name. Unfortunately, Dick has a dark side. He's short-tempered, a control freak, perhaps even (you'll find this out as he speaks and acts) a paranoid. Jane tries mightily to overlook Dick's faults and make the marriage work (why she tries so hard is something you will also find out; she will come onstage and tell you). They have a child, and for awhile things seem better. Then, when the little girl is three or so, the abuse and the jealous tirades begin again. The abuse is verbal at first, then physical. Dick is convinced that Jane is sleeping with someone, perhaps someone from her job. Is it someone specific? I don't know and don't care. Eventually Dick may tell you who he suspects. If he does, we'll both know, won't we?

At last poor Jane can't take it anymore. She divorces the schmuck and gets custody of their daughter, Little Nell. Dick begins to stalk her. Jane responds by getting a restraining order, a document about as useful as a parasol in a hurricane, as many abused women will tell you. Finally, after an incident which you will write in vivid and scary detail—a public beating, perhaps—Richard the Schmuck is arrested and jailed. All of this is back story. How you work it in—and *how much* of it you work in—is up to you. In any case, it's not the situation. What follows is the situation.

One day shortly after Dick's incarceration in the city jail, Jane picks up Little Nell at the daycare center and ferries her to a friend's house for a birthday party. Jane then takes herself home, looking forward to two or three hours' unaccustomed peace and quiet. Perhaps, she thinks, I'll take a nap. It's a house she's going to, even though she's a young working woman—the situation sort of demands it. How she came by this house and why she has the afternoon off are things the story will tell you and which will look neatly plotted if you come up with good reasons (perhaps the house belongs to her parents; perhaps she's house-sitting; perhaps another thing entirely).

Something pings at her, just below the level of consciousness, as she lets herself in, something that makes her uneasy. She can't isolate it and tells herself it's just nerves, a little fall-out from her five years of hell with Mr. Congeniality. What else *could* it be? Dick is under lock and key, after all.

Before taking her nap, Jane decides to have a cup of herbal tea and watch the news. (Can you use that pot of boiling water on the stove later on? Perhaps, perhaps.) The lead item on *Action News at Three* is a shocker: that morning, three men escaped from the city jail, killing a guard in the process. Two of the three bad guys were recaptured almost at once, but the third is still at large. None of the prisoners are identified by name (not in *this* newscast, at least), but Jane, sitting in her empty house (which you will now have plausibly explained), knows beyond a shadow of a doubt that one of them was Dick. She knows because she has finally identified that ping of unease she felt in the foyer. It was the smell, faint and fading, of Vitalis hair-tonic. *Dick's* hair-tonic. Jane sits in her chair, her muscles lax with fright, unable to get up. And as she hears Dick's footfalls begin to descend the stairs, she thinks: *Only Dick would make sure he had hair-tonic, even in jail.* She must get up, must run, but she can't move . . .

It's a pretty good story, yes? I think so, but not exactly unique. As I've already pointed out, ESTRANGED HUBBY BEATS UP (or MURDERS) EX-WIFE makes the paper every other week, sad but true. What I want you to do in this exercise is *change the sexes of the antagonist and protagonist* before beginning to work out the situation in your narrative—make the ex-wife the stalker, in other words (perhaps it's a mental institution she's escaped from instead of the city jail), the husband the victim. Narrate this without plotting—let the situation and that one unexpected inversion carry you along. I predict you will succeed swimmingly . . . if, that is, you are honest about how your characters speak and behave. Honesty in story-telling makes up for a great many stylistic faults, as the work of wooden-prose writers like Theodore Dreiser and Ayn Rand shows, but lying is the great unrepairable fault. Liars prosper, no question about it, but only in the grand sweep of things, never down in the jungles of actual composition, where you must take your objective one bloody word at a time. If you begin to lie about what you know and feel while you're down there, everything falls down.

When you finish your exercise, drop me a line at www.stephenking.com and tell me how it worked for you. I can't promise to vet every reply, but I *can* promise to read at least some of your adventures with great interest. I'm curious to know what kind of fossil you dig up, and how much of it you are able to retrieve from the ground intact.

– 6 –

Description is what makes the reader a sensory participant in the story. Good description is a learned skill, one of the prime reasons why you cannot succeed unless you read a lot and write a lot. It's not just a question of *how-to,* you see; it's also a question of *how much to.* Reading will help you answer how much, and only reams of writing will help you with the how. You can learn only by doing.

Description begins with visualization of what it is you want the reader to experience. It ends with your translating what you see in your mind into words on the page. It's far from easy. As I've said, we've all heard someone say, "Man, it was so great (or so horrible/strange/funny) . . . I just can't describe it!" If you want to be a successful writer, you *must* be able to describe it, and in a way that will cause your reader to prickle with recognition. If you can do this, you will be paid for your labors, and deservedly so. If you can't, you're going to collect a lot of rejection slips and perhaps explore a career in the fascinating world of telemarketing.

Thin description leaves the reader feeling bewildered and nearsighted. Overdescription buries him or her in details and images. The trick is to find a happy medium. It's also important to know *what* to describe and what can be left alone while you get on with your main job, which is telling a story.

I'm not particularly keen on writing which exhaustively describes the physical characteristics of the people in the story and what they're wearing (I find wardrobe inventory particularly irritating; if I want to read descriptions of clothes, I can always get a J. Crew catalogue). I can't remember many cases where I felt I had to describe what the people in a story of mine looked like—I'd rather let the reader supply the faces, the builds, and the clothing as well. If I tell you that Carrie White is a high school outcast with a bad complexion and a fashion-victim wardrobe, I think you can do the rest, can't you? I don't need to give you a pimple-by-pimple, skirt-by-skirt rundown. We all remember one or more high school losers, after all; if I describe mine, it freezes out yours, and I lose a little bit of the bond of understanding I want to forge between us. Description begins in the writer's imagination, but should finish in the reader's. When it comes to actually pulling this off, the writer is much more fortunate than the filmmaker, who is almost always doomed to show too much . . . including, in nine cases out of ten, the zipper running up the monster's back.

I think locale and texture are much more important to the reader's sense of actually being *in* the story than any physical description of the players. Nor do I think that physical description should be a shortcut to character. So spare me, if you please, the hero's **sharply intelligent blue eyes** and **outthrust determined chin;** likewise the heroine's **arrogant cheekbones.** This sort of thing is bad technique and lazy writing, the equivalent of all those tiresome adverbs.

For me, good description usually consists of a few well-chosen details that will stand for everything else. In most cases, these details will be the first ones that come to mind. Certainly they will do for a start. If you decide later on that you'd like to change, add, or delete, you can do so—it's what rewrite was invented for. But I think you will find that, in most cases, your first visualized details will be the truest and best. You should remember (and your reading will prove it over and over again should you begin to doubt) that it's as easy to overdescribe as to underdescribe. Probably easier.

One of my favorite restaurants in New York is the steakhouse Palm Too on Second Avenue. If I decide to set a scene in Palm Too, I'll certainly be writing about what I know, as I've been there on a number of occasions. Before beginning to write, I'll take a moment to call up an image of the place, drawing from my memory and filling my mind's eye, an eye whose vision grows sharper the more it is used. I call it a mental eye because that's the phrase with which we're all familiar, but what I actually want to do is open *all* my senses. This memory search will be brief but intense, a kind of hypnotic recall. And, as with actual hypnosis, you'll find it easier to accomplish the more you attempt it.

The first four things which come to my mind when I think of Palm Too are: (a) the darkness of the bar and the contrasting brightness of the backbar mirror, which catches and reflects light from the street; (b) the sawdust on the floor; (c) the funky cartoon caricatures on the walls; (d) the smells of cooking steak and fish.

If I think longer I can come up with more stuff (what I don't remember I'll make up—during the visualization process, fact and fiction become entwined), but there's no need for more. This isn't the Taj Mahal we're visiting, after all, and I don't want to sell you the place. It's also important to remember it's not about the setting, anyway—it's about the story, and it's *always* about the story. It will not behoove me (or you) to wander off into thickets of description just because it would be easy to do. We have other fish (and steak) to fry.

Bearing that in mind, here's a sample bit of narration which takes a character into Palm Too:

> The cab pulled up in front of Palm Too at quarter to four on a bright summer afternoon. Billy paid the driver, stepped out onto the sidewalk, and took a quick look around for Martin. Not in sight. Satisfied, Billy went inside.
>
> After the hot clarity of Second Avenue, Palm Too was as dark as a cave. The backbar mirror picked up some of the street-glare and glimmered in the gloom like a mirage. For a moment it was all Billy could see, and then his eyes began to adjust. There were a few solitary drinkers at the bar. Beyond them, the maître d', his tie undone and his shirt cuffs rolled back to show his hairy wrists, was talking with the bartender. There was still

sawdust sprinkled on the floor, Billy noted, as if this were a twenties speakeasy instead of a millennium eatery where you couldn't smoke, let alone spit a gob of tobacco between your feet. And the cartoons dancing across the walls—gossip-column caricatures of downtown political hustlers, newsmen who had long since retired or drunk themselves to death, celebrities you couldn't quite recognize—still gambolled all the way to the ceiling. The air was redolent of steak and fried onions. All of it the same as it ever was.

The maître d' stepped forward. "Can I help you, sir? We don't open for dinner until six, but the bar—"

"I'm looking for Richie Martin," Billy said.

Billy's arrival in the cab is narration—action, if you like that word better. What follows after he steps through the door of the restaurant is pretty much straight description. I got in almost all of the details which first came to mind when I accessed my memories of the real Palm Too, and I added a few other things, as well—the maître d' between shifts is pretty good, I think; I love the undone tie and the cuffs rolled up to expose the hairy wrists. It's like a photograph. The smell of fish is the only thing not here, and that's because the smell of the onions was stronger.

We come back to actual storytelling with a bit of narration (the maître d' steps forward to center stage) and then the dialogue. By now we see our location clearly. There are plenty of details I could have added—the narrowness of the room, Tony Bennett on the sound system, the Yankees bumper-sticker on the cash register—but what would be the point? When it comes to scene-setting and all sorts of description, a meal is as good as a feast. We want to know if Billy has located Richie Martin—that's the story we paid our twenty-four bucks to read. More about the restaurant would slow the pace of that story, perhaps annoying us enough to break the spell good fiction can weave. In many cases when a reader puts a story aside because it "got boring," the boredom arose because the writer grew enchanted with his powers of description and lost sight of his priority, which is to keep the ball rolling. If the reader wants to know more about Palm Too than can be found above, he or she can either visit the next time he or she is in New York, or send for a brochure. I've already spilled enough ink here for me to indicate Palm Too will be a major setting for my story. If it turns out not to be, I'd do well to revise the descriptive stuff down by a few lines in the next draft. Certainly I couldn't keep it in on the grounds that it's good; it *should* be good, if I'm being paid to do it. What I'm not being paid to do is be self-indulgent.

There is straight description ("a few solitary drinkers at the bar") and a bit of rather more poetic description ("The backbar mirror . . . glimmered in the gloom like a mirage") in my central descriptive paragraph about Palm Too. Both are okay, but I like the figurative stuff. The use of simile and other figurative language is one of the chief delights of fiction—reading it and writing it, as well. When it's on target, a simile delights us in much the same way meeting an old friend in a crowd of strangers does. By comparing two seemingly unrelated objects—a restaurant bar and a cave, a mirror and a mirage—we are sometimes able to see an old thing in a new and vivid way.* Even if the result is mere clarity

---

*Although "dark as a cave" isn't all that riveting; certainly we've heard it before. It is, truth to tell, a bit lazy, not quite a cliché but certainly in the neighborhood.

instead of beauty, I think writer and reader are participating together in a kind of miracle. Maybe that's drawing it a little strong, but yeah—it's what I believe.

When a simile or metaphor *doesn't* work, the results are sometimes funny and sometimes embarrassing. Recently I read this sentence in a forthcoming novel I prefer not to name: "He sat stolidly beside the corpse, waiting for the medical examiner as patiently as a man waiting for a turkey sandwich." If there is a clarifying connection here, I wasn't able to make it. I consequently closed the book without reading further. If a writer knows what he or she is doing, I'll go along for the ride. If he or she doesn't . . . well, I'm in my fifties now, and there are a lot of books out there. I don't have time to waste with the poorly written ones.

The Zen simile is only one potential pitfall of figurative language. The most common—and again, landing in this trap can usually be traced back to not enough reading—is the use of clichéd similes, metaphors, and images. He ran **like a madman,** she was pretty **as a summer day,** the guy was **a hot ticket,** Bob fought **like a tiger** . . . don't waste my time (or anyone's) with such chestnuts. It makes you look either lazy or ignorant. Neither description will do your reputation as a writer much good.

My all-time favorite similes, by the way, come from the hardboiled-detective fiction of the forties and fifties, and the literary descendants of the dime-dreadful writers. These favorites include "It was darker than a carload of assholes" (George V. Higgins) and "I lit a cigarette [that] tasted like a plumber's handkerchief" (Raymond Chandler).

The key to good description begins with clear seeing and ends with clear writing, the kind of writing that employs fresh images and simple vocabulary. I began learning my lessons in this regard by reading Chandler, Hammett, and Ross MacDonald; I gained perhaps even more respect for the power of compact, descriptive language from reading T. S. Eliot (those ragged claws scuttling across the ocean floor; those coffee spoons), and William Carlos Williams (white chickens, red wheelbarrow, the plums that were in the ice box, so sweet and so cold).

As with all other aspects of the narrative art, you will improve with practice, but practice will never make you perfect. Why should it? What fun would that be? And the harder you try to be clear and simple, the more you will learn about the complexity of our American dialect. It be slippery, precious; aye, it be very slippery, indeed. Practice the art, always reminding yourself that your job is to say what you see, and then to get on with your story.

– 7 –

Let us now talk a little bit about dialogue, the audio portion of our programme. It's dialogue that gives your cast their voices, and is crucial in defining their characters—only what people do tells us more about what they're like, and talk is sneaky: what people say often conveys their character to others in ways of which they—the speakers—are completely unaware.

You can tell me via straight narration that your main character, Mistuh Butts, never did well in school, never even *went* much to school, but you can convey the same thing, and much more vividly, by his speech . . . and one of the cardinal rules of good fiction is never tell us a thing if you can show us, instead:

"What you reckon?" the boy asked. He doodled a stick in the dirt without looking up. What he drew could have been a ball, or a planet, or nothing but a circle. "You reckon the earth goes around the sun like they say?"

"I don't know what they say," Mistuh Butts replied. "I ain't never studied what thisun or thatun says, because eachun says a different thing until your head is finally achin and you lose your aminite."

"What's aminite?" the boy asked.

"You don't never shut up the questions!" Mistuh Butts cried. He seized the boy's stick and snapped it. "Aminite is in your belly when it's time to eat! Less you sick! And folks say *I'm* ignorant!"

"Oh, *appetite,*" the boy said placidly, and began drawing again, this time with his finger.

Well-crafted dialogue will indicate if a character is smart or dumb (Mistuh Butts isn't necessarily a moron just because he can't say *appetite;* we must listen to him awhile longer before making up our minds on that score), honest or dishonest, amusing or an old sobersides. Good dialogue, such as that written by George V. Higgins, Peter Straub, or Graham Greene, is a delight to read; bad dialogue is deadly.

Writers have different skill levels when it comes to dialogue. Your skills in this area can be improved, but, as a great man once said (actually it was Clint Eastwood), "A man's got to know his limitations." H. P. Lovecraft was a genius when it came to tales of the macabre, but a terrible dialogue writer. He seems to have known it, too, because in the millions of words of fiction he wrote, fewer than *five thousand* are dialogue. The following passage from "The Colour Out of Space," in which a dying farmer describes the alien presence which has invaded his well, showcases Lovecraft's dialogue problems. Folks, people just don't talk like this, even on their deathbeds:

> "Nothin' . . . nothin' . . . the colour . . . it burns . . . cold an' wet . . . but it burns . . . it lived in the well . . . I seen it . . . a kind o' smoke . . . jest like the flowers last spring . . . the well shone at night . . . everything alive . . . sucked the life out of everything . . . in the stone . . . it must a'come in that stone . . . pizened the whole place . . . dun't know what it wants . . . that round thing the men from the college dug out'n the stone . . . it was that same colour . . . jest the same, like the flowers an' plants . . . seeds . . . I seen it the fust time this week . . . it beats down your mind an' then gets ye . . . burns ye up . . . It come from some place whar things ain't as they is here . . . one o' them professors said so . . ."

And so on and so forth, in carefully constructed elliptical bursts of information. It's hard to say exactly what's wrong with Lovecraft's dialogue, other than the obvious: it's stilted and lifeless, brimming with country cornpone ("some place whar things ain't as they is here"). When dialogue is right, we know. When it's wrong we also know—it jags on the ear like a badly tuned musical instrument.

Lovecraft was, by all accounts, both snobbish and painfully shy (a galloping racist as well, his stories full of sinister Africans and the sort of scheming Jews my Uncle Oren always worried about after four or five beers), the kind of writer who maintains a voluminous correspondence but gets along poorly with others in person—were he alive today, he'd likely exist most vibrantly in various Internet chatrooms. Dialogue is a skill best learned by people who enjoy talking and listening to others—particularly listening, picking up the accents, rhythms, dialect, and slang of various groups. Loners such as Lovecraft often write it badly, or with the care of someone who is composing in a language other than his or her native tongue.

I don't know if contemporary novelist John Katzenbach is a loner or not, but his novel *Hart's War* contains some memorably bad dialogue. Katzenbach is the sort of novelist who drives creative-writing teachers mad, a wonderful storyteller whose art is marred by self-repetition (a fault which is curable) and an ear for talk that is pure tin (a fault which probably isn't). *Hart's War* is a murder mystery set in a World War II POW camp—a neat idea, but problematic in Katzenbach's hands once he really gets the pot boiling. Here is Wing Commander Phillip Pryce talking to his friends just before the Germans in charge of Stalag Luft 13 take him away, not to be repatriated as they claim, but probably to be shot in the woods.

> Pryce grabbed at Tommy once again. "Tommy," he whispered, "this is not a coincidence! Nothing is what it seems! Dig deeper! Save him, lad, save him! For more than ever, now, I believe Scott is innocent! . . . You're on your own now, boys. And remember, I'm counting on you to live through this! Survive! Whatever happens!"
>
> He turned back to the Germans. "All right, *Hauptmann*," he said with a sudden, exceedingly calm determination. "I'm ready now. Do with me what you will."

Either Katzenbach does not realize that every line of the Wing Commander's dialogue is a cliché from a late-forties war movie or he's trying to use that similarity deliberately to awaken feelings of pity, sadness, and perhaps nostalgia in his audience. Either way, it doesn't work. The only feeling the passage evokes is a kind of impatient incredulity. You wonder if any editor ever saw it, and if so, what stayed his or her blue pencil. Given Katzenbach's considerable talents in other areas, his failure here tends to reinforce my idea that writing good dialogue is art as well as craft.

Many good dialogue writers simply seem to have been born with a well-tuned ear, just as some musicians and singers have perfect or near-perfect pitch. Here's a passage from Elmore Leonard's novel *Be Cool.* You might compare it to the Lovecraft and Katzenbach passages above, noting first of all that here we've got an honest-to-God exchange going on, and not a stilted soliloquy:

Chili . . . looked up again as Tommy said, "You doing okay?"

"You want to know if I'm making out?"

"I mean in your business. How's it going? I know you did okay with *Get Leo,* a terrific picture, terrific. And you know what else? It was good. But the sequel—what was it called?"

"Get Lost."

"Yeah, well that's what happened before I got a chance to see it, it disappeared."

"It didn't open big so the studio walked away. I was against doing a sequel to begin with. But the guy running production at Tower says they're making the picture, with me or without me. I thought, well, if I can come up with a good story . . ."

On Writing

Two guys at lunch in Beverly Hills, and right away we know they're both players. They may be phonies (and maybe they're not), but they're an instant buy within the context of Leonard's story; in fact, we welcome them with open arms. Their talk is so real that part of what we feel is the guilty pleasure of anyone first tuning in and then eavesdropping on an interesting conversation. We're getting a sense of character, as well, although only in faint strokes. This is early on in the novel (page two, actually), and Leonard is an old pro. He knows he doesn't have to do it all at once. Still, don't we learn something about Tommy's character when he assures Chili that *Get Leo* is not only terrific, but also good?

We could ask ourselves if such dialogue is true to life or only to a certain *idea* of life, a certain stereotyped image of Hollywood players, Hollywood lunches, Hollywood deals. This is a fair enough question, and the answer is, perhaps not. Yet the dialogue *does* ring true to our ear; at his best (and although *Be Cool* is quite entertaining, it is far from Leonard's best), Elmore Leonard is capable of a kind of street poetry. The skill necessary to write such dialogue comes from years of practice; the art comes from a creative imagination which is working hard and having fun.

As with all other aspects of fiction, the key to writing good dialogue is honesty. And if you *are* honest about the words coming out of your characters' mouths, you'll find that you've let yourself in for a fair amount of criticism. Not a week goes by that I don't receive at least one pissed-off letter (most weeks there are more) accusing me of being foul-mouthed, bigoted, homophobic, murderous, frivolous, or downright psychopathic. In the majority of cases what my correspondents are hot under the collar about relates to something in the dialogue: "Let's get the fuck out of Dodge" or "We don't cotton much to niggers around here" or "What do you think you're doing, you fucking faggot?"

My mother, God rest her, didn't approve of profanity or any such talk; she called it "the language of the ignorant." This did not, however, keep her from yelling "Oh shit!" if she burned the roast or nailed her thumb a good one while hammering a picture-hook in the wall. Nor does it preclude most people, Christian as well as heathen, from saying something similar (or even stronger) when the dog barfs on the shag carpet or the car slips off the jack. It's important to tell the truth; so much depends upon it, as William Carlos Williams almost said when he was writing about that red wheelbarrow. The Legion of Decency might not like the word *shit,* and you might not like it much, either, but sometimes you're just stuck with it—no kid ever ran to his mother and said that his little sister just *defecated* in the tub. I suppose he might say *pushed* or *went woowoo,* but *took a shit* is, I fear, very much in the ballpark (little pitchers have big ears, after all).

You *must* tell the truth if your dialogue is to have the resonance and realism that *Hart's War,* good story though it is, so sadly lacks—and that holds true all the way down to what folks say when they hit their thumb with the hammer. If you substitute "Oh sugar!" for "Oh shit!" because you're thinking about the Legion of Decency, you are breaking the unspoken contract that exists between writer and reader—your promise to express the truth of how people act and talk through the medium of a made-up story.

On the other hand, one of your characters (the protagonist's old maid aunt, for instance) really *might* say *Oh sugar* instead of *Oh shit* after pounding her thumb with the hammer.

You'll know which to use if you know your character, and we'll learn something about the speaker that will make him or her more vivid and interesting. The point is to let each character speak freely, without regard to what the Legion of Decency or the Christian Ladies' Reading Circle may approve of. To do otherwise would be cowardly as well as dishonest, and believe me, writing fiction in America as we enter the twenty-first century is no job for intellectual cowards. There are lots of would-be censors out there, and although they may have different agendas, they all want basically the same thing: for you to see the world they see . . . or to at least shut up about what you *do* see that's different. They are agents of the status quo. Not necessarily bad guys, but dangerous guys if you happen to believe in intellectual freedom.

As it happens, I agree with my mother: profanity and vulgarity *is* the language of the ignorant and the verbally challenged. *Mostly,* that is; there are exceptions, including profane aphorisms of great color and vitality. *They always fuck you at the drive-thru; I'm busier than a one-legged man in an ass-kicking contest; wish in one hand, shit in the other, see which one fills up first*—these phrases and others like them aren't for the drawing-room, but they *are* striking and pungent. Or consider this passage from *Brain Storm,* by Richard Dooling, where vulgarity becomes poetry:

> "Exhibit A: One loutish, headstrong penis, a barbarous cuntivore without a flyspeck of decency in him. The capscallion of all rapscallions. A scurvy, vermiform scug with a serpentine twinkle in his solitary eye. An orgulous Turk who strikes in the dark vaults of flesh like a penile thunderbolt. A greedy cur seeking shadows, slick crevices, tuna fish ecstasy, and sleep . . ."

Although not offered as dialogue, I want to reproduce another passage from Dooling here, because it speaks to the converse: that one can be quite admirably graphic without resorting to vulgarity or profanity at all:

> She straddled him and prepared to make the necessary port connections, male and female adapters ready, I/O enabled, server/client, master/slave. Just a couple of high-end biological machines preparing to hot-dock with cable modems and access each other's front-end processors.

If I were a Henry James or Jane Austen sort of guy, writing only about toffs or smart college folks, I'd hardly ever have to use a dirty word or a profane phrase; I might never have had a book banned from America's school libraries or gotten a letter from some helpful fundamentalist fellow who wants me to know that I'm going to burn in hell, where all my millions of dollars won't buy me so much as a single drink of water. I did not, however, grow up among folks of that sort. I grew up as a part of America's lower middle class, and they're the people I can write about with the most honesty and knowledge. It means that they say shit more often than sugar when they bang their thumbs, but I've made my peace with that. Was never much at war with it in the first place, as a matter of fact.

When I get one of Those Letters, or face another review that accuses me of being a vulgar lowbrow—which to some extent I am—I take comfort from the words of turn-of-the-century social realist Frank Norris, whose novels include *The Octopus, The Pit,* and *McTeague,* an authentically great book. Norris wrote about working-class guys on ranches, in city laboring jobs, in factories. McTeague, the main character of Norris's finest work, is an unschooled dentist. Norris's books provoked a good deal of public outrage, to which Norris responded coolly and disdainfully: "What do I care for their opinions? I never truckled. I told them the truth."

Some people don't want to hear the truth, of course, but that's not your problem. What would be is wanting to be a writer without wanting to shoot straight. Talk, whether ugly or beautiful, is an index of character; it can also be a breath of cool, refreshing air in a room some people would prefer to keep shut up. In the end, the important question has nothing to do with whether the talk in your story is sacred or profane; the only question is how it rings on the page and in the ear. If you expect it to ring true, then you must talk yourself. Even more important, you must shut up and listen to others talk.

– 8 –

Everything I've said about dialogue applies to building characters in fiction. The job boils down to two things: paying attention to how the real people around you behave and then telling the truth about what you see. You may notice that your next-door neighbor picks his nose when he thinks no one is looking. This is a great detail, but noting it does you no good as a writer unless you're willing to dump it into a story at some point.

Are fictional characters drawn directly from life? Obviously not, at least on a one-to-one basis—you'd *better* not, unless you want to get sued or shot on your way to the mailbox some fine morning. In many cases, such as *roman à clef* novels like *Valley of the Dolls,* characters are drawn *mostly* from life, but after readers get done playing the inevitable guessing game about who's who, these stories tend to be unsatisfying, stuffed with shadowbox celebrities who bonk each other and then fade quickly from the reader's mind. I read *Valley of the Dolls* shortly after it came out (I was a cook's boy at a western Maine resort that summer), gobbling it up as eagerly as everyone else who bought it, I suppose, but I can't remember much of what it was about. On the whole, I think I prefer the weekly codswallop served up by *The National Enquirer,* where I can get recipes and cheesecake photographs as well as scandal.

For me, what happens to characters as a story progresses depends solely on what I discover about them as I go along—how they grow, in other words. Sometimes they grow a little. If they grow a lot, they begin to influence the course of the story instead of the other way around. I almost always start with something that's situational. I don't say that's right, only that it's the way I've always worked. If a story ends up that same way, however, I count it something of a failure no matter how interesting it may be to me or to others. I think the best stories always end up being about the people rather than the event, which is to say character-driven. Once you get beyond the short story, though (two to four thousand words, let's say), I'm not much of a believer in the so-called character study; I think that in the end, the story should always be the boss. Hey, if you want a character study, buy a biography or get season tickets to your local college's theater-lab productions. You'll get all the character you can stand.

It's also important to remember that no one is "the bad guy" or "the best friend" or "the whore with a heart of gold" in real life; in real life we each of us regard ourselves as the main character, the protagonist, the big cheese; the camera is on *us,* baby. If you can bring this attitude into your fiction, you may not find it easier to create *brilliant* characters, but it will be harder for you to create the sort of one-dimensional dopes that populate so much pop fiction.

Annie Wilkes, the nurse who holds Paul Sheldon prisoner in *Misery,* may seem psychopathic to us, but it's important to remember that she seems perfectly sane and reasonable to herself—heroic, in fact, a beleaguered woman trying to survive in a hostile world filled with cockadoodie brats. We see her go through dangerous mood-swings, but I tried never to come right out and say "Annie was depressed and possibly suicidal that day" or "Annie seemed particularly happy that day." If I have to tell you, I lose. If, on the other hand, I can show you a silent, dirty-haired woman who compulsively gobbles cake and candy, then have you draw the conclusion that Annie is in the depressive part of a manic-depressive cycle, I win. And if I am able, even briefly, to give you a Wilkes'-eye-view of the world—if I can make you understand her madness—then perhaps I can make her someone you sympathize with or even identify with. The result? She's more frightening than ever, because she's close to real. If, on the other hand, I turn her into a cackling old crone, she's just another pop-up bogeylady. In that case I lose bigtime, and so does the reader. Who would want to visit with such a stale shrew? That version of Annie was old when *The Wizard of Oz* was in its first run.

It would be fair enough to ask, I suppose, if Paul Sheldon in *Misery* is me. Certainly *parts* of him are . . . but I think you will find that, if you continue to write fiction, every character you create is partly you. When you ask yourself what a certain character will do given a certain set of circumstances, you're making the decision based on what you yourself would (or, in the case of a bad guy, wouldn't) do. Added to these versions of yourself are the character traits, both lovely and unlovely, which you observe in others (a guy who picks his nose when he thinks no one is looking, for instance). There is also a wonderful third element: pure blue-sky imagination. This is the part which allowed me to be a psychotic nurse for a little while when I was writing *Misery*. And being Annie was not, by and large, hard at all. In fact, it was sort of fun. I think being Paul was harder. He was sane, I'm sane, no four days at Disneyland there.

My novel *The Dead Zone* arose from two questions: Can a political assassin ever be right? And if he is, could you make him the protagonist of a novel? The good guy? These ideas called for a dangerously unstable politician, it seemed to me—a fellow who could climb the political ladder by showing the world a jolly, jes'-folks face and charming the voters by refusing to play the game in the usual way. (Greg Stillson's campaign tactics as I imagined them twenty years ago were very similar to the ones Jesse Ventura used in his successful campaign for the governor's seat in Minnesota. Thank goodness Ventura doesn't seem like Stillson in any other ways.)

The Dead Zone's protagonist, Johnny Smith, is also an everyday, jes'-folks sort of guy, only with Johnny it's no act. The one thing that sets him apart is a limited ability to see the future, gained as the result of a childhood accident. When Johnny shakes Greg Stillson's hand at a political rally, he has a vision of Stillson becoming the President of the United States and subsequently starting World War III. Johnny comes to the conclusion that the only way he can keep this from happening—the only way he can save the world, in other words—is by putting a bullet in Stillson's head. Johnny is different from other violent, paranoid mystics in only one way: he really *can* see the future. Only don't they all say that?

The situation had an edgy, outlaw feel to it that appealed to me. I thought the story would work if I could make Johnny a genuinely decent guy without turning him into a plaster saint. Same thing with Stillson, only backwards: I wanted him to be authentically nasty and really scare the reader, not just because Stillson is always boiling with potential violence but because he is so goddam *persuasive.* I wanted the reader to constantly be thinking: "This guy is out of control—how come somebody can't see through him?" The fact that Johnny *does* see through him would, I thought, put the reader even more firmly in Johnny's corner.

When we first meet the potential assassin, he's taking his girl to the county fair, riding the rides and playing the games. What could be more normal or likable? The fact that he's on the verge of proposing to Sarah makes us like him even more. Later, when Sarah suggests they cap a perfect date by sleeping together for the first time, Johnny tells her he wants to wait until they're married. I felt I was walking a fine line on that one—I wanted readers to see Johnny as sincere and sincerely in love, a straight shooter but not a tight-assed prude. I was able to cut his principled behavior a bit by giving him a childish sense of humor; he greets Sarah wearing a glow-in-the-dark Halloween mask (the mask hopefully works in a symbolic way, too; certainly Johnny is perceived as a monster when he points a gun at candidate Stillson). "Same old Johnny," Sarah says, laughing, and by the time the two of them are headed back from the fair in Johnny's old Volkswagen Bug, I think Johnny Smith has become our friend, just an average American guy who's hoping to live happily ever after. The sort of guy who'd return your wallet with the money still in it if he found it on the street or stop and help you change your flat tire if he came upon you broke down by the side of the road. Ever since John F. Kennedy was shot in Dallas, the great American bogeyman has been the guy with the rifle in a high place. I wanted to make this guy into the reader's friend.

Johnny was hard. Taking an average guy and making him vivid and interesting always is. Greg Stillson (like most villains) was easier and a lot more fun. I wanted to nail his dangerous, divided character in the first scene of the book. Here, several years before he runs for the U.S. House of Representatives in New Hampshire, Stillson is a young travelling salesman hawking Bibles to midwest country folk. When he stops at one farm, he is menaced by a snarling dog. Stillson remains friendly and smiling—Mr. Jes' Folks—until he's positive no one's home at the farm. Then he sprays teargas into the dog's eyes and kicks it to death.

If one is to measure success by reader response, the opening scene of *The Dead Zone* (my first number-one hardcover bestseller) was one of my most successful ever. Certainly it struck a raw nerve; I was deluged with letters, most of them protesting my outrageous cruelty to animals. I wrote back to these folks, pointing out the usual things: (a) Greg Stillson wasn't real; (b) the *dog* wasn't real; (c) I myself had never in my life put the boot to one of my pets, or anyone else's. I also pointed out what might have been a little less obvious—it was important to establish, right up front, that Gregory Ammas Stillson was an extremely dangerous man, and very good at camouflage.

I continued to build the characters of Johnny and Greg in alternating scenes until the confrontation at the end of the book, when things resolve themselves in what I hoped would be an unexpected way. The characters of my protagonist and antagonist were determined by the story I had to tell—by the fossil, the found object, in other words. My job (and yours, if you decide this is a viable approach to storytelling) is to make sure these fictional folks behave in ways that will both help the story and seem reasonable to us, given what we know about them (and what we know about real life, of course). Sometimes villains feel self-doubt (as Greg Stillson does); sometimes they feel pity (as Annie Wilkes does). And sometimes the good guy tries to turn away from doing the right thing, as Johnny Smith does . . . as Jesus Christ himself did, if you think about that prayer ("take this cup from my lips") in the Garden of Gethsemane. And if you do your job, your characters will come to life and start doing stuff on their own. I know that sounds a little creepy if you haven't actually experienced it, but it's terrific fun when it happens. And it will solve a lot of your problems, believe me.

– 9 –

We've covered some basic aspects of good storytelling, all of which return to the same core ideas: that practice is invaluable (and should feel good, really not like practice at all) and that honesty is indispensable. Skills in description, dialogue, and character development all boil down to seeing or hearing clearly and then transcribing what you see or hear with equal clarity (and without using a lot of tiresome, unnecessary adverbs).

There are lots of bells and whistles, too—onomatopoeia, incremental repetition, stream of consciousness, interior dialogue, changes of verbal tense (it has become quite fashionable to tell stories, especially shorter ones, in the present tense), the sticky question of back story (how do you get it in and how much of it belongs), theme, pacing (we'll touch on these last two), and a dozen other topics, all of which are covered—sometimes at exhausting length—in writing courses and standard writing texts.

My take on all these things is pretty simple. It's all on the table, every bit of it, and you should use anything that improves the quality of your writing and doesn't get in the way of your story. If you like an alliterative phrase—the knights of nowhere battling the nabobs of nullity—by all means throw it in and see how it looks on paper. If it seems to work, it can stay. If it doesn't (and to me this one sounds pretty bad, like Spiro Agnew crossed with Robert Jordan), well, that DELETE key is on your machine for a good reason.

There is absolutely no need to be hidebound and conservative in your work, just as you are under no obligation to write experimental, nonlinear prose because *The Village Voice* or *The New York Review of Books* says the novel is dead. Both the traditional and the modern are available to you. Shit, write upside down if you want to, or do it in Crayola pictographs. But no matter how you do it, there comes a point when you must judge what you've written and how well you wrote it. I don't believe a story or a novel should be allowed outside the door of your study or writing room unless you feel confident that it's reasonably reader-friendly. You can't please all of the readers all of the time; you can't please even *some* of the readers all of the time, but you really ought to try to please at least some of the readers some of the time. I think William Shakespeare said that. And now that I've waved that caution flag, duly satisfying all OSHA, MENSA, NASA, and Writers' Guild guidelines, let me reiterate that it's all on the table, all up for grabs. Isn't that an intoxicating thought? I think it is. Try any goddam thing you like, no matter how boringly normal or outrageous. If it works, fine. If it doesn't, toss it. Toss it even if you love it. Sir Arthur Quiller-Couch once said, "Murder your darlings," and he was right.

I most often see chances to add the grace-notes and ornamental touches after my basic storytelling job is done. Once in awhile it comes earlier; not long after I began *The Green Mile* and realized my main character was an innocent man likely to be executed for the crime of another, I decided to give him the initials J.C., after the most famous innocent man of all time. I first saw this done in *Light in August* (still my favorite Faulkner novel), where the sacrificial lamb is named Joe Christmas. Thus death-row inmate John Bowes became John Coffey. I wasn't sure, right up to the end of the book, if my J.C. would live or die. I *wanted* him to live because I liked and pitied him, but I figured those initials couldn't hurt, one way or the other.*

Mostly I don't see stuff like that until the story's done. Once it is, I'm able to kick back, read over what I've written, and look for underlying patterns. If I see some (and I almost always do), I can work at bringing them out in a second, more fully realized, draft of the story. Two examples of the sort of work second drafts were made for are symbolism and theme.

If in school you ever studied the symbolism of the color white in *Moby-Dick* or Hawthorne's symbolic use of the forest in such stories as "Young Goodman Brown" and came away from those classes feeling like a stupidnik, you may even now be backing off with your hands raised protectively in front of you, shaking your head and saying *gee, no thanks, I gave at the office.*

---

*A few critics accused me of being symbolically simplistic in the matter of John Coffey's initials. And I'm like, "What is this, rocket science?" I mean, come *on*, guys.

But wait. Symbolism doesn't have to be difficult and relentlessly brainy. Nor does it have to be consciously crafted as a kind of ornamental Turkish rug upon which the furniture of the story stands. If you can go along with the concept of the story as a pre-existing thing, a fossil in the ground, then symbolism must also be pre-existing, right? Just another bone (or set of them) in your new discovery. That's if it's there. If it isn't, so what? You've still got the story itself, don't you?

If it *is* there and if you notice it, I think you should bring it out as well as you can, polishing it until it shines and then cutting it the way a jeweler would cut a precious or semi-precious stone.

Carrie, as I've already noted, is a short novel about a picked-on girl who discovers a telekinetic ability within herself—she can move objects by thinking about them. To atone for a vicious shower-room prank in which she has participated, Carrie's classmate Susan Snell persuades her boyfriend to invite Carrie to the Senior Prom. They are elected King and Queen. During the celebration, another of Carrie's classmates, the unpleasant Christine Hargensen, pulls a second prank on Carrie, this one deadly. Carrie takes her revenge by using her telekinetic power to kill most of her classmates (and her atrocious mother) before dying herself. That's the whole deal, really; it's as simple as a fairy-tale. There was no need to mess it up with bells and whistles, although I *did* add a number of epistolary interludes (passages from fictional books, a diary entry, letters, teletype bulletins) between narrative segments. This was partly to inject a greater sense of realism (I was thinking of Orson Welles's radio adaptation of *War of the Worlds*) but mostly because the first draft of the book was so damned short it barely seemed like a novel.

On Writing

When I read *Carrie* over prior to starting the second draft, I noticed there was blood at all three crucial points of the story: beginning (Carrie's paranormal ability is apparently brought on by her first menstrual period), climax (the prank which sets Carrie off at the prom involves a bucket of pig's blood— "pig's blood for a pig," Chris Hargensen tells her boyfriend), and end (Sue Snell, the girl who tries to help Carrie, discovers she is not pregnant as she had half-hoped and half-feared when she gets her own period).

There's plenty of blood in most horror stories, of course— it is our stock-in-trade, you might say. Still, the blood in *Carrie* seemed more than just splatter to me. It seemed to *mean* something. That meaning wasn't consciously created, however. While writing *Carrie* I never once stopped to think: "Ah, all this blood symbolism will win me Brownie Points with the critics" or "Boy oh boy, *this* should certainly get me in a college bookstore or two!" For one thing, a writer would have to be a lot crazier than I am to think of *Carrie* as anyone's intellectual treat.

Intellectual treat or not, the significance of all that blood was hard to miss once I started reading over my beer- and tea-splattered first-draft manuscript. So I started to play with the idea, image, and emotional connotations of blood, trying to think of as many associations as I could. There were lots, most of them pretty heavy. Blood is strongly linked to the idea of sacrifice; for young women it's associated with reaching physical maturity and the ability to bear children; in the Christian religion (plenty of others, as well), it's symbolic of both sin and salvation. Finally, it is associated with the handing down of family traits and talents. We are said to look like this or behave like that because "it's in our blood." We know this isn't very scientific, that those things are really in our genes and DNA patterns, but we use the one to summarize the other.

It is that ability to summarize and encapsulate that makes symbolism so interesting, useful, and—when used well—arresting. You could argue that it's really just another kind of figurative language.

Does that make it necessary to the success of your story or novel? Indeed not, and it can actually hurt, especially if you get carried away. Symbolism exists to adorn and enrich, not to create a sense of artificial profundity. *None* of the bells and whistles are about story, all right? Only *story* is about story. (Are you tired of hearing that yet? I hope not, 'cause I'm not even *close* to getting tired of saying it.)

Symbolism (and the other adornments, too) *does* serve a useful purpose, though—it's more than just chrome on the grille. It can serve as a focusing device for both you and your reader, helping to create a more unified and pleasing work. I think that, when you read your manuscript over (and when you *talk* it over), you'll see if symbolism, or the potential for it, exists. If it doesn't, leave well enough alone. If it does, however—if it's clearly a part of the fossil you're working to unearth—go for it. Enhance it. You're a monkey if you don't.

– 10 –

The same things are true of theme. Writing and literature classes can be annoyingly preoccupied by (and pretentious about) theme, approaching it as the most sacred of sacred cows, but (don't be shocked) it's really no big deal. If you write a novel, spend weeks and then months catching it word by word, you owe it both to the book and to yourself to lean back (or take a long walk) when you've finished and ask yourself why you bothered—why you spent all that time, why it seemed so important. In other words, what's it all about, Alfie?

When you write a book, you spend day after day scanning and identifying the trees. When you're done, you have to step back and look at the forest. Not every book has to be loaded with symbolism, irony, or musical language (they call it prose for a reason, y'know), but it seems to me that every book—at least every one worth reading—is about *something*. Your job during or just after the first draft is to decide what something or somethings yours is about. Your job in the second draft— one of them, anyway—is to make that something even more clear. This may necessitate some big changes and revisions. The benefits to you and your reader will be clearer focus and a more unified story. It hardly ever fails.

The book that took me the longest to write was *The Stand*. This is also the one my longtime readers still seem to like the best (there's something a little depressing about such a united opinion that you did your best work twenty years ago, but we won't go into that just now, thanks). I finished the first draft about sixteen months after I started it. *The Stand* took an especially long time because it nearly died going into the third turn and heading for home.

I'd wanted to write a sprawling, multi-character sort of novel—a fantasy epic, if I could manage it—and to that end I employed a shifting-perspective narrative, adding a major character in each chapter of the long first section. Thus Chapter One concerned itself with Stuart Redman, a blue-collar factory worker from Texas; Chapter Two first concerned itself with Fran Goldsmith, a pregnant college girl from Maine, and then returned to Stu; Chapter Three began with Larry Underwood, a rock-and-roll singer in New York, before going back first to Fran, then to Stu Redman again.

My plan was to link all these characters, the good, the bad, and the ugly, in two places: Boulder and Las Vegas. I thought they'd probably end up going to war against one another. The first half of the book also told the story of a man-made virus which sweeps America and the world, wiping out ninety-nine per cent of the human race and utterly destroying our technology-based culture.

I was writing this story near the end of the so-called Energy Crisis in the 1970s, and I had an absolutely marvellous time envisioning a world that went smash during the course of one horrified, infected summer (really not much more than a month). The view was panoramic, detailed, nationwide, and (to me, at least) breathtaking. Rarely have I seen so clearly with the eye of my imagination, from the traffic jam plugging the dead tube of New York's Lincoln Tunnel to the sinister, Nazi-ish rebirth of Las Vegas under the watchful (and often amused) red eye of Randall Flagg. All this sounds terrible, *is* terrible, but to me the vision was also strangely optimistic. No more energy crisis, for one thing, no more famine, no more massacres in Uganda, no more acid rain or hole in the ozone layer. *Finito* as well to saber-rattling nuclear superpowers, and certainly no more overpopulation. Instead, there was a chance for humanity's remaining shred to start over again in a God-centered world to which miracles, magic, and prophecy had returned. I liked my story. I liked my characters. And still there came a point when I couldn't write any longer because I didn't know what to write. Like Pilgrim in John Bunyan's epic, I had come to a place where the straight way was lost. I wasn't the first writer to discover this awful place, and I'm a long way from being the last; this is the land of writer's block.

If I'd had two or even three hundred pages of single-spaced manuscript instead of more than five hundred, I think I would have abandoned *The Stand* and gone on to something else—God knows I had done it before. But five hundred pages was too great an investment, both in time and in creative energy; I found it impossible to let go. Also, there was this little voice whispering to me that the book was really good, and if I didn't finish I would regret it forever. So instead of moving on to another project, I started taking long walks (a habit which would, two decades later, get me in a lot of trouble). I took a book or magazine on these walks but rarely opened it, no matter how bored I felt looking at the same old trees and the same old chattering, ill-natured jays and squirrels. Boredom can be a very good thing for someone in a creative jam. I spent those walks being bored and thinking about my gigantic boondoggle of a manuscript.

For weeks I got exactly nowhere in my thinking—it all just seemed too hard, too fucking complex. I had run out too many plotlines, and they were in danger of becoming snarled. I circled the problem again and again, beat my fists on it, knocked my head against it . . . and then one day when I was thinking of nothing much at all, the answer came to me. It arrived whole and complete—gift-wrapped, you could say—in a single bright flash. I ran home and jotted it down on paper, the only time I've done such a thing, because I was terrified of forgetting.

What I saw was that the America in which *The Stand* took place might have been depopulated by the plague, but the world of my story had become dangerously overcrowded—a veritable Calcutta. The solution to where I was stuck, I saw, could be pretty much the same as the situation that got me going—an explosion instead of a plague, but still one quick, hard slash of the Gordian knot. I would send the survivors west from Boulder to Las Vegas on a redemptive quest—they would go at once, with no supplies and no plan, like Biblical characters seeking a vision or to know the will of God. In Vegas they would meet Randall Flagg, and good guys and bad guys alike would be forced to make their stand.

At one moment I had none of this; at the next I had all of it. If there is any one thing I love about writing more than the rest, it's that sudden flash of insight when you see how everything connects. I have heard it called "thinking above the curve," and it's that; I've heard it called "the over-logic," and it's that, too. Whatever you call it, I wrote my page or two of notes in a frenzy of excitement and spent the next two or three days turning my solution over in my mind, looking for flaws and holes (also working out the actual narrative flow, which involved two supporting characters placing a bomb in a major character's closet), but that was mostly out of a sense of this-is-too-good-to-be-true unbelief. Too good or not, I knew it *was* true at the moment of revelation: that bomb in Nick Andros's closet was going to solve all my narrative problems. It did, too. The rest of the book ran itself off in nine weeks.

Later, when my first draft of *The Stand* was done, I was able to get a better fix on what had stopped me so completely in mid-course; it was a lot easier to think without that voice in the middle of my head constantly yammering *"I'm losing my book! Ah shit, five hundred pages and I'm losing my book! Condition red! CONDITION RED!!"* I was also able to analyze what got me going again and appreciate the irony of it: I saved my book by blowing approximately half its major characters to smithereens (there actually ended up being *two* explosions, the one in Boulder balanced by a similar act of sabotage in Las Vegas).

The real source of my malaise, I decided, had been that in the wake of the plague, my Boulder characters—the good guys—were starting up the same old technological deathtrip. The first hesitant CB broadcasts, beckoning people to Boulder, would soon lead to TV; infomercials and 900 numbers would be back in no time. Same deal with the power plants. It certainly didn't take my Boulder folks long to decide that seeking the will of the God who spared them was a lot less important than getting the refrigerators and air conditioners up and running again. In Vegas, Randall Flagg and his friends were learning how to fly jets and bombers as well as getting the lights back on, but that was okay—to be expected—because they were the bad guys. What had stopped me was realizing, on some level of my mind, that the good guys and bad guys were starting to look perilously alike, and what got me going again was realizing the good guys were worshipping an electronic golden calf and needed a wake-up call. A bomb in the closet would do just fine.

All this suggested to me that violence as a solution is woven through human nature like a damning red thread. That became the theme of *The Stand,* and I wrote the second draft with it fixed firmly in my mind. Again and again characters (the bad ones like Lloyd Henreid as well as the good ones like Stu Redman and Larry Underwood) mention the fact that "all that stuff [i.e., weapons of mass destruction] is just lying around, waiting to be picked up." When the Boulderites propose—innocently, meaning only the best—to rebuild the same old neon Tower of Babel, they are wiped out by more violence. The folks who plant the bomb are doing what Randall Flagg told them to, but Mother Abagail, Flagg's opposite number, says again and again that "all things serve God." If this is true—and within the context of *The Stand* it certainly is—then the bomb is actually a stern message from the guy upstairs, a way of saying "I didn't bring you all this way just so you could start up the same old shit."

Near the end of the novel (it *was* the end of the first, shorter version of the story), Fran asks Stuart Redman if there's any hope at all, if people ever learn from their mistakes. Stu replies, "I don't know," and then pauses. In story-time, that pause lasts only as long as it takes the reader to flick his or her eye to the last line. In the writer's study, it went on a lot longer. I searched my mind and heart for something else Stu could say, some clarifying statement. I wanted to find it because at that moment if at no other, Stu was speaking for me. In the end, however, Stu simply repeats what he has already said: *I don't know.* It was the best I could do. Sometimes the book gives you answers, but not always, and I didn't want to leave the readers who had followed me through hundreds of pages with nothing but some empty platitude I didn't believe myself. There is no *moral* to *The Stand,* no "We'd *better* learn or we'll probably destroy the whole damned planet next time"—but if the theme stands out clearly enough, those discussing it may offer their own morals and conclusions. Nothing wrong with that; such discussions are one of the great pleasures of the reading life.

Although I'd used symbolism, imagery, and literary homage before getting to my novel about the big plague (without *Dracula,* for instance, I think there is no *'Salem's Lot*), I'm quite sure that I never thought much about theme before getting roadblocked on *The Stand.* I suppose I thought such things were for Better Minds and Bigger Thinkers. I'm not sure I would have gotten to it as soon as I did, had I not been desperate to save my story.

I was astounded at how really useful "thematic thinking"

turned out to be. It wasn't just a vaporous idea that English professors made you write about on midterm essay exams ("Discuss the thematic concerns of *Wise Blood* in three well-reasoned paragraphs—30 pts"), but another handy gadget to keep in the toolbox, this one something like a magnifying glass.

Since my revelation on the road concerning the bomb in the closet, I have never hesitated to ask myself, either before starting the second draft of a book or while stuck for an idea in the first draft, just what it is I'm writing about, why I'm spending the time when I could be playing my guitar or riding my motorcycle, what got my nose down to the grindstone in the first place and then kept it there. The answer doesn't always come right away, but there usually is one, and it's usually not too hard to find, either.

I don't believe any novelist, even one who's written forty-plus books, has too many thematic concerns; I have many interests, but only a few that are deep enough to power novels. These deep interests (I won't quite call them obsessions) include how difficult it is—perhaps impossible!—to close Pandora's technobox once it's open *(The Stand, The Tommy-knockers, Firestarter)*; the question of why, if there is a God, such terrible things happen *(The Stand, Desperation, The Green Mile)*; the thin line between reality and fantasy *(The Dark Half, Bag of Bones, The Drawing of the Three)*; and most of all, the terrible attraction violence sometimes has for fundamentally good people *(The Shining, The Dark Half)*. I've also written again and again about the fundamental differences between children and adults, and about the healing power of the human imagination.

And I repeat: *no big deal.* These are just interests which have grown out of my life and thought, out of my experiences as a boy and a man, out of my roles as a husband, a father, a writer, and a lover. They are questions that occupy my mind when I turn out the lights for the night and I'm alone with myself, looking up into the darkness with one hand tucked beneath the pillow.

You undoubtedly have your own thoughts, interests, and concerns, and they have arisen, as mine have, from your experiences and adventures as a human being. Some are likely similar to those I've mentioned above and some are likely very different, but you have them, and you should use them in your work. That's not all those ideas are there for, perhaps, but surely it's one of the things they are good for.

I should close this little sermonette with a word of warning—starting with the questions and thematic concerns is a recipe for bad fiction. Good fiction always begins with story and progresses to theme; it almost never begins with theme and progresses to story. The only possible exceptions to this rule that I can think of are allegories like George Orwell's *Animal Farm* (and I have a sneaking suspicion that with *Animal Farm* the story idea may indeed have come first; if I see Orwell in the afterlife, I mean to ask him).

But once your basic story is on paper, you need to think about what it means and enrich your following drafts with your conclusions. To do less is to rob your work (and eventually your readers) of the vision that makes each tale you write uniquely your own.

– 11 –

So far, so good. Now let's talk about revising the work—how much and how many drafts? For me the answer has always been two drafts and a polish (with the advent of word-processing technology, my polishes have become closer to a third draft).

You should realize that I'm only talking about my own personal mode of writing here; in actual practice, rewriting varies greatly from writer to writer. Kurt Vonnegut, for example, rewrote each page of his novels until he got them exactly the way he wanted them. The result was days when he might only manage a page or two of finished copy (and the wastebasket would be full of crumpled, rejected page seventy-ones and seventy-twos), but when the manuscript was finished, the *book* was finished, by gum. You could set it in type. Yet I think certain things hold true for most writers, and those are the ones I want to talk about now. If you've been writing awhile, you won't need me to help you much with this part; you'll have your own established routine. If you're a beginner, though, let me urge that you take your story through at least two drafts; the one you do with the study door closed and the one you do with it open.

With the door shut, downloading what's in my head directly to the page, I write as fast as I can and still remain comfortable. Writing fiction, especially a long work of fiction, can be a difficult, lonely job; it's like crossing the Atlantic Ocean in a bathtub. There's plenty of opportunity for self-doubt. If I write rapidly, putting down my story exactly as it comes into my mind, only looking back to check the names of my characters and the relevant parts of their back stories, I find that I can keep up with my original enthusiasm and at the same time outrun the self-doubt that's always waiting to settle in.

This first draft—the All-Story Draft—should be written with no help (or interference) from anyone else. There may come a point when you want to show what you're doing to a close friend (very often the close friend you think of first is the one who shares your bed), either because you're proud of what you're doing or because you're doubtful about it. My best advice is to resist this impulse. Keep the pressure on; don't lower it by exposing what you've written to the doubt, the praise, or even the well-meaning questions of someone from the Outside World. Let your hope of success (and your fear of failure) carry you on, difficult as that can be. There'll be time to show off what you've done when you finish . . . but even after finishing I think you must be cautious and give yourself a chance to think while the story is still like a field of freshly fallen snow, absent of any tracks save your own.

The great thing about writing with the door shut is that you find yourself forced to concentrate on story to the exclusion of practically everything else. No one can ask you "What were you trying to express with Garfield's dying words?" or "What's the significance of the green dress?" You may not have been trying to express *anything* with Garfield's dying words, and Maura could be wearing green only because that's what you saw when she came into sight in your mind's eye. On the other hand, perhaps those things *do* mean something (or will, when you get a chance to look at the forest instead of the trees). Either way, the first draft is the wrong place to think about it.

Here's something else—if no one says to you, "Oh Sam (or Amy)! This is *wonderful!,*" you are a lot less apt to slack off or to start concentrating on the wrong thing . . . *being wonderful,* for instance, instead of *telling the goddam story.*

Now let's say you've finished your first draft. Congratulations! Good job! Have a glass of champagne, send out for pizza, do whatever it is you do when you've got something to celebrate. If you have someone who has been impatiently waiting to read your novel—a spouse, let's say, someone who has perhaps been working nine to five and helping to pay the bills while you chase your dream—then this is the time to give up the goods . . . if, that is, your first reader or readers will promise not to talk to you about the book until *you* are ready to talk to *them* about it.

This may sound a little high-handed, but it's really not. You've done a lot of work and you need a period of time (how much or how little depends on the individual writer) to rest. Your mind and imagination—two things which are related, but not really the same—have to recycle themselves, at least in regard to this one particular work. My advice is that you take a couple of days off—go fishing, go kayaking, do a jig-saw puzzle—and then go to work on something else. Something shorter, preferably, and something that's a complete change of direction and pace from your newly finished book. (I wrote some pretty good novellas, "The Body" and "Apt Pupil" among them, between drafts of longer works like *The Dead Zone* and *The Dark Half*.)

How long you let your book rest—sort of like bread dough between kneadings—is entirely up to you, but I think it should be a minimum of six weeks. During this time your manuscript will be safely shut away in a desk drawer, aging and (one hopes) mellowing. Your thoughts will turn to it frequently, and you'll likely be tempted a dozen times or more to take it out, if only to re-read some passage that seems particularly fine in your memory, something you'd like to go back to so you can re-experience what a really excellent writer you are.

Resist temptation. If you don't, you'll very likely decide you didn't do as well on that passage as you thought and you'd better retool it on the spot. This is bad. The only thing worse would be for you to decide the passage is even *better* than you remembered—why not drop everything and read the whole book over right then? Get back to work on it! Hell, you're ready! You're fuckin Shakespeare!

You're not, though, and you're not ready to go back to the old project until you've gotten so involved in a new one (or re-involved in your day-to-day life) that you've almost forgotten the unreal estate that took up three hours of your every morning or afternoon for a period of three or five or seven months.

When you come to the correct evening (which you well may have marked on your office calendar), take your manuscript out of the drawer. If it looks like an alien relic bought at a junk-shop or yard sale where you can hardly remember stopping, you're ready. Sit down with your door shut (you'll be opening it to the world soon enough), a pencil in your hand, and a legal pad by your side. Then read your manuscript over.

Do it all in one sitting, if that's possible (it won't be, of course, if your book is a four- or five-hundred-pager). Make all the notes you want, but concentrate on the mundane housekeeping jobs, like fixing misspellings and picking up inconsistencies. There'll be plenty; only God gets it right the first time and only a slob says, "Oh well, let it go, that's what copyeditors are for."

If you've never done it before, you'll find reading your book over after a six-week layoff to be a strange, often exhilarating experience. It's yours, you'll recognize it as yours, even be able to remember what tune was on the stereo when you wrote certain lines, and yet it will also be like reading the work of someone else, a soul-twin, perhaps. This is the way it should be, the reason you waited. It's always easier to kill someone else's darlings than it is to kill your own.

With six weeks' worth of recuperation time, you'll also be able to see any glaring holes in the plot or character development. I'm talking about holes big enough to drive a truck through. It's amazing how some of these things can elude the writer while he or she is occupied with the daily work of composition. And listen—if you spot a few of these big holes, you are *forbidden* to feel depressed about them or to beat up on yourself. Screw-ups happen to the best of us. There's a story that the architect of the Flatiron Building committed suicide when he realized, just before the ribbon-cutting ceremony, that he had neglected to put any men's rooms in his prototypical skyscraper. Probably not true, but remember this: someone *really did* design the *Titanic* and then label it unsinkable.

For me, the most glaring errors I find on the re-read have to do with character motivation (related to character development but not quite the same). I'll smack myself upside the head with the heel of my palm, then grab my legal pad and write something like **p. 91: Sandy Hunter filches a buck from Shirley's stash in the dispatch office. Why? God's sake, Sandy would NEVER do anything like this!** I also mark the page in the manuscript with a big ✗ symbol, meaning that cuts and/or changes are needed on this page, and reminding myself to check my notes for the exact details if I don't remember them.

I love this part of the process (well, I love *all* the parts of the process, but this one is especially nice) because I'm rediscovering my own book, and usually liking it. That changes. By the time a book is actually in print, I've been over it a dozen times or more, can quote whole passages, and only wish the damned old smelly thing would go away. That's later, though; the first read-through is usually pretty fine.

During that reading, the top part of my mind is concentrating on story and toolbox concerns: knocking out pronouns with unclear antecedents (I hate and mistrust pronouns, every one of them as slippery as a fly-by-night personal-injury lawyer), adding clarifying phrases where they seem necessary, and of course, deleting all the adverbs I can bear to part with (never all of them; never enough).

Underneath, however, I'm asking myself the Big Questions. The biggest: Is this story coherent? And if it is, what will turn coherence into a song? What are the recurring elements? Do they entwine and make a theme? I'm asking myself What's it all about, Stevie, in other words, and what I can do to make those underlying concerns even clearer. What I want most of all is *resonance*, something that will linger for a little while in Constant Reader's mind (and heart) after he or she has closed the book and put it up on the shelf. I'm looking for ways to do that without spoon-feeding the reader or selling my birthright for a plot of message. Take all those messages and those morals and stick em where the sun don't shine, all right? I want resonance. Most of all, *I'm looking for what I meant,* because in the second draft I'll want to add scenes and incidents that reinforce that meaning. I'll also want to delete stuff that goes in other directions. There's apt to be a lot of that stuff, especially near the beginning of a story, when I have a tendency to flail. All that thrashing around has to go if I am to achieve anything like a unified effect. When I've finished reading and making all my little anal-retentive revisions, it's time to open the door and show what I've written to four or five close friends who have indicated a willingness to look.

Someone—I can't remember who, for the life of me—once wrote that all novels are really letters aimed at one person. As it happens, I believe this. I think that every novelist has a single ideal reader; that at various points during the composition of a story, the writer is thinking, "I wonder what he/she will think when he/she reads *this* part?" For me that first reader is my wife, Tabitha.

She has always been an extremely sympathetic and supportive first reader. Her positive reaction to difficult books like *Bag of Bones* (my first novel with a new publisher after twenty good years with Viking that came to an end in a stupid squabble about money) and relatively controversial ones like *Gerald's Game* meant the world to me. But she's also unflinching when she sees something she thinks is wrong. When she does, she lets me know loud and clear.

In her role as critic and first reader, Tabby often makes me think of a story I read about Alfred Hitchcock's wife, Alma Reville. Ms. Reville was the equivalent of Hitch's first reader, a sharp-eyed critic who was totally unimpressed with the suspense-master's growing reputation as an *auteur*. Lucky for him. Hitch say he want to fly, Alma say, "First eat your eggs."

Not long after finishing *Psycho*, Hitchcock screened it for a few friends. They raved about it, declaring it to be a suspense masterpiece. Alma was quiet until they'd all had their say, then spoke very firmly: "You can't send it out like that."

There was a thunderstruck silence, except for Hitchcock himself, who only asked why not. "Because," his wife responded, "Janet Leigh swallows when she's supposed to be dead." It was true. Hitchcock didn't argue any more than I do when Tabby points out one of my lapses. She and I may argue about many aspects of a book, and there have been times when I've gone against her judgment on subjective matters, but when she catches me in a goof, I know it, and thank God I've got someone around who'll tell me my fly's unzipped before I go out in public that way.

In addition to Tabby's first read, I usually send manuscripts to between four and eight other people who have critiqued my stories over the years. Many writing texts caution against asking friends to read your stuff, suggesting you're not apt to get a very unbiased opinion from folks who've eaten dinner at your house and sent their kids over to play with your kids in your backyard. It's unfair, according to this view, to put a pal in such a position. What happens if he/she feels he/she has to say, "I'm sorry, good buddy, you've written some great yarns in the past but this one sucks like a vacuum cleaner"?

The idea has some validity, but I don't think an unbiased opinion is exactly what I'm looking for. And I believe that most people smart enough to read a novel are also tactful enough to find a gentler mode of expression than "This sucks." (Although most of us know that "I think this has a few problems" actually means "This sucks," don't we?) Besides, if you really did write a stinker—it happens; as the author of *Maximum Overdrive* I'm qualified to say so—wouldn't you rather hear the news from a friend while the entire edition consists of a half-dozen Xerox copies?

When you give out six or eight copies of a book, you get back six or eight highly subjective opinions about what's good and what's bad in it. If all your readers think you did a pretty good job, you probably did. This sort of unanimity does happen, but it's rare, even with friends. More likely, they'll think that some parts are good and some parts are . . . well, not so good. Some will feel Character A works but Character B is far-fetched. If others feel that Character B is believable but Character A is overdrawn, it's a wash. You can safely relax and leave things the way they are (in baseball, tie goes to the runner; for novelists, it goes to the writer). If some people love your ending and others hate it, same deal—it's a wash, and tie goes to the writer.

Some first readers specialize in pointing out factual errors, which are the easiest to deal with. One of my first-reader smart guys, the late Mac McCutcheon, a wonderful high school English teacher, knew a lot about guns. If I had a character toting a Winchester .330, Mac might jot in the margin that Winchester didn't make that caliber but Remington did. In such cases you've got two for the price of one—the error and the fix. It's a good deal, because you come off looking like you're an expert and your first reader will feel flattered to have been of help. And the best catch Mac ever made for me had nothing to do with guns. One day while reading a piece of a manuscript in the teachers' room, he burst out laughing—laughed so hard, in fact, that tears went rolling down his bearded cheeks. Because the story in question, *'Salem's Lot,* had not been intended as a laff riot, I asked him what he had found. I had written a line that went something like this: **Although deer season doesn't start until November in Maine, the fields of October are often alive with gunshots; the locals are shooting as many peasants as they think their families will eat.** A copyeditor would no doubt have picked up the mistake, but Mac spared me that embarrassment.

Subjective evaluations are, as I say, a little harder to deal with, but listen: if everyone who reads your book says you have a problem (Connie comes back to her husband too easily, Hal's cheating on the big exam seems unrealistic given what we know about him, the novel's conclusion seems abrupt and arbitrary), you've got a problem and you better do something about it.

Plenty of writers resist this idea. They feel that revising a story according to the likes and dislikes of an audience is somehow akin to prostitution. If you really feel that way, I won't try to change your mind. You'll save on charges at Copy Cop, too, because you won't have to show anyone your story in the first place. In fact (he said snottily), if you *really* feel that way, why bother to publish at all? Just finish your books and then pop them in a safe-deposit box, as J. D. Salinger is reputed to have been doing in his later years.

And yes, I can relate, at least a bit, to that sort of resentment. In the film business, where I have had a quasi-professional life, first-draft showings are called "test screenings." These have become standard practice in the industry, and they drive most filmmakers absolutely bugshit. Maybe they should. The studio shells out somewhere between fifteen and a hundred million dollars to make a film, then asks the director to recut it based on the opinions of a Santa Barbara multiplex audience composed of hairdressers, meter maids, shoe-store clerks, and out-of-work pizza-delivery guys. And the worst, most maddening thing about it? If you get the demographic right, test screenings seem to work.

I'd hate to see novels revised on the basis of test audiences—a lot of good books would never see the light of day if it was done that way—but come on, we're talking about half a dozen people you know and respect. If you ask the right ones (and if they agree to read your book), they can tell you a lot.

Do all opinions weigh the same? Not for me. In the end I listen most closely to Tabby, because she's the one I write for, the one I want to wow. If you're writing primarily for one person besides yourself, I'd advise you to pay very close attention to that person's opinion (I know one fellow who says he writes mostly for someone who's been dead fifteen years, but the majority of us aren't in that position). And if what you hear makes sense, then make the changes. You can't let the whole world into your story, but you can let in the ones that matter the most. And you should.

Call that one person you write for Ideal Reader. He or she is going to be in your writing room all the time: in the flesh once you open the door and let the world back in to shine on the bubble of your dream, in spirit during the sometimes troubling and often exhilarating days of the first draft, when the door is closed. And you know what? You'll find yourself bending the story even before Ideal Reader glimpses so much as the first sentence. I.R. will help you get outside yourself a little, to actually read your work in progress as an audience would while you're still working. This is perhaps the best way of all to make sure you stick to story, a way of playing to the audience even while there's no audience there and you're totally in charge.

When I write a scene that strikes me as funny (like the pie-eating contest in "The Body" or the execution rehearsal in *The Green Mile*), I am also imagining my I.R. finding it funny. I love it when Tabby laughs out of control—she puts her hands up as if to say *I surrender* and these big tears go rolling down her cheeks. I love it, that's all, fucking adore it, and when I get hold of something with that potential, I twist it as hard as I can. During the actual writing of such a scene (door closed), the thought of making her laugh—or cry—is in the back of my mind. During the rewrite (door open), the question—*is it funny enough yet? scary enough?*—is right up front. I try to watch her when she gets to a particular scene, hoping for at least a smile or—jackpot, baby!—that big belly-laugh with the hands up, waving in the air.

This isn't always easy on her. I gave her the manuscript of

my novella *Hearts in Atlantis* while we were in North Carolina, where we'd gone to see a Cleveland Rockers–Charlotte Sting WNBA game. We drove north to Virginia the following day, and it was during this drive that Tabby read my story. There are some funny parts in it—at least *I* thought so—and I kept peeking over at her to see if she was chuckling (or at least smiling). I didn't think she'd notice, but of course she did. On my eighth or ninth peek (I guess it *could* have been my fifteenth), she looked up and snapped: "Pay attention to your driving before you crack us up, will you? Stop being so goddam *needy!*"

I paid attention to my driving and stopped sneaking peeks (well . . . almost). About five minutes later, I heard a snort of laughter from my right. Just a little one, but it was enough for me. The truth is that most writers *are* needy. Especially between the first draft and the second, when the study door swings open and the light of the world shines in.

– 12 –

Ideal Reader is also the best way for you to gauge whether or not your story is paced correctly and if you've handled the back story in satisfactory fashion.

Pace is the speed at which your narrative unfolds. There is a kind of unspoken (hence undefended and unexamined) belief in publishing circles that the most commercially successful stories and novels are fast-paced. I guess the underlying thought is that people have so many things to do today, and are so easily distracted from the printed word, that you'll lose them unless you become a kind of short-order cook, serving up sizzling burgers, fries, and eggs over easy just as fast as you can.

On Writing

Like so many unexamined beliefs in the publishing business, this idea is largely bullshit . . . which is why, when books like Umberto Eco's *The Name of the Rose* or Charles Frazier's *Cold Mountain* suddenly break out of the pack and climb the best-seller lists, publishers and editors are astonished. I suspect that most of them ascribe these books' unexpected success to unpredictable and deplorable lapses into good taste on the part of the reading public.

Not that there's anything wrong with rapidly paced novels. Some pretty good writers—Nelson DeMille, Wilbur Smith, and Sue Grafton, to name just three—have made millions writing them. But you can overdo the speed thing. Move too fast and you risk leaving the reader behind, either by confusing or by wearing him/her out. And for myself, I *like* a slower pace and a bigger, higher build. The leisurely luxury-liner experience of a long, absorbing novel like *The Far Pavilions* or *A Suitable Boy* has been one of the form's chief attractions since the first examples—endless, multipart epistolary tales like *Clarissa.* I believe each story should be allowed to unfold at its own pace, and that pace is not always double time. Nevertheless, you need to beware—if you slow the pace down too much, even the most patient reader is apt to grow restive.

The best way to find the happy medium? Ideal Reader, of course. Try to imagine whether he or she will be bored by a certain scene—if you know the tastes of your I.R. even half as well as I know the tastes of mine, that shouldn't be too hard. Is I.R. going to feel there's too much pointless talk in this place or that? That you've underexplained a certain situation . . . or overexplained it, which is one of my chronic failings? That you forgot to resolve some important plot point? Forgot an entire *character,* as Raymond Chandler once did? (When asked about the murdered chauffeur in *The Big Sleep,*

Chandler—who liked his tipple—replied, "Oh, him. You know, I forgot all about him.") These questions should be in your mind even with the door closed. And once it's open— once your Ideal Reader has actually read your manuscript— you should ask your questions out loud. Also, needy or not, you might want to watch and see when your I.R. puts your manuscript down to do something else. What scene was he or she reading? What was so easy to put down?

Mostly when I think of pacing, I go back to Elmore Leonard, who explained it so perfectly by saying he just left out the boring parts. This suggests cutting to speed the pace, and that's what most of us end up having to do (kill your darlings, kill your darlings, even when it breaks your egocentric little scribbler's heart, kill your darlings).

As a teenager, sending out stories to magazines like *Fantasy and Science Fiction* and *Ellery Queen's Mystery Magazine,* I got used to the sort of rejection note that starts *Dear Contributor* (might as well start off *Dear Chump*), and so came to relish any little personal dash on these printed pink-slips. They were few and far between, but when they came they never failed to lighten my day and put a smile on my face.

In the spring of my senior year at Lisbon High—1966, this would've been—I got a scribbled comment that changed the way I rewrote my fiction once and forever. Jotted below the machine-generated signature of the editor was this *mot:* "Not bad, but PUFFY. You need to revise for length. Formula: 2nd Draft = 1st Draft – 10%. Good luck."

I wish I could remember who wrote that note—Algis Budrys, perhaps. Whoever it was did me a hell of a favor. I copied the formula out on a piece of shirt-cardboard and taped it to the wall beside my typewriter. Good things started to happen for me shortly after. There was no sudden golden flood of magazine sales, but the number of personal notes on the rejection slips went up fast. I even got one from Durant Imboden, the fiction editor at *Playboy*. That communiqué almost stopped my heart. *Playboy* paid two thousand dollars and up for short stories, and two grand was a quarter of what my mother made each year in her housekeeping job at Pineland Training Center.

The Rewrite Formula probably wasn't the only reason I started to get some results; I suspect another was that it was just my time, coming around at last (sort of like Yeats's rough beast). Still, the Formula was surely part of it. Before the Formula, if I produced a story that was four thousand words or so in first draft, it was apt to be five thousand in second (some writers are taker-outers; I'm afraid I've always been a natural putter-inner). After the Formula, that changed. Even today I will aim for a second-draft length of thirty-six hundred words if the first draft of a story ran four thousand . . . and if the first draft of a novel runs three hundred and fifty thousand words, I'll try my damndest to produce a second draft of no more than three hundred and fifteen thousand . . . three hundred, if possible. Usually it is possible. What the Formula taught me is that every story and novel is collapsible to some degree. If you can't get out ten per cent of it while retaining the basic story and flavor, you're not trying very hard. The effect of judicious cutting is immediate and often amazing—literary Viagra. You'll feel it and your I.R. will, too.

Back story is all the stuff that happened before your tale began but which has an impact on the front story. Back story helps define character and establish motivation. I think it's important to get the back story in as quickly as possible, but it's also important to do it with some grace. As an example of what's not graceful, consider this line of dialogue:

"Hello, ex-wife," Tom said to Doris as she entered the room.

Now, it may be important to the story that Tom and Doris are divorced, but there *has* to be a better way to do it than the above, which is about as graceful as an axe-murder. Here is one suggestion:

"Hi, Doris," Tom said. His voice sounded natural enough—to his own ears, at least—but the fingers of his right hand crept to the place where his wedding ring had been until six months ago.

Still no Pulitzer winner, and quite a bit longer than *Hello, ex-wife,* but it's not all about speed, as I've already tried to point out. And if you think it's all about information, you ought to give up fiction and get a job writing instruction manuals—Dilbert's cubicle awaits.

You've probably heard the phrase *in medias res,* which means "into the midst of things." This technique is an ancient and honorable one, but I don't like it. *In medias res* necessitates flashbacks, which strike me as boring and sort of corny. They always make me think of those movies from the forties and fifties where the picture gets all swimmy, the voices get all echoey, and suddenly it's sixteen months ago and the mud-splashed convict we just saw trying to outrun the bloodhounds is an up-and-coming young lawyer who hasn't yet been framed for the murder of the crooked police chief.

As a reader, I'm a lot more interested in what's *going* to happen than what already *did.* Yes, there are brilliant novels that run counter to this preference (or maybe it's a prejudice)—*Rebecca,* by Daphne du Maurier, for one; *A Dark-Adapted Eye,* by Barbara Vine, for another—but I like to start at square one, dead even with the writer. I'm an A-to-Z man; serve me the appetizer first and give me dessert if I eat my veggies.

Even when you tell your story in this straightforward manner, you'll discover you can't escape at least *some* back story. In a very real sense, every life is *in medias res.* If you introduce a forty-year-old man as your main character on page one of your novel, and if the action begins as the result of some brand-new person or situation's exploding onto the stage of this fellow's life—a road accident, let's say, or doing a favor for a beautiful woman who keeps looking sexily back over her shoulder (did you note the awful adverb in this sentence which I could not bring myself to kill?)—you'll *still* have to deal with the first forty years of the guy's life at some point. How much and how well you deal with those years will have a lot to do with the level of success your story achieves, with whether readers think of it as "a good read" or "a big fat bore." Probably J. K. Rowling, author of the Harry Potter stories, is the current champ when it comes to back story. You could do worse than read these, noting how effortlessly each new book recaps what has gone before. (Also, the Harry Potter novels are just *fun,* pure story from beginning to end.)

Your Ideal Reader can be of tremendous help when it comes to figuring out how well you did with the back story and how much you should add or subtract on your next draft. You need to listen very carefully to the things I.R. didn't understand, and then ask yourself if *you* understand them. If you do and just didn't put those parts across, your job on the second draft is to clarify. If you don't—if the parts of the back story your Ideal Reader queried are hazy to you, as well—then you need to think a lot more carefully about the past events that cast a light on your characters' present behavior.

You also need to pay close attention to those things in the back story that bored your Ideal Reader. In *Bag of Bones,* for instance, main character Mike Noonan is a fortyish writer who, as the book opens, has just lost his wife to a brain aneurysm. We start on the day of her death, but there's still a hell of a lot of back story here, much more than I usually have in my fiction. This includes Mike's first job (as a newspaper reporter), the sale of his first novel, his relations with his late wife's sprawling family, his publishing history, and especially the matter of their summer home in western Maine—how they came to buy it and some of its pre–Mike-and-Johanna history. Tabitha, my I.R., read all this with apparent enjoyment, but there was also a two- or three-page section about Mike's community-service work in the year after his wife dies, a year in which his grief is magnified by a severe case of writer's block. Tabby didn't like the community-service stuff.

"Who cares?" she asked me. "I want to know more about his bad dreams, not how he ran for city council in order to help get the homeless alcoholics off the street."

"Yeah, but he's got *writer's block,*" I said. (When a novelist is challenged on something he likes—one of his darlings—the first two words out of his mouth are almost always *Yeah but.*) "This block goes on for a year, maybe more. He has to do *something* in all that time, doesn't he?"

"I guess so," Tabby said, "but you don't have to bore me with it, do you?"

Ouch. Game, set, and match. Like most good I.R.s, Tabby can be ruthless when she's right.

I cut down Mike's charitable contributions and community

functions from two pages to two paragraphs. It turned out that Tabby was right—as soon as I saw it in print, I knew. Three million people or so have read *Bag of Bones,* I've gotten at least four thousand letters concerning it, and so far not a single one has said, "Hey, turkey! What was Mike doing for community-service work during the year he couldn't write?"

The most important things to remember about back story are that (a) everyone has a history and (b) most of it isn't very interesting. Stick to the parts that are, and don't get carried away with the rest. Long life stories are best received in bars, and only then an hour or so before closing time, and if you are buying.

– 13 –

We need to talk a bit about research, which is a specialized kind of back story. And please, if you *do* need to do research because parts of your story deal with things about which you know little or nothing, remember that word *back.* That's where research belongs: as far in the background and the back story as you can get it. *You* may be entranced with what you're learning about flesh-eating bacteria, the sewer system of New York, or the I.Q. potential of collie pups, but your readers are probably going to care a lot more about your characters and your story.

Exceptions to the rule? Sure, aren't there always? There have been very successful writers—Arthur Hailey and James Michener are the first ones that come to my mind—whose novels rely heavily on fact and research. Hailey's are barely disguised manuals about how things work (banks, airports, hotels), and Michener's are combination travelogues, geography lessons, and history texts. Other popular writers, like Tom Clancy and Patricia Cornwell, are more story-oriented but still deliver large (and sometimes hard to digest) dollops of factual information along with the melodrama. I sometimes think that these writers appeal to a large segment of the reading population who feel that fiction is somehow immoral, a low taste which can only be justified by saying, "Well, ahem, yes, I *do* read {Fill in author's name here}, but only on airplanes and in hotel rooms that don't have CNN; also, I learned a great deal about {Fill in appropriate subject here}."

For every successful writer of the factoid type, however, there are a hundred (perhaps even a thousand) wannabes, some published, most not. On the whole, I think story belongs in front, but some research is inevitable; you shirk it at your peril.

In the spring of 1999 I drove from Florida, where my wife and I had wintered, back to Maine. My second day on the road, I stopped for gas at a little station just off the Pennsylvania Turnpike, one of those amusingly antique places where a fellow still comes out, pumps your gas, and asks how you're doing and who you like in the NCAA tournament.

I told this one I was doing fine and liked Duke in the tournament. Then I went around back to use the men's room. There was a brawling stream full of snowmelt beyond the station, and when I came out of the men's, I walked a little way down the slope, which was littered with cast-off tire-rims and engine parts, for a closer look at the water. There were still patches of snow on the ground. I slipped on one and started to slide down the embankment. I grabbed a piece of someone's old engine block and stopped myself before I got fairly started, but I realized as I got up that if I'd fallen just right, I could have slid all the way down into that stream and been swept away. I found myself wondering, had that happened, how long it would have taken the gas station attendant to call the State Police if my car, a brand-new Lincoln Navigator, just continued to stand there in front of the pumps. By the time I got back on the turnpike again, I had two things: a wet ass from my fall behind the Mobil station, and a great idea for a story.

In it, a mysterious man in a black coat—likely not a human being at all but some creature inexpertly disguised to look like one—abandons his vehicle in front of a small gas station in rural Pennsylvania. The vehicle looks like an old Buick Special from the late fifties, but it's no more a Buick than the guy in the black coat was a human being. The vehicle falls into the hands of some State Police officers working out of a fictional barracks in western Pennsylvania. Twenty years or so later, these cops tell the story of the Buick to the grief-stricken son of a State Policeman who has been killed in the line of duty.

It was a grand idea and has developed into a strong novel about how we hand down our knowledge and our secrets; it's also a grim and frightening story about an alien piece of machinery that sometimes reaches out and swallows people whole. Of course there *were* a few minor problems—the fact that I knew absolutely zilch about the Pennsylvania State Police, for one thing—but I didn't let any of that bother me. I simply made up all the stuff I didn't know.

I could do that because I was writing with the door shut—writing only for myself and the Ideal Reader in my mind (my mental version of Tabby is rarely as prickly as my real-life wife can be; in my daydreams she usually applauds and urges me ever onward with shining eyes). One of my most memorable sessions took place in a fourth-floor room of Boston's Eliot Hotel—me sitting at the desk by the window, writing about an autopsy on an alien bat-creature while the Boston Marathon flowed exuberantly by just below me and rooftop boomboxes blasted out "Dirty Water," by The Standells. There were a thousand people down there below me in the streets, but not a single one in my room to be a party-pooper and tell me I got this detail wrong or the cops don't do things that way in western Pennsylvania, so nyah-nyah-nyah.

The novel—it's called *From a Buick Eight*—has been set aside in a desk drawer since late May of 1999, when the first draft was finished. Work on it has been delayed by circumstances beyond my control, but eventually I hope and expect to spend a couple of weeks in western Pennsylvania, where I've been given conditional permission to do some ride-alongs with the State Police (the condition—which seems eminently reasonable to me—was that I not make them look like meanies, maniacs, or idiots). Once I've done that, I should be able to correct the worst of my howlers and add some really nice detail-work.

Not much, though; research is back story, and the key word in back story is *back*. The tale I have to tell in *Buick Eight* has to do with monsters and secrets. It is *not* a story about police procedure in western Pennsylvania. What I'm looking for is nothing but a touch of verisimilitude, like the handful of spices you chuck into a good spaghetti sauce to really finish her off. That sense of reality is important in any work of fiction, but I think it is particularly important in a story dealing with the abnormal or paranormal. Also, enough details— always assuming they are the correct ones—can stem the tide of letters from picky-ass readers who apparently live to tell writers that they messed up (the tone of these letters is unvaryingly gleeful). When you step away from the "write what you know" rule, research becomes inevitable, and it can add a lot to your story. Just don't end up with the tail wagging the dog; remember that you are writing a novel, not a research paper. The story always comes first. I think that even James Michener and Arthur Hailey would have agreed with that.

– 14 –

I'm often asked if I think the beginning writer of fiction can benefit from writing classes or seminars. The people who ask are, all too often, looking for a magic bullet or a secret ingredient or possibly Dumbo's magic feather, none of which can be found in classrooms or at writing retreats, no matter how enticing the brochures may be. As for myself, I'm doubtful about writing classes, but not entirely against them.

In T. Coraghessan Boyle's wonderful tragicomic novel *East Is East,* there is a description of a writer's colony in the woods that struck me as fairy-tale perfect. Each attendee has his or her own little cabin where he or she supposedly spends the day writing. At noon, a waiter from the main lodge brings these fledgling Hemingways and Cathers a box lunch and puts it on the front stoop of the cottage. Very *quietly* puts it on the stoop, so as not to disturb the creative trance of the cabin's occupant. One room of each cabin is the writing room. In the other is a cot for that all-important afternoon nap . . . or, perhaps, for a revivifying bounce with one of the other attendees.

In the evening, all members of the colony gather in the lodge for dinner and intoxicating conversation with the writers in residence. Later, before a roaring fire in the parlor, marshmallows are toasted, popcorn is popped, wine is drunk, and the stories of the colony attendees are read aloud and then critiqued.

To me, this sounded like an absolutely enchanted writing environment. I especially liked the part about having your lunch left at the front door, deposited there as quietly as the tooth fairy deposits a quarter under a kid's pillow. I imagine it appealed because it's so far from my own experience, where the creative flow is apt to be stopped at any moment by a message from my wife that the toilet is plugged up and would I try to fix it, or a call from the office telling me that I'm in imminent danger of blowing yet another dental appointment. At times like that I'm sure all writers feel pretty much the same, no matter what their skill and success level: *God, if only I were in the right writing environment, with the right understanding people, I just KNOW I could be penning my masterpiece.*

In truth, I've found that any day's routine interruptions and distractions don't much hurt a work in progress and may actually help it in some ways. It is, after all, the dab of grit that seeps into an oyster's shell that makes the pearl, not pearl-making seminars with other oysters. And the larger the work looms in my day—the more it seems like an *I hafta* instead of just an *I wanna*—the more problematic it can become. One serious problem with writers' workshops is that *I hafta* becomes the rule. You didn't come, after all, to wander lonely as a cloud, experiencing the beauty of the woods or the grandeur of the mountains. You're supposed to be *writing,* dammit, if only so that your colleagues will have something to critique as they toast their goddam marshmallows there in the main lodge. When, on the other hand, making sure the kid gets to his basketball camp on time is every bit as important as your work in progress, there's a lot less pressure to produce.

And what *about* those critiques, by the way? How valuable

are they? Not very, in my experience, sorry. A lot of them are maddeningly vague. *I love the feeling of Peter's story,* someone may say. *It had something . . . a sense of I don't know . . . there's a loving kind of you know . . . I can't exactly describe it . . .*

Other writing-seminar gemmies include *I felt like the tone thing was just kind of you know; The character of Polly seemed pretty much stereotypical; I loved the imagery because I could see what he was talking about more or less perfectly.*

And, instead of pelting these babbling idiots with their own freshly toasted marshmallows, everyone else sitting around the fire is often *nodding* and *smiling* and looking *solemnly thoughtful.* In too many cases the teachers and writers in residence are nodding, smiling, and looking solemnly thoughtful right along with them. It seems to occur to few of the attendees that if you have a feeling you just can't describe, you might just be, I don't know, kind of like, my sense of it is, maybe in the wrong fucking class.

Non-specific critiques won't help when you sit down to your second draft, and may hurt. Certainly none of the comments above touch on the language of your piece, or its narrative sense; these comments are just wind, offering no factual input at all.

Also, daily critiques force you to write with the door constantly open, and in my mind that sort of defeats the purpose. What good does it do you to have the waiter tiptoe soundlessly up to the stoop of your cabin with your lunch and then tiptoe away with equal solicitous soundlessness, if you are reading your current work aloud every night (or handing it out on Xeroxed sheets) to a group of would-be writers who are telling you they like the way you handle tone and mood but want to know if Dolly's cap, the one with the bells on it, is symbolic? The pressure to explain is always on, and a lot of your creative energy, it seems to me, is therefore going in the wrong direction. You find yourself constantly questioning your prose and your purpose when what you should probably be doing is writing as fast as the Gingerbread Man runs, getting that first draft down on paper while the shape of the fossil is still bright and clear in your mind. Too many writing classes make *Wait a minute, explain what you meant by that* a kind of bylaw.

In all fairness, I must admit to a certain prejudice here: one of the few times I suffered a full-fledged case of writer's block was during my senior year at the University of Maine, when I was taking not one but two creative-writing courses (one was the seminar in which I met my future wife, so it can hardly be counted as a dead loss). Most of my fellow students that semester were writing poems about sexual yearning or stories in which moody young men whose parents did not understand them were preparing to go off to Vietnam. One young woman wrote a good deal about the moon and her menstrual cycle; in these poems *the moon* always appeared as *th m'n.* She could not explain just why this had to be, but we all kind of felt it: th m'n, yeah, dig it, sister.

I brought poems of my own to class, but back in my dorm room was my dirty little secret: the half-completed manuscript of a novel about a teenage gang's plan to start a race-riot. They would use this for cover while ripping off two dozen loan-sharking operations and illegal drug-rings in the city of Harding, my fictional version of Detroit (I had never been within six hundred miles of Detroit, but I didn't let that stop or even slow me down). This novel, *Sword in the Darkness,* seemed very tawdry to me when compared to what my fellow students were trying to achieve; which is why, I suppose, I never brought any of it to class for a critique. The fact that it was also better and somehow truer than all my poems about sexual yearning and post-adolescent angst only made things worse. The result was a four-month period in which I could write almost nothing at all. What I did instead was drink beer, smoke Pall Malls, read John D. MacDonald paperbacks, and watch afternoon soap operas.

Writing courses and seminars do offer at least one undeniable benefit: in them, the desire to write fiction or poetry is taken seriously. For aspiring writers who have been looked upon with pitying condescension by their friends and relatives ("You better not quit your day job just yet!" is a popular line, usually delivered with a hideous Bob's-yer-uncle grin), this is a wonderful thing. In writing classes, if nowhere else, it is entirely permissible to spend large chunks of your time off in your own little dreamworld. Still—do you really need permission and a hall-pass to go there? Do you need someone to make you a paper badge with the word WRITER on it before you can believe you *are* one? God, I hope not.

Another argument in favor of writing courses has to do with the men and women who teach them. There are thousands of talented writers at work in America, and only a few of them (I think the number might be as low as five per cent) can support their families and themselves with their work. There's always some grant money available, but it's never enough to go around. As for government subsidies for creative writers, perish the thought. Tobacco subsidies, sure. Research grants to study the motility of unpreserved bull sperm, of course. Creative-writing subsidies, never. Most voters would agree, I think. With the exception of Norman Rockwell and Robert Frost, America has never much revered her creative people; as a whole, we're more interested in commemorative plates from the Franklin Mint and Internet greeting-cards. And if you don't like it, it's a case of tough titty said the kitty, 'cause that's just the way things are. Americans are a lot more interested in TV quiz shows than in the short fiction of Raymond Carver.

The solution for a good many underpaid creative writers is to teach what they know to others. This can be a nice thing, and it's nice when beginning writers have a chance to meet with and listen to veteran writers they may have long admired. It's also great when writing classes lead to business contacts. I got my first agent, Maurice Crain, courtesy of my sophomore comp teacher, the noted regional short story writer Edwin M. Holmes. After reading a couple of my stories in Eh-77 (a comp class emphasizing fiction), Professor Holmes asked Crain if he would look at a selection of my work. Crain agreed, but we never had much of an association—he was in his eighties, unwell, and died shortly after our first correspondence. I can only hope it wasn't my initial batch of stories that killed him.

You don't *need* writing classes or seminars any more than you need this or any other book on writing. Faulkner learned his trade while working in the Oxford, Mississippi, post office. Other writers have learned the basics while serving in the Navy, working in steel mills, or doing time in America's finer crossbar hotels. I learned the most valuable (and commercial) part of my life's work while washing motel sheets and restaurant tablecloths at the New Franklin Laundry in Bangor. You learn best by reading a lot and writing a lot, and the most valuable lessons of all are the ones you teach yourself. These lessons almost always occur with the study door closed. Writing-class discussions can often be intellectually stimulating and great fun, but they also often stray far afield from the actual nuts-and-bolts business of writing.

Still, I suppose you might end up in a version of that sylvan writer's colony in *East Is East:* your own little cottage in the pines, complete with word processor, fresh disks (what is so delicately exciting to the imagination as a box of fresh computer disks or a ream of blank paper?), the cot in the other room for that afternoon nap, and the lady who tiptoes to your stoop, leaves your lunch, and then tiptoes away again. That would be okay, I guess. If you got a chance to participate in a deal like that, I'd say go right ahead. You might not learn The Magic Secrets of Writing (there aren't any—bummer, huh?), but it would certainly be a grand time, and grand times are something I'm *always* in favor of.

– 15 –

Other than *Where do you get your ideas?,* the questions any publishing writer hears most frequently from those who want to publish are *How do you get an agent?* and *How do you make contact with people in the world of publishing?*

The tone in which these questions are asked is often bewildered, sometimes chagrined, and frequently angry. There is a commonly held suspicion that most newcomers who actually succeed in getting their books published broke through because they had an in, a contact, a rabbi in the business. The underlying assumption is that publishing is just one big, happy, incestuously closed family.

It's not true. Neither is it true that agents are a snooty, superior bunch that would die before allowing their ungloved fingers to touch an unsolicited manuscript. (Well okay, yeah, there are a *few* like that.) The fact is that agents, publishers, and editors are all looking for the next hot writer who can sell a lot of books and make lots of money . . . and not just the next hot *young* writer, either; Helen Santmyer was in a retirement home when she published . . . *And Ladies of the Club.* Frank McCourt was quite a bit younger when he published *Angela's Ashes,* but he's still no spring chicken.

As a young man just beginning to publish some short fiction in the t&a magazines, I was fairly optimistic about my chances of getting published; I knew that I had some game, as the basketball players say these days, and I also felt that time was on my side; sooner or later the best-selling writers of the sixties and seventies would either die or go senile, making room for newcomers like me.

Still, I was aware that I had worlds to conquer beyond the pages of *Cavalier, Gent,* and *Juggs.* I wanted my stories to find the right markets, and that meant finding a way around the troubling fact that a good many of the best-paying ones (*Cosmopolitan,* for instance, which at that time published lots of short stories) wouldn't look at unsolicited fiction. The answer, it seemed to me, was to have an agent. If my fiction was good, I thought in my unsophisticated but not entirely illogical way, an agent would solve all my problems.

I didn't discover until much later that not all agents are good agents, and that a good agent is useful in many other ways than getting the fiction editor at *Cosmo* to look at your short stories. But as a young man I did not yet realize that there are people in the publishing world—more than a few, actually—who would steal the pennies off a dead man's eyes. For me, that didn't really matter, because before my first couple of novels actually succeeded in finding an audience, I had little to steal.

You *should* have an agent, and if your work is salable, you will have only a moderate amount of trouble finding one.

You'll probably be able to find one even if your work *isn't* salable, as long as it shows promise. Sports agents represent minor leaguers who are basically playing for meal-money, in hopes that their young clients will make it to the bigs; for the same reason, literary agents are often willing to handle writers with only a few publishing credits. You'll very likely find someone to handle your work even if your publishing credits are limited strictly to the "little magazines," which pay only in copies—these magazines are often regarded by agents and book publishers as proving-grounds for new talent.

You must begin as your own advocate, which means reading the magazines publishing the kind of stuff you write. You should also pick up the writers' journals and buy a copy of *Writer's Market,* the most valuable of tools for the writer new to the marketplace. If you're really poor, ask someone to give it to you for Christmas. Both the mags and *WM* (it's a whopper of a volume, but reasonably priced) list book and magazine publishers, and include thumbnail descriptions of the sort of stories each market uses. You'll also find the most salable lengths and the names of editorial staffs.

As a beginning writer, you'll be most interested in the "little magazines," if you're writing short stories. If you're writing or have written a novel, you'll want to note the lists of literary agents in the writing magazines and in *Writer's Market.* You may also want to add a copy of the *LMP (Literary Market Place)* to your reference shelf. You need to be canny, careful, and assiduous in your search for an agent or a publisher, but—this bears repeating—the most important thing you can do for yourself is *read the market.* Looking at the thumbnail rundowns in *Writer's Digest* may help (". . . publishes mostly mainstream fiction, 2,000–4,000 words, steer clear of stereotyped characters and hackneyed romance situations"), but a thumbnail is, leave us face it, just a thumbnail. Submitting stories without first reading the market is like playing darts in a dark room—you might hit the target every now and then, but you don't deserve to.

Here is the story of an aspiring writer I'll call Frank. Frank is actually a composite of three young writers I know, two men and one woman. All have enjoyed some success in their twenties as writers; none, as of this writing, are driving Rolls-Royces. All three will probably break through, which is to say that by the age of forty, I believe, all three will be publishing regularly (and probably one will have a drinking problem).

The three faces of Frank all have different interests and write in different styles and voices, but their approaches to the hurdles between them and becoming published writers are similar enough for me to feel comfortable about putting them together. I also feel that other beginning writers—you, for instance, dear Reader—could do worse than follow in Frank's footsteps.

Frank was an English major (you don't *have* to be an English major to become a writer, but it sure doesn't hurt) who began submitting his stories to magazines as a college student. He took several creative-writing courses, and many of the magazines to which he made submissions were recommended to him by his creative-writing teachers. Recommended or not, Frank carefully read the stories in each magazine, and submitted his own stories according to his sense of where each would fit best. "For three years I read every story *Story* magazine published," he says, then laughs. "I may be the only person in America who can make that statement."

Careful reading or not, Frank didn't publish any stories in

those markets while attending college, although he *did* publish half a dozen or so in the campus literary magazine (we'll call it *The Quarterly Pretension*). He received personal notes of rejection from readers at several of the magazines to which he submitted, including *Story* (the female version of Frank said, "They *owed* me a note!") and *The Georgia Review.* During this time Frank subscribed to *Writer's Digest* and *The Writer,* reading them carefully and paying attention to articles about agents and the accompanying agency lists. He circled the names of several who mentioned literary interests he felt he shared. Frank took particular note of agents who talked about liking stories of "high conflict," an arty way of saying suspense stories. Frank is attracted to suspense stories, also to stories of crime and the supernatural.

A year out of college, Frank gets his first acceptance letter—oh happy day. It is from a little magazine available at a few newsstands but mostly by subscription; let's call it *Kingsnake.* The editor offers to buy Frank's twelve-hundred-word vignette, "The Lady in the Trunk," for twenty-five dollars plus a dozen cc's—contributor's copies. Frank is, of course, delirious; way past Cloud Nine. All the relatives get a call, even the ones he doesn't like (*especially* the ones he doesn't like, is my guess). Twenty-five bucks won't pay the rent, won't even buy a week's worth of groceries for Frank and his wife, but it's a validation of his ambition, and that— any newly published writer would agree, I think—is priceless: *Someone wants something I did! Yippee!* Nor is that the only benefit. It is a *credit,* a small snowball which Frank will now begin rolling downhill, hoping to turn it into a snow-boulder by the time it gets to the bottom.

Six months later, Frank sells another story to a magazine called *Lodgepine Review* (like *Kingsnake, Lodgepine* is a composite). Only "sell" is probably too strong a word; proposed payment for Frank's "Two Kinds of Men" is twenty-five contributor's copies. Still, it's another credit. Frank signs the acceptance form (loving that line beneath the blank for his signature almost to death—PROPRIETOR OF THE WORK, by God!) and sends it back the following day.

Tragedy strikes a month later. It comes in the form of a form letter, the salutation of which reads *Dear **Lodgepine Review** Contributor.* Frank reads it with a sinking heart. A grant was not renewed, and *Lodgepine Review* has gone to that great writer's workshop in the sky. The forthcoming summer issue will be the last. Frank's story, unfortunately, was slated for fall. The letter closes by wishing Frank good luck in placing his story elsewhere. In the lower lefthand corner, someone has scribbled four words: AWFULLY SORRY *about this.*

Frank is AWFULLY SORRY, too (after getting loaded on cheap wine and waking up with cheap wine hangovers, he and his wife are SORRIER STILL), but his disappointment doesn't prevent him from getting his almost-published short story right back into circulation. At this point he has half a dozen of them making the rounds. He keeps a careful record of where they have been and what sort of response they got during their visit at each stop. He also keeps track of magazines where he has established some sort of personal contact, even if that contact consists of nothing but two scribbled lines and a coffee-stain.

A month after the bad news about *Lodgepine Review,* Frank gets some very good news; it arrives in a letter from a man he's never heard of. This fellow is the editor of a brand-new little magazine called *Jackdaw.* He is now soliciting stories for the first issue, and an old school friend of his—editor of the recently defunct *Lodgepine Review,* as a matter of fact—mentioned Frank's cancelled story. If Frank hasn't placed it, the *Jackdaw* editor would certainly like a look. No promises, but . . .

Frank doesn't *need* promises; like most beginning writers, all he needs is a little encouragement and an unlimited supply of take-out pizza. He mails the story off with a letter of thanks (and a letter of thanks to the ex–*Lodgepine* editor, of course). Six months later "Two Kinds of Men" appears in the premiere issue of *Jackdaw.* The Old Boy Network, which plays as large a part in publishing as it does in many other white-collar/pink-collar businesses, has triumphed again. Frank's pay for this story is fifteen dollars, ten contributor's copies, and another all-important credit.

In the next year, Frank lands a job teaching high school English. Although he finds it extremely difficult to teach literature and correct student themes in the daytime and then work on his own stuff at night, he continues to do so, writing new short stories and getting them into circulation, collecting rejection slips and occasionally "retiring" stories he's sent to all the places he can think of. "They'll look good in my collection when it finally comes out," he tells his wife. Our hero has also picked up a second job, writing book and film reviews for a newspaper in a nearby city. He's a busy, busy boy. Nevertheless, in the back of his mind, he has begun to think about writing a novel.

When asked what is the most important thing for a young writer who's just beginning to submit his or her fiction to remember, Frank pauses only a few seconds before replying, "Good presentation."

Say what?

He nods. "Good presentation, absolutely. When you send your story out, there ought to be a very brief cover-letter on top of the script, telling the editor where you've published other stories and just a line or two on what this one's about. And you should close by thanking him for the reading. That's especially important.

"You should submit on a good grade of white bond paper— none of that slippery erasable stuff. Your copy should be double-spaced, and on the first page you should put your address in the upper lefthand corner—it doesn't hurt to include your telephone number, too. In the righthand corner, put an approximate word-count." Frank pauses, laughs, and says: "Don't cheat, either. Most magazine editors can tell how long a story is just by looking at the print and riffling the pages."

I'm still a bit surprised at Frank's answer; I expected something that was a little less nuts-and-bolts.

"Nah," he says. "You get practical in a hurry once you're out of school and trying to find a place for yourself in the business. The very first thing I learned was that you don't get any kind of hearing at all unless you go in looking like a professional." Something in his tone makes me think he believes I've forgotten a lot about how tough things are at the entry-level, and perhaps he's right. It's been almost forty years since I had a stack of rejection-slips pinned to a spike in my bedroom, after all. "You can't make them like your story," Frank finishes, "but you can at least make it easy for them to try to like it."

As I write this, Frank's own story is still a work in progress, but his future looks bright. He has published a total of six shorts now, and won a fairly prestigious prize for one of them—we'll call it the Minnesota Young Writers' Award, although no part of my Frank composite actually lives in Minnesota. The cash prize was five hundred dollars, by far his biggest paycheck for a story. He has begun work on his novel, and when it's finished—in the early spring of 2001, he esti-mates—a reputable young agent named Richard Chams (also a pseudonym) has agreed to handle it for him.

Frank got serious about finding an agent at about the same time he got serious about his novel. "I didn't want to put in all that work and then be faced with not knowing how to sell the damn thing when I was done," he told me.

Based on his explorations of the *LMP* and the lists of agents in *Writer's Market,* Frank wrote an even dozen letters, each exactly the same except for the salutation. Here is the template:

June 19, 1999

Dear   :

I am a young writer, twenty-eight years old, in search of an agent. I got your name in a *Writer's Digest* article titled "Agents of the New Wave," and thought we might fit each other. I have published six stories since getting serious about my craft. They are:

"The Lady in the Trunk," *Kingsnake,* Winter 1996 ($25 plus copies)

"Two Kinds of Men," *Jackdaw,* Summer 1997 ($15 plus copies)

"Christmas Smoke," *Mystery Quarterly,* Fall 1997 ($35)

"Big Thumps, Charlie Takes His Lumps," *Cemetery Dance,* January–February 1998 ($50 plus copies)

"Sixty Sneakers," *Puckerbrush Review,* April–May 1998 (copies)

"A Long Walk in These 'Yere Woods," *Minnesota Review*, Winter 1998–1999 ($70 plus copies)

I would be happy to send any of these stories (or any of the half dozen or so I'm currently flogging around) for you to look at, if you'd like. I'm particularly proud of "A Long Walk in These 'Yere Woods," which won the Minnesota Young Writers' Award. The plaque looks good on our living room wall, and the prize money—$500—looked excellent for the week or so it was actually in our bank account (I have been married for four years; my wife, Marjorie, and I teach school).

The reason I'm seeking representation now is that I'm at work on a novel. It's a suspense story about a man who gets arrested for a series of murders which occurred in his little town twenty years before. The first eighty pages or so are in pretty good shape, and I'd also be delighted to show you these.

Please be in touch and tell me if you'd like to see some of my material. In the meantime, thank you for taking the time to read my letter.

Sincerely yours,

Frank included his telephone number as well as his address, and one of his target agents (not Richard Chams) actually called to chat. Three wrote back asking to look at the prize-winning story about the hunter lost in the woods. Half a dozen asked to see the first eighty pages of his novel. The response was big, in other words—only one agent to whom he wrote expressed no interest in Frank's work, citing a full roster of clients. Yet outside of his slight acquaintances in the world of the "little magazines," Frank knows absolutely nobody in the publishing business—has not a single personal contact.

"It was amazing," he says, "absolutely amazing. I expected to take whoever wanted to take *me*—if anybody did—and count myself lucky. Instead, I got to pick and choose." He puts down his bumper crop of possible agents to several things. First, the letter he sent around was literate and well-spoken ("It took four drafts and two arguments with my wife to get that casual tone just right," Frank says). Second, he could supply an actual list of published short stories, and a fairly substantial one. No big money, but the magazines were reputable. Third, there was the prize-winner. Frank thinks that may have been key. I don't know if it was or not, but it certainly didn't hurt.

Frank was also intelligent enough to ask Richard Chams and all the other agents he queried for a list of *their* bona fides—not a list of clients (I don't know if an agent who gave out the names of his clients would even be ethical), but a list of the publishers to whom the agent had sold books and the magazines to which he had sold short stories. It's easy to con a writer who's desperate for representation. Beginning writers need to remember that anyone with a few hundred dollars to invest can place an ad in *Writer's Digest,* calling himself or herself a literary agent—it isn't as if you have to pass a bar exam, or anything.

You should be especially wary of agents who promise to read your work for a fee. A few such agents are reputable (the Scott Meredith Agency used to read for fees; I don't know if they still do or not), but all too many are unscrupulous fucks. I'd suggest that if you're that anxious to get published, you skip agent-hunting or query-letters to publishers and go directly to a vanity press. There you will at least get a semblance of your money's worth.

– 16 –

We're nearly finished. I doubt if I've covered everything you need to know to become a better writer, and I'm sure I haven't answered all your questions, but I *have* talked about those aspects of the writing life which I can discuss with at least some confidence. I must tell you, though, that confidence during the actual writing of this book was a commodity in remarkably short supply. What I was long on was physical pain and self-doubt.

When I proposed the idea of a book on writing to my publisher at Scribner, I felt that I knew a great deal about the subject; my head all but burst with the different things I wanted to say. And perhaps I *do* know a lot, but some of it turned out to be dull and most of the rest, I've discovered, has more to do with instinct than with anything resembling "higher thought." I found the act of articulating those instinctive truths painfully difficult. Also, something happened halfway through the writing of *On Writing*—a life-changer, as they say. I'll tell you about it presently. For now, just please know that I did the best I could.

One more matter needs to be discussed, a matter that bears directly on that life-changer and one that I've touched on already, but indirectly. Now I'd like to face it head-on. It's a question that people ask in different ways—sometimes it comes out polite and sometimes it comes out rough, but it always amounts to the same: *Do you do it for the money, honey?*

The answer is no. Don't now and never did. Yes, I've made

a great deal of dough from my fiction, but I never set a single word down on paper with the thought of being paid for it. I have done some work as favors for friends—logrolling is the slang term for it—but at the very worst, you'd have to call that a crude kind of barter. I have written because it fulfilled me. Maybe it paid off the mortgage on the house and got the kids through college, but those things were on the side—I did it for the buzz. I did it for the pure joy of the thing. And if you can do it for joy, you can do it forever.

There have been times when for me the act of writing has been a little act of faith, a spit in the eye of despair. The second half of this book was written in that spirit. I gutted it out, as we used to say when we were kids. Writing is not life, but I think that sometimes it can be a way back to life. That was something I found out in the summer of 1999, when a man driving a blue van almost killed me.

ON LIVING:
A POSTSCRIPT

– 1 –

When we're at our summer house in western Maine—a house very much like the one Mike Noonan comes back to in *Bag of Bones*—I walk four miles every day, unless it's pouring down rain. Three miles of this walk are on dirt roads which wind through the woods; a mile of it is on Route 5, a two-lane blacktop highway which runs between Bethel and Fryeburg.

The third week in June of 1999 was an extraordinarily happy one for my wife and me; our kids, now grown and scattered across the country, were all home. It was the first time in nearly six months that we'd all been under the same roof. As an extra bonus, our first grandchild was in the house, three months old and happily jerking at a helium balloon tied to his foot.

On the nineteenth of June, I drove our younger son to the Portland Jetport, where he caught a flight back to New York City. I drove home, had a brief nap, and then set out on my usual walk. We were planning to go *en famille* to see *The General's Daughter* in nearby North Conway, New Hampshire, that evening, and I thought I just had time to get my walk in before packing everybody up for the trip.

I set out on that walk around four o'clock in the afternoon, as well as I can remember. Just before reaching the main road (in western Maine, any road with a white line running down the middle of it is a main road), I stepped into the woods and urinated. It was two months before I was able to take another leak standing up.

When I reached the highway I turned north, walking on the gravel shoulder, against traffic. One car passed me, also headed north. About three-quarters of a mile farther along, the woman driving the car observed a light blue Dodge van heading south. The van was looping from one side of the road to the other, barely under the driver's control. The woman in the car turned to her passenger when they were safely past the wandering van and said, "That was Stephen King walking back there. I sure hope that guy in the van doesn't hit him."

Most of the sightlines along the mile of Route 5 which I walk are good, but there is one stretch, a short steep hill, where a pedestrian walking north can see very little of what might be coming his way. I was three-quarters of the way up this hill when Bryan Smith, the owner and operator of the Dodge van, came over the crest. He wasn't on the road; he was on the shoulder. *My* shoulder. I had perhaps three-quarters of a second to register this. It was just time enough to think, *My God, I'm going to be hit by a schoolbus.* I started to turn to my left. There is a break in my memory here. On the other side of it I'm on the ground, looking at the back of the van, which is now pulled off the road and tilted to one side. This recollection is very clear and sharp, more like a snapshot than a memory. There is dust around the van's taillights. The license plate and the back windows are dirty. I register these things with no thought that I have been in an accident, or of anything else. It's a snapshot, that's all. I'm not thinking; my head has been swopped clean.

There's another little break in my memory here, and then I am very carefully wiping palmfuls of blood out of my eyes with my left hand. When my eyes are reasonably clear, I look around and see a man sitting on a nearby rock. He has a cane drawn across his lap. This is Bryan Smith, forty-two years of age, the man who hit me with his van. Smith has got quite the driving record; he has racked up nearly a dozen vehicle-related offenses.

Smith wasn't looking at the road on the afternoon our lives came together because his rottweiler had jumped from the very rear of his van into the back-seat area, where there was an Igloo cooler with some meat stored inside. The rott-weiler's name is Bullet (Smith has another rottweiler at home; that one is named Pistol). Bullet started to nose at the lid of the cooler. Smith turned around and tried to push Bul-let away. He was still looking at Bullet and pushing his head away from the cooler when he came over the top of the knoll; still looking and pushing when he struck me. Smith told friends later that he thought he'd hit "a small deer" until he noticed my bloody spectacles lying on the front seat of his van. They were knocked from my face when I tried to get out of Smith's way. The frames were bent and twisted, but the lenses were unbroken. They are the lenses I'm wearing now, as I write this.

– 2 –

Smith sees I'm awake and tells me help is on the way. He speaks calmly, even cheerily. His look, as he sits on his rock with his cane drawn across his lap, is one of pleasant commiseration: *Ain't the two of us just had the shittiest luck?* it says. He and Bullet left the campground where they were staying, he later tells an investigator, because he wanted "some of those Marzes-bars they have up to the store." When I hear this little detail some weeks later, it occurs to me that I have nearly been killed by a character right out of one of my own novels. It's almost funny.

Help is on the way, I think, and that's probably good because I've been in a hell of an accident. I'm lying in the ditch and there's blood all over my face and my right leg hurts. I look down and see something I don't like: my lap now appears to be on sideways, as if my whole lower body had been wrenched half a turn to the right. I look back up at the man with the cane and say, "Please tell me it's just dislocated."

"Nah," he says. Like his face, his voice is cheery, only mildly interested. He could be watching all this on TV while he noshes on one of those Marzes-bars. "It's broken in five I'd say maybe six places."

"I'm sorry," I tell him—God knows why—and then I'm gone again for a little while. It isn't like blacking out; it's more as if the film of memory has been spliced here and there.

When I come back this time, an orange-and-white van is idling at the side of the road with its flashers going. An emergency medical technician—Paul Fillebrown is his name—is kneeling beside me. He's doing something. Cutting off my jeans, I think, although that might have come later.

I ask him if I can have a cigarette. He laughs and says not hardly. I ask him if I'm going to die. He tells me no, I'm not going to die, but I need to go to the hospital, and fast. Which one would I prefer, the one in Norway–South Paris or the one in Bridgton? I tell him I want to go to Northern Cumberland

Hospital in Bridgton, because my youngest child—the one I just took to the airport—was born there twenty-two years before. I ask Fillebrown again if I'm going to die, and he tells me again that I'm not. Then he asks me if I can wiggle the toes on my right foot. I wiggle them, thinking of an old rhyme my mother used to recite sometimes: *This little piggy went to market, this little piggy stayed home.* I should have stayed home, I think; going for a walk today was a really bad idea. Then I remember that sometimes when people are paralyzed, they think they're moving but really aren't.

"My toes, did they move?" I ask Paul Fillebrown. He says they did, a good healthy wiggle. "Do you swear to God?" I ask him, and I think he does. I'm starting to pass out again. Fillebrown asks me, very slowly and loudly, bending down into my face, if my wife is at the big house on the lake. I can't remember. I can't remember where any of my family is, but I'm able to give him the telephone numbers of both our big house and the cottage on the far side of the lake where my daughter sometimes stays. Hell, I could give him my Social Security number, if he asked. I've got all my numbers. It's just everything else that's gone.

Other people are arriving now. Somewhere a radio is crackling out police calls. I'm put on a stretcher. It hurts, and I scream. I'm lifted into the back of the EMT truck, and the police calls are closer. The doors shut and someone up front says, "You want to really hammer it." Then we're rolling.

Paul Fillebrown sits down beside me. He has a pair of clippers and tells me he's going to have to cut the ring off the third finger of my right hand—it's a wedding ring Tabby gave me in 1983, twelve years after we were actually married. I try to tell Fillebrown that I wear it on my right hand because the real wedding ring is still on the third finger of my left—the original two-ring set cost me $15.95 at Day's Jewelers in Bangor. That first ring only cost eight bucks, in other words, but it seems to have worked.

Some garbled version of this comes out, probably nothing Paul Fillebrown can actually understand, but he keeps nodding and smiling as he cuts that second, more expensive, wedding ring off my swollen right hand. Two months or so later, I call Fillebrown to thank him; by then I understand that he probably saved my life by administering the correct on-scene medical aid and then getting me to the hospital at a speed of roughly one hundred and ten miles an hour, over patched and bumpy back roads.

Fillebrown assures me that I'm more than welcome, then suggests that perhaps someone was watching out for me. "I've been doing this for twenty years," he tells me over the phone, "and when I saw the way you were lying in the ditch, plus the extent of the impact injuries, I didn't think you'd make it to the hospital. You're a lucky camper to still be with the program."

The extent of the impact injuries is such that the doctors at Northern Cumberland Hospital decide they cannot treat me there; someone summons a LifeFlight helicopter to take me to Central Maine Medical Center in Lewiston. At this point my wife, older son, and daughter arrive. The kids are allowed a brief visit; my wife is allowed to stay longer. The doctors have assured her that I'm banged up, but I'll make it. The lower half of my body has been covered. She isn't allowed to look at the interesting way my lap has shifted around to the right, but she is allowed to wash the blood off my face and pick some of the glass out of my hair.

There's a long gash in my scalp, the result of my collision with Bryan Smith's windshield. This impact came at a point less than two inches from the steel driver's-side support post. Had I struck that, I likely would have been killed or rendered permanently comatose, a vegetable with legs. Had I struck the rocks jutting out of the ground beyond the shoulder of Route 5, I likely also would have been killed or permanently paralyzed. I didn't hit them; I was thrown over the van and fourteen feet in the air, but landed just shy of the rocks.

"You must have pivoted to the left just a little at the last second," Dr. David Brown tells me later. "If you hadn't, we wouldn't be having this conversation."

The LifeFlight helicopter lands in the parking lot of Northern Cumberland Hospital, and I am wheeled out to it. The sky is very bright, very blue. The clatter of the helicopter's rotors is very loud. Someone shouts into my ear, "Ever been in a helicopter before, Stephen?" The speaker sounds jolly, all excited for me. I try to answer yes, I've been in a helicopter before—twice, in fact—but I can't. All at once it's very tough to breathe.

They load me into the helicopter. I can see one brilliant wedge of blue sky as we lift off; not a cloud in it. Beautiful. There are more radio voices. This is my afternoon for hearing voices, it seems. Meanwhile, it's getting even harder to breathe. I gesture at someone, or try to, and a face bends upside down into my field of vision.

"Feel like I'm drowning," I whisper.

Somebody checks something, and someone else says, "His lung has collapsed."

There's a rattle of paper as something is unwrapped, and then the someone else speaks into my ear, loudly so as to be heard over the rotors. "We're going to put a chest tube in you, Stephen. You'll feel some pain, a little pinch. Hold on."

It's been my experience (learned when I was just a wee lad

with infected ears) that if a medical person tells you you're going to feel a little pinch, they're going to hurt you really bad. This time it isn't as bad as I expected, perhaps because I'm full of painkiller, perhaps because I'm on the verge of passing out again. It's like being thumped very high up on the right side of the chest by someone holding a short sharp object. Then there's an alarming whistle in my chest, as if I've sprung a leak. In fact, I suppose I have. A moment later the soft in-out of normal respiration, which I've listened to my whole life (mostly without being aware of it, thank God), has been replaced by an unpleasant *shloop-shloop-shloop* sound. The air I'm taking in is very cold, but it's air, at least, *air,* and I keep breathing it. I don't want to die. I love my wife, my kids, my afternoon walks by the lake. I also love to write; I have a book on writing that's sitting back home on my desk, half-finished. I don't want to die, and as I lie in the helicopter looking out at the bright blue summer sky, I realize that I am actually lying in death's doorway. Someone is going to pull me one way or the other pretty soon; it's mostly out of my hands. All I can do is lie there, look at the sky, and listen to my thin, leaky breathing: *shloop-shloop-shloop.*

Ten minutes later we set down on the concrete landing pad at CMMC. To me, it seems to be at the bottom of a concrete well. The blue sky is blotted out and the *whap-whap-whap* of the helicopter rotors becomes magnified and echoey, like the clapping of giant hands.

Still breathing in great leaky gulps, I am lifted out of the helicopter. Someone bumps the stretcher and I scream. "Sorry, sorry, you're okay, Stephen," someone says—when you're badly hurt, everyone calls you by your first name, everyone is your pal.

"Tell Tabby I love her very much," I say as I am first lifted and then wheeled, very fast, down some sort of descending concrete walkway. All at once I feel like crying.

"You can tell her that yourself," the someone says. We go through a door; there is air-conditioning and lights flowing past overhead. Speakers issue pages. It occurs to me, in a muddled sort of way, that an hour before I was taking a walk and planning to pick some berries in a field that overlooks Lake Kezar. I wouldn't pick for long, though; I'd have to be home by five-thirty because we were all going to the movies. *The General's Daughter,* starring John Travolta. Travolta was in the movie made out of *Carrie,* my first novel. He played the bad guy. That was a long time ago.

"When?" I ask. "When can I tell her?"

"Soon," the voice says, and then I pass out again. This time it's no splice but a great big whack taken out of the memory-film; there are a few flashes, confused glimpses of faces and operating rooms and looming X-ray machinery; there are delusions and hallucinations fed by the morphine and Dilaudid being dripped into me; there are echoing voices and hands that reach down to paint my dry lips with swabs that taste of peppermint. Mostly, though, there is darkness.

– 3 –

Bryan Smith's estimate of my injuries turned out to be conservative. My lower leg was broken in at least nine places—the orthopedic surgeon who put me together again, the formidable David Brown, said that the region below my right knee had been reduced to "so many marbles in a sock." The extent of those lower-leg injuries necessitated two deep incisions—they're called medial and lateral fasciotomies—to release the pressure caused by the exploded tibia and also to allow blood to flow back into the lower leg. Without the fasciatomies (or if the fasciotomies had been delayed), it probably would have been necessary to amputate the leg. My right knee itself was split almost directly down the middle; the technical term for the injury is "comminuted intra-articular tibial fracture." I also suffered an acetabular fracture of the right hip—a serious derailment, in other words—and an open femoral intertrochanteric fracture in the same area. My spine was chipped in eight places. Four ribs were broken. My right collarbone held, but the flesh above it was stripped raw. The laceration in my scalp took twenty or thirty stitches.

Yeah, on the whole I'd say Bryan Smith was a tad conservative.

– 4 –

Mr. Smith's driving behavior in this case was eventually examined by a grand jury, who indicted him on two counts: driving to endanger (pretty serious) and aggravated assault (very serious, the kind of thing that means jail time). After due consideration, the District Attorney responsible for prosecuting such cases in my little corner of the world allowed Smith to plead out to the lesser charge of driving to endanger. He received six months of county jail time (sentence suspended) and a year's suspension of his privilege to drive. He was also put on probation for a year with restrictions on other motor vehicles, such as snowmobiles and ATVs. It is conceivable that Bryan Smith could be legally back on the road in the fall or winter of 2001.

– 5 –

David Brown put my leg back together in five marathon surgical procedures that left me thin, weak, and nearly at the end of my endurance. They also left me with at least a fighting chance to walk again. A large steel and carbon-fiber apparatus called an external fixator was clamped to my leg. Eight large steel pegs called Schanz pins run through the fixator and into the bones above and below my knee. Five smaller steel rods radiate out from the knee. These look sort of like a child's drawing of sunrays. The knee itself was locked in place. Three times a day, nurses would unwrap the smaller pins and the much larger Schanz pins and swab the holes out with hydrogen peroxide. I've never had my leg dipped in kerosene and then lit on fire, but if that ever happens, I'm sure it will feel quite a bit like daily pin-care.

I entered the hospital on June nineteenth. Around the twenty-fifth I got up for the first time, staggering three steps to a commode, where I sat with my hospital johnny in my lap and my head down, trying not to weep and failing. You try to tell yourself that you've been lucky, most incredibly lucky, and usually that works because it's true. Sometimes it doesn't work, that's all. Then you cry.

A day or two after those initial steps, I started physical therapy. During my first session I managed ten steps in a downstairs corridor, lurching along with the help of a walker. One other patient was learning to walk again at the same time, a wispy eighty-year-old woman named Alice who was recovering from a stroke. We cheered each other on when we had enough breath to do so. On our third day in the downstairs hall, I told Alice that her slip was showing.

"Your *ass* is showing, sonnyboy," she wheezed, and kept going.

By the Fourth of July I was able to sit up in a wheelchair long enough to go out to the loading dock behind the hospital and watch some of the fireworks. It was a fiercely hot night, the streets filled with people eating snacks, drinking beer and soda, watching the sky. Tabby stood next to me, holding my hand, as the sky lit up red and green, blue and yellow. She was staying in a condo apartment across the street from the hospital, and each morning she brought me poached eggs and tea. I could use the nourishment, it seemed. In 1997, after returning from a motorcycle trip across the Australian desert, I weighed two hundred and sixteen pounds. On the day I was released from Central Maine Medical Center, I weighed a hundred and sixty-five.

I came home to Bangor on July ninth, after a hospital stay of three weeks. I began a daily rehab program which includes stretching, bending, and crutch-walking. I tried to keep my courage and my spirits up. On August fourth I went back to CMMC for another operation. Inserting an IV into my arm, the anesthesiologist said, "Okay, Stephen—you're going to feel a little like you just had a couple of cocktails." I opened my mouth to tell him that would be interesting, since I hadn't had a cocktail in eleven years, but before I could get anything out, I was gone again. When I woke up this time, the Schanz pins in my upper thigh were gone. I could bend my knee again. Dr. Brown pronounced my recovery "on course" and sent me home for more rehab and physical therapy (those of us undergoing P.T. know that the letters actually stand for Pain and Torture). And in the midst of all this, something else happened.

On July twenty-fourth, five weeks after Bryan Smith hit me with his Dodge van, I began to write again.

– 6 –

I actually began *On Writing* in November or December of 1997, and although it usually takes me only three months to finish the first draft of a book, this one was still only half-completed eighteen months later. That was because I'd put it aside in February or March of 1998, not sure how to continue, or if I should continue at all. Writing fiction was almost as much fun as it had ever been, but every word of the nonfiction book was a kind of torture. It was the first book I had put aside uncompleted since *The Stand,* and *On Writing* spent a lot longer in the desk drawer.

In June of 1999, I decided to spend the summer finishing the damn writing book—let Susan Moldow and Nan Graham at Scribner decide if it was good or bad, I thought. I read the manuscript over, prepared for the worst, and discovered I actually sort of liked what I had. The road to finishing it seemed clear-cut, too. I had finished the memoir ("C.V."), which attempted to show some of the incidents and life-situations which made me into the sort of writer I turned out to be, and I had covered the mechanics—those that seemed most important to me, at least. What remained to be done was the key section, "On Writing," where I'd try to answer some of the questions I'd been asked in seminars and at speaking engagements, plus all those I *wish* I'd been asked . . . those questions about the language.

On the night of June seventeenth, blissfully unaware that I was now less than forty-eight hours from my little date with Bryan Smith (not to mention Bullet the rottweiler), I sat down at our dining room table and listed all the questions I wanted to answer, all the points I wanted to address. On the eighteenth, I wrote the first four pages of the "On Writing" section. That was where the work still stood in late July, when I decided I'd better get back to work . . . or at least try.

I didn't *want* to go back to work. I was in a lot of pain, unable to bend my right knee, and restricted to a walker. I couldn't imagine sitting behind a desk for long, even in my wheelchair. Because of my cataclysmically smashed hip, sitting was torture after forty minutes or so, impossible after an hour and a quarter. Added to this was the book itself, which seemed more daunting than ever—how was I supposed to write about dialogue, character, and getting an agent when the most pressing thing in my world was how long until the next dose of Percocet?

Yet at the same time I felt I'd reached one of those crossroads moments when you're all out of choices. And I had been in terrible situations before which the writing had helped me get over—had helped me forget myself for at least a little while. Perhaps it would help me again. It seemed ridiculous to think it might be so, given the level of my pain and physical incapacitation, but there was that voice in the back of my mind, both patient and implacable, telling me that, in the words of the Chambers Brothers, Time Has Come Today. It's possible for me to disobey that voice, but very difficult to disbelieve it.

In the end it was Tabby who cast the deciding vote, as she so often has at crucial moments in my life. I'd like to think I've done the same for her from time to time, because it seems to me that one of the things marriage is about is casting the tiebreaking vote when you just can't decide what you should do next.

My wife is the person in my life who's most likely to say I'm working too hard, it's time to slow down, stay away from that damn PowerBook for a little while, Steve, give it a rest. When I told her on that July morning that I thought I'd better go back to work, I expected a lecture. Instead, she asked me where I wanted to set up. I told her I didn't know, hadn't even thought about it.

She thought about it, then said: "I can rig a table for you in the back hall, outside the pantry. There are plenty of plug-ins—you can have your Mac, the little printer, and a fan." The fan was certainly a must—it had been a terrifically hot summer, and on the day I went back to work, the temperature outside was ninety-five. It wasn't much cooler in the back hall.

Tabby spent a couple of hours putting things together, and that afternoon at four o'clock she rolled me out through the kitchen and down the newly installed wheelchair ramp into the back hall. She had made me a wonderful little nest there: laptop and printer connected side by side, table lamp, manuscript (with my notes from the month before placed neatly on top), pens, reference materials. Standing on the corner of the desk was a framed picture of our younger son, which she had taken earlier that summer.

"Is it all right?" she asked.

"It's gorgeous," I said, and hugged her. It *was* gorgeous. So is she.

The former Tabitha Spruce of Oldtown, Maine, knows when I'm working too hard, but she also knows that sometimes it's the work that bails me out. She got me positioned at the table, kissed me on the temple, and then left me there to find out if I had anything left to say. It turned out I did, a little, but without her intuitive understanding that yes, it *was* time, I'm not sure either of us would ever have found that out for sure.

That first writing session lasted an hour and forty minutes, by far the longest period I'd spent sitting upright since being struck by Smith's van. When it was over, I was dripping with sweat and almost too exhausted to sit up straight in my wheelchair. The pain in my hip was just short of apocalyptic. And the first five hundred words were uniquely terrifying—it was as if I'd never written anything before them in my life. All my old tricks seemed to have deserted me. I stepped from one word to the next like a very old man finding his way across a stream on a zigzag line of wet stones. There was no inspiration that first afternoon, only a kind of stubborn determination and the hope that things would get better if I kept at it.

Tabby brought me a Pepsi—cold and sweet and good— and as I drank it I looked around and had to laugh despite the pain. I'd written *Carrie* and *'Salem's Lot* in the laundry room of a rented trailer. The back hall of our house in Bangor resembled it enough to make me feel almost as if I'd come full circle.

There was no miraculous breakthrough that afternoon, unless it was the ordinary miracle that comes with any attempt to create something. All I know is that the words started coming a little faster after awhile, then a little faster still. My hip still hurt, my back still hurt, my leg, too, but those hurts began to seem a little farther away. I started to get on top of them. There was no sense of exhilaration, no buzz—not that day—but there was a sense of accomplishment that was almost as good. I'd gotten going, there was that much. The scariest moment is always just before you start.

After that, things can only get better.

– 7 –

For me, things have continued to get better. I've had two more operations on my leg since that first sweltering afternoon in the back hall, I've had a fairly serious bout of infection, and I continue to take roughly a hundred pills a day, but the external fixator is now gone and I continue to write. On some days that writing is a pretty grim slog. On others—more and more of them as my leg begins to heal and my mind reaccustoms itself to its old routine—I feel that buzz of happiness, that sense of having found the right words and put them in a line. It's like lifting off in an airplane: you're on the ground, on the ground, on the ground . . . and then you're up, riding on a magical cushion of air and prince of all you survey. That makes me happy, because it's what I was made to do. I still don't have much strength—I can do a little less than half of what I used to be able to do in a day—but I've had enough to get me to the end of this book, and for that I'm grateful. Writing did not save my life—Dr. David Brown's skill and my wife's loving care did that—but it has continued to do what it always has done: it makes my life a brighter and more pleasant place.

Writing isn't about making money, getting famous, getting dates, getting laid, or making friends. In the end, it's about enriching the lives of those who will read your work, and enriching your own life, as well. It's about getting up, getting well, and getting over. Getting happy, okay? Getting happy.

Some of this book—perhaps too much—has been about how I learned to do it. Much of it has been about how you can do it better. The rest of it—and perhaps the best of it—is a permission slip: you can, you should, and if you're brave enough to start, *you will.* Writing is magic, as much the water of life as any other creative art. The water is free. So drink.

Drink and be filled up.

And Furthermore, Part I: Door Shut, Door Open

Earlier in this book, when writing about my brief career as a sports reporter for the Lisbon *Weekly Enterprise* (I was, in fact, the entire sports department; a small-town Howard Cosell), I offered an example of how the editing process works. That example was necessarily brief, and dealt with nonfiction. The passage that follows is fiction. It is completely raw, the sort of thing I feel free to do with the door shut—it's the story undressed, standing up in nothing but its socks and undershorts. I suggest that you look at it closely before going on to the edited version.

The Hotel Story

Mike Enslin was still in the revolving door when he saw Ostermeyer, the manager of the Hotel Dolphin, sitting in one of the overstuffed lobby chairs. Mike's heart sank a little. *Maybe should have brought the damned lawyer along again, after all,* he thought. Well, too late now. And even if Ostermeyer had decided to throw up another roadblock or two between Mike and room 1408, that wasn't all bad; it would simply add to the story when he finally told it.

Ostermeyer saw him, got up, and was crossing the room with one pudgy hand held out as Mike left the revolving door. The Dolphin was on Sixty-first Street, around the corner from Fifth Avenue; small but smart. A man and woman dressed in evening clothes passed Mike as he reached out and took Ostermeyer's hand, switching his small overnight case to his left hand in order to do it. The woman was blonde, dressed in black, of course, and the light, flowery smell of her perfume seemed to summarize New York. On the mezzanine level, someone was playing "Night and Day" in the bar, as if to underline the summary.

"Mr. Enslin. Good evening."

"Mr. Ostermeyer. Is there a problem?"

Ostermeyer looked pained. For a moment he glanced around the small, smart lobby, as if for help. At the concierge's stand, a man was discussing theater tickets with his wife while the concierge himself watched them with a small, patient smile. At the front desk, a man with the rumpled look one only got after long hours in Business Class was discussing his reservation with a woman in a smart black suit that could itself have doubled for evening wear. It was business as usual at the Hotel Dolphin. There was help for everyone except poor Mr. Ostermeyer, who had fallen into the writer's clutches.

"Mr. Ostermeyer?" Mike repeated, feeling a little sorry for the man.

"No," Ostermeyer said at last. "No problem. But, Mr. Enslin . . . could I speak to you for a moment in my office?"

So, Mike thought. *He wants to try one more time.*

Under other circumstances he might have been impatient. Now he was not. It would help the section on room 1408, offer the proper ominous tone the readers of his books seemed to crave—it was to be One Final Warning—but that wasn't all. Mike Enslin hadn't been sure until now, in spite of all the backing and filling; now he was. Ostermeyer wasn't playing a part. Ostermeyer was really afraid of room 1408, and what might happen to Mike there tonight.

"Of course, Mr. Ostermeyer. Should I leave my bag at the desk, or bring it?"

"Oh, we'll bring it along, shall we?" Ostermeyer, the good host, reached for it. Yes, he still held out some hope of persuading Mike not to stay in the room. Otherwise, he would have directed Mike to the desk . . . or taken it there himself. "Allow me."

"I'm fine with it," Mike said. "Nothing but a change of clothes and a toothbrush."

"Are you sure?"

"Yes," Mike said, holding his eyes. "I'm afraid I am."

For a moment Mike thought Ostermeyer was going to give up. He sighed, a little round man in a dark cutaway coat and a neatly knotted tie, and then he squared his shoulders again. "Very good, Mr. Enslin. Follow me."

The hotel manager had seemed tentative in the lobby, depressed, almost beaten. In his oak-paneled office, with the pictures of the hotel on the walls (the Dolphin had opened in October of 1910—Mike might publish without the benefit of reviews in the journals or the big-city papers, but he did his research), Ostermeyer seemed to gain assurance again. There was a Persian carpet on the floor. Two standing lamps cast a mild yellow light. A desk-lamp with a green lozenge-shaped shade stood on the desk, next to a humidor. And next to the humidor were Mike Enslin's last three books. Paperback editions, of course; there had been no hardbacks. Yet he did quite well. *Mine host has been doing a little research of his own,* Mike thought.

Mike sat down in one of the chairs in front of the desk. He expected Ostermeyer to sit behind the desk, where he could draw authority from it, but Ostermeyer surprised him. He sat in the other chair on what he probably thought of as the employees' side of the desk, crossed his legs, then leaned forward over his tidy little belly to touch the humidor.

"Cigar, Mr. Enslin? They're not Cuban, but they're quite good."

"No, thank you. I don't smoke."

Ostermeyer's eyes shifted to the cigarette behind Mike's right ear—parked there on a jaunty jut the way an oldtime wisecracking New York reporter might have parked his next smoke just below his fedora with the PRESS tag stuck in the band. The cigarette had become so much a part of him that for a moment Mike honestly didn't know what Ostermeyer was looking at. Then he remembered, laughed, took it down, looked at it himself, then looked back at Ostermeyer.

"Haven't had a cigarette in nine years," he said. "I had an older brother who died of lung cancer. I quit shortly after he died. The cigarette behind the ear . . ." He shrugged. "Part affectation, part superstition, I guess. Kind of like the ones you sometimes see on people's desks or walls, mounted in a little box with a sign saying BREAK GLASS IN CASE OF EMERGENCY. I sometimes tell people I'll light up in case of nuclear war. Is 1408 a smoking room, Mr. Ostermeyer? Just in case nuclear war breaks out?"

"As a matter of fact, it is."

"Well," Mike said heartily, "that's one less worry in the watches of the night."

Mr. Ostermeyer sighed again, unamused, but this one didn't have the disconsolate quality of his lobby-sigh. Yes, it was the room, Mike reckoned. *His* room. Even this afternoon, when Mike had come accompanied by Robertson, the lawyer, Ostermeyer had seemed less flustered once they were in here. At the time Mike had thought it was partly because they were no longer drawing stares from the passing public, partly because Ostermeyer had given up. Now he knew better. It was the room. And why not? It was a room with good pictures on the walls, a good rug on the floor, and good cigars—although not Cuban—in the humidor. A lot of managers had no doubt conducted a lot of business in here since October of 1910; in its own way it was as New York as the blonde woman in her black off-the-shoulder dress, her smell of perfume and her unarticulated promise of sleek sex in the small hours of the morning—New York sex. Mike himself was from Omaha, although he hadn't been back there in a lot of years.

"You still don't think I can talk you out of this idea of yours, do you?" Ostermeyer asked.

"I know you can't," Mike said, replacing the cigarette behind his ear.

What follows is revised copy of this same opening passage—it's the story putting on its clothes, combing its hair, maybe adding just a small dash of cologne. Once these changes are incorporated into my document, I'm ready to open the door and face the world.

~~The Hotel Story~~ **1408** ①

By Stephen King

② Mike Enslin was still in the revolving door when he saw ~~Ostermeyer~~ **Olin** the manager of the Hotel Dolphin, sitting in one of the overstuffed lobby chairs. Mike's heart sank ~~a little~~. *Maybe should have brought the damned lawyer along again, after all,* he thought. Well, too late now. And even if ~~Ostermeyer~~ **Olin** had decided to throw up another roadblock or two between Mike and room 1408, that wasn't all bad; ~~it would simply add to the story when he finally told it~~ **there were compensations.** ~~Ostermeyer~~ **Olin** saw him, got up, and was crossing the room with one pudgy hand held out as Mike left the revolving door. The Dolphin was on Sixty-first Street, around the corner from Fifth Avenue, small but smart. A man and woman dressed in evening clothes passed Mike as he reached out and took ~~Ostermeyer's~~ **Olin's** hand, switching his small overnight case to his left hand in order to do it. The woman was blonde, dressed in black, of course, and the light, flowery smell of her perfume seemed to summarize New York. On the mezzanine level, someone was playing "Night and Day" in the bar, as if to underline the summary.

"Mr. Enslin. Good evening."

"Mr. ~~Ostermeyer.~~ Olin. Is there a problem?"

~~Ostermeyer~~ Olin looked pained. For a moment he glanced around the small, smart lobby, as if for help. At the concierge's stand, a man was discussing theater tickets with his wife while the concierge himself watched ~~them~~ with a small, patient smile. At the front desk, a man with the rumpled look one only got after long hours in Business Class was discussing his reservation with a woman in a smart black suit that could itself have doubled for evening wear. It was business as usual at the Hotel Dolphin. There was help for everyone except poor Mr. ~~Ostermeyer,~~ Olin who had fallen into the writer's clutches.

 "Mr. ~~Ostermeyer?~~ Olin" Mike repeated~~, feeling a little sorry for the man.~~

277

"No," Ostermeyer said at last. ~~"No problem. But,~~ [R] " Mr. Enslin . . . could I speak to you for a moment in my office?"

So, Mike thought. ~~He wants to try one more time~~ [& well, and why not?] ~~Under other circumstances he might have been impatient. Now he was not.~~ It would help the section on room 1408, ~~offer~~ [add to] the ~~proper~~ ominous tone the readers of his books seemed to crave~~, it was to be One Final Warning—but that wasn't all,~~ [and that wasn't all.] Mike Enslin hadn't been sure until now, in spite of all the backing and filling; now he was. ~~Ostermeyer~~ [Olin] wasn't playing a part. ~~Ostermeyer~~ [Olin] was really afraid of room 1408, and what might happen to Mike there tonight.

"Of course, Mr. ~~Ostermeyer Should I leave my bag at the desk, or bring it?~~ [Olin." "Olin,]

"Oh, we'll bring it along, shall we?" ~~Ostermeyer, the good host, reached for~~ it. [Mike's bag.] ~~Yes, he still held out some hope of persuading Mike not to stay in the room. Otherwise, he would have directed Mike to the desk . . . or taken it there himself.~~ "Allow me."

"I'm fine with it," Mike said. "Nothing but a change of clothes and a toothbrush."

"Are you sure?"

"Yes," Mike said, holding his eyes. "I'm ~~afraid I~~ already wearing my lucky Hawaiian shirt." He smiled. "It's the one with ~~am.~~ the ghost repellent."

~~For a moment Mike thought Ostermeyer was~~ A Olin ~~going to give up. He~~ sighed, a little round man in a dark cutaway coat and a neatly knotted tie, ~~and then he squared his shoulders again.~~ "Very good, Mr. Enslin. Follow me."

The hotel manager had seemed tentative in the lobby, ~~depressed,~~ almost beaten. In his oak-paneled office, with the pictures of the hotel on the walls (the Dolphin had opened in October of 1910—Mike might publish without the benefit of reviews in the journals or the big-city papers, but he did his research), ~~Ostermeyer~~ Olin seemed to gain assurance again. There was a Persian carpet on the floor. Two standing lamps cast a mild yellow light. A desk-lamp with a green lozenge-shaped shade stood on the desk, next to a humidor. And next to the humidor were Mike Enslin's last three books. Paperback editions, of course; there had been no hardbacks. ~~Yet he did quite well.~~ *Mine host has been doing a little research of his own,* Mike thought.

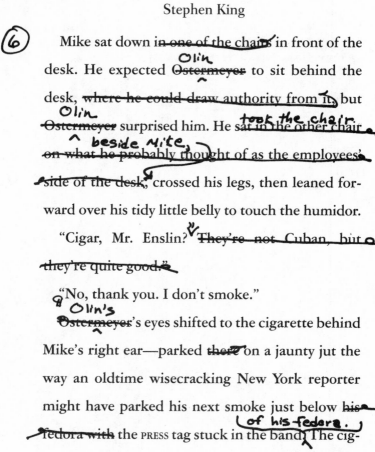

⑥ Mike sat down ~~in one of the chairs~~ in front of the desk. He expected ~~Ostermeyer~~ Olin to sit behind the desk, ~~where he could draw authority from it,~~ but ~~Ostermeyer~~ Olin surprised him. He sat ~~in the other chair~~ took the chair beside Mike, ~~on what he probably thought of as the employees' side of the desk,~~ crossed his legs, then leaned forward over his tidy little belly to touch the humidor.

"Cigar, Mr. Enslin? ~~They're not Cuban, but they're quite good.~~"

"No, thank you. I don't smoke."

~~Ostermeyer~~ Olin's eyes shifted to the cigarette behind Mike's right ear—parked ~~there~~ on a jaunty jut the way an oldtime wisecracking New York reporter might have parked his next smoke just below ~~his fedora with~~ the PRESS tag stuck in the band of his fedora. The cigarette had become so much a part of him that for a moment Mike honestly didn't know what ~~Ostermeyer~~ Olin was looking at. Then he ~~remembered,~~ laughed, took it down, looked at it himself, then looked back at ~~Ostermeyer~~ Olin.

"Haven't had ~~a cigarette~~ one in nine years," he said. "I had an older brother who died of lung cancer. I ⑦ quit ~~shortly~~ after he died. The cigarette behind the ear . . ." He shrugged. "Part affectation, part super-

~~Like the Hawaiian shirt. Or the cigarettes~~

stition, I guess. ~~Kind of like the ones~~ you some-

times see on people's desks or walls, mounted in a

little box with a sign saying BREAK GLASS IN CASE OF

EMERGENCY. ~~I sometimes tell people I'll light up in~~ ~~case of nuclear war.~~ Is 1408 a smoking room, Mr.

~~Ostermeyer~~ Olin? Just in case nuclear war breaks out?"

"As a matter of fact, it is."

"Well," Mike said heartily, "that's one less worry

in the watches of the night."

Mr. ~~Ostermeyer~~ Olin sighed again, ~~unamused~~ but

this ~~one~~ sigh didn't have the disconsolate quality of his

lobby-sigh. Yes, it was the ~~room,~~ office, Mike reckoned.

His ~~room~~ office. Even this afternoon, when Mike had

come accompanied by Robertson, the lawyer,

~~Ostermeyer~~ Olin had seemed less flustered once they

were in here. ~~At the time Mike had thought it was~~

~~partly because they were no longer drawing stares~~

~~from the passing public, partly because Oster-~~

~~meyer had given up. Now he knew better. It was~~

Where else could you feel in charge, if not in your special place?

~~the room.~~ Olin's office. And why not? ~~It~~ was a room with good

pictures on the walls, a good rug on the floor, and

good cigars—~~although not Cuban~~—in the humidor. A lot of managers had no doubt conducted a lot of business in here since ~~October of~~ 1910; in its own way it was as New York as the blonde ~~woman~~ in her black off-the-shoulder dress, her smell of perfume and her unarticulated promise of sleek (New York) sex in the small hours of the morning. ~~New York~~ ~~sex.~~ Mike himself was from Omaha, although he hadn't been back there in ~~a lot of~~ years.

"You still don't think I can talk you out of this idea of yours, do you?" ~~Ostermeyer~~ Olin asked.

"I know you can't," Mike said, replacing the cigarette behind his ear.

The reasons for the majority of the changes are self-evident; if you flip back and forth between the two versions, I'm confident that you'll understand almost all of them, and I'm hopeful that you'll see how raw the first-draft work of even a so-called "professional writer" is once you really examine it.

Most of the changes are cuts, intended to speed the story. I have cut with Strunk in mind—"Omit needless words"— and also to satisfy the formula stated earlier: 2nd Draft = 1st Draft − 10%.

I have keyed a few changes for brief explanation:

1. Obviously, "The Hotel Story" is never going to replace "Killdozer!" or *Norma Jean, the Termite Queen* as a title. I simply slotted it into the first draft, knowing a better one would occur as I went along. (If a better title doesn't occur, an edi-

tor will usually supply his or her idea of a better one, and the results are usually ugly.) I like "1408" because this is a "thirteenth floor" story, and the numbers add up to thirteen.

2. Ostermeyer is a long and gallumphing name. By changing it to Olin via global replace, I was able to shorten my story by about fifteen lines at a single stroke. Also, by the time I finished "1408," I had realized it was probably going to be part of an audio collection. I would read the stories myself, and didn't want to sit there in the little recording booth, saying Ostermeyer, Ostermeyer, Ostermeyer all day long. So I changed it.

3. I'm doing a lot of the reader's thinking for him here. Since most readers can think for themselves, I felt free to cut this from five lines to just two.

4. Too much stage direction, too much belaboring of the obvious, and too much clumsy back story. Out it goes.

5. Ah, here is the lucky Hawaiian shirt. It shows up in the first draft, but not until about page thirty. That's too late for an important prop, so I stuck it up front. There's an old rule of theater that goes, "If there's a gun on the mantel in Act I, it must go off in Act III." The reverse is also true; if the main character's lucky Hawaiian shirt plays a part at the end of a story, it must be introduced early. Otherwise it looks like a *deus ex machina* (which of course it is).

6. The first-draft copy reads "Mike sat down in one of the chairs in front of the desk." Well, duh—where else is he going to sit? On the floor? I don't think so, and out it goes. Also out is the business of the Cuban cigars. This is not only trite, it's the sort of thing bad guys are always saying in bad movies. "Have a cigar! They're Cuban!" Fuhgeddaboudit!

7. The first- and second-draft ideas and basic information are the same, but in the second draft, things have been cut to

the bone. And look! See that wretched adverb, that "shortly"? Stomped it, didn't I? No mercy!

8. And here's one I didn't cut . . . not just an adverb but a Swiftie: **"Well," Mike said heartily** . . . But I stand behind my choice not to cut in this case, would argue that it's the exception which proves the rule. "Heartily" has been allowed to stand because I want the reader to understand that Mike is making fun of poor Mr. Olin. Just a little, but yes, he's making fun.

9. This passage not only belabors the obvious but repeats it. Out it goes. The concept of a person's feeling comfortable in one's own special place, however, seemed to clarify Olin's character, and so I added it.

I toyed with the idea of including the entire finished text of "1408" in this book, but the idea ran counter to my determination to be brief, for once in my life. If you would like to listen to the entire thing, it's available as part of a three-story audio collection, *Blood and Smoke*. You may access a sample on the Simon and Schuster Web site, http://www.SimonSays.com. And remember, for our purposes here, you don't need to finish the story. This is about engine maintenance, not joyriding.

And Furthermore, Part II:
A Booklist

When I talk about writing, I usually offer my audiences an abbreviated version of the "On Writing" section which forms the second half of this book. That includes the Prime Rule, of course: Write a lot and read a lot. In the Q-and-A period which follows, someone invariably asks: "What do *you* read?"

I've never given a very satisfactory answer to that question, because it causes a kind of circuit overload in my brain. The easy answer—"Everything I can get my hands on"—is true enough, but not helpful. The list that follows provides a more specific answer to that question. These are the best books I've read over the last three or four years, the period during which I wrote *The Girl Who Loved Tom Gordon, Hearts in Atlantis, On Writing,* and the as-yet-unpublished *From a Buick Eight.* In some way or other, I suspect each book in the list had an influence on the books I wrote.

As you scan this list, please remember that I'm not Oprah and this isn't my book club. These are the ones that worked for me, that's all. But you could do worse, and a good many of these might show you some new ways of doing your work.

Even if they don't, they're apt to entertain you. They certainly entertained me.

Abrahams, Peter: *A Perfect Crime*
Abrahams, Peter: *Lights Out*
Abrahams, Peter: *Pressure Drop*
Abrahams, Peter: *Revolution #9*
Agee, James: *A Death in the Family*
Bakis, Kirsten: *Lives of the Monster Dogs*
Barker, Pat: *Regeneration*
Barker, Pat: *The Eye in the Door*
Barker, Pat: *The Ghost Road*
Bausch, Richard: *In the Night Season*
Blauner, Peter: *The Intruder*
Bowles, Paul: *The Sheltering Sky*
Boyle, T. Coraghessan: *The Tortilla Curtain*
Bryson, Bill: *A Walk in the Woods*
Buckley, Christopher: *Thank You for Smoking*
Carver, Raymond: *Where I'm Calling From*
Chabon, Michael: *Werewolves in Their Youth*
Chorlton, Windsor: *Latitude Zero*
Connelly, Michael: *The Poet*
Conrad, Joseph: *Heart of Darkness*
Constantine, K. C.: *Family Values*
DeLillo, Don: *Underworld*
DeMille, Nelson: *Cathedral*
DeMille, Nelson: *The Gold Coast*
Dickens, Charles: *Oliver Twist*
Dobyns, Stephen: *Common Carnage*
Dobyns, Stephen: *The Church of Dead Girls*
Doyle, Roddy: *The Woman Who Walked into Doors*
Elkin, Stanley: *The Dick Gibson Show*
Faulkner, William: *As I Lay Dying*
Garland, Alex: *The Beach*

On Writing

George, Elizabeth: *Deception on His Mind*
Gerritsen, Tess: *Gravity*
Golding, William: *Lord of the Flies*
Gray, Muriel: *Furnace*
Greene, Graham: *A Gun for Sale* (aka *This Gun for Hire*)
Greene, Graham: *Our Man in Havana*
Halberstam, David: *The Fifties*
Hamill, Pete: *Why Sinatra Matters*
Harris, Thomas: *Hannibal*
Haruf, Kent: *Plainsong*
Hoeg, Peter: *Smilla's Sense of Snow*
Hunter, Stephen: *Dirty White Boys*
Ignatius, David: *A Firing Offense*
Irving, John: *A Widow for One Year*
Joyce, Graham: *The Tooth Fairy*
Judd, Alan: *The Devil's Own Work*
Kahn, Roger: *Good Enough to Dream*
Karr, Mary: *The Liars' Club*
Ketchum, Jack: *Right to Life*
King, Tabitha: *Survivor*
King, Tabitha: *The Sky in the Water* (unpublished)
Kingsolver, Barbara: *The Poisonwood Bible*
Krakauer, Jon: *Into Thin Air*
Lee, Harper: *To Kill a Mockingbird*
Lefkowitz, Bernard: *Our Guys*
Little, Bentley: *The Ignored*
Maclean, Norman: *A River Runs Through It and Other Stories*
Maugham, W. Somerset: *The Moon and Sixpence*
McCarthy, Cormac: *Cities of the Plain*
McCarthy, Cormac: *The Crossing*
McCourt, Frank: *Angela's Ashes*
McDermott, Alice: *Charming Billy*
McDevitt, Jack: *Ancient Shores*
McEwan, Ian: *Enduring Love*

McEwan, Ian: *The Cement Garden*

McMurtry, Larry: *Dead Man's Walk*

McMurtry, Larry, and Diana Ossana: *Zeke and Ned*

Miller, Walter M.: *A Canticle for Leibowitz*

Oates, Joyce Carol: *Zombie*

O'Brien, Tim: *In the Lake of the Woods*

O'Nan, Stewart: *The Speed Queen*

Ondaatje, Michael: *The English Patient*

Patterson, Richard North: *No Safe Place*

Price, Richard: *Freedomland*

Proulx, Annie: *Close Range: Wyoming Stories*

Proulx, Annie: *The Shipping News*

Quindlen, Anna: *One True Thing*

Rendell, Ruth: *A Sight for Sore Eyes*

Robinson, Frank M.: *Waiting*

Rowling, J. K.: *Harry Potter and the Chamber of Secrets*

Rowling, J. K.: *Harry Potter and the Prisoner of Azakaban*

Rowling, J. K.: *Harry Potter and the Sorcerer's Stone*

Russo, Richard: *Mohawk*

Schwartz, John Burnham: *Reservation Road*

Seth, Vikram: *A Suitable Boy*

Shaw, Irwin: *The Young Lions*

Slotkin, Richard: *The Crater*

Smith, Dinitia: *The Illusionist*

Spencer, Scott: *Men in Black*

Stegner, Wallace: *Joe Hill*

Tartt, Donna: *The Secret History*

Tyler, Anne: *A Patchwork Planet*

Vonnegut, Kurt: *Hocus Pocus*

Waugh, Evelyn: *Brideshead Revisited*

Westlake, Donald E.: *The Ax*

Further to Furthermore, Part III

At the end of the original edition of *On Writing*, I listed about a hundred books which entertained and taught me. The publishers suggested I update the list for this new edition, so here are eighty-plus more—the best things I've read between 2001 and 2009. As I said in the 2000 edition of the book . . . you could do worse.

Abrahams, Peter: *End of Story*
Abrahams, Peter: *The Tutor*
Adiga, Aravind: *The White Tiger*
Atkinson, Kate: *One Good Turn*
Atwood, Margaret: *Oryx and Crake*
Berlinski, Mischa: *Fieldwork*
Black, Benjamin [pseudo.]: *Christine Falls*
Blauner, Peter: *The Last Good Day*
Bolaño, Roberto: *2666*
Carr, David: *The Night of the Gun*
Casey, John: *Spartina*
Chabon, Michael: *The Yiddish Policemen's Union*
Child, Lee: The Jack Reacher novels, starting with *Killing Floor*
Connelly, Michael: *The Narrows*

Costello, Mark: *Big If*
Cunningham, Michael: *The Hours*
Danielewski, Mark Z.: *House of Leaves*
Díaz, Junot: *The Brief Wondrous Life of Oscar Wao*
Dooling, Richard: *White Man's Grave*
Downing, David: *Zoo Station*
Dubus, Andre: *The Garden of Last Days*
Enger, Leif: *Peace Like a River*
Exley, Frederick: *A Fan's Notes*
Ferris, Joshua: *Then We Came to the End*
Franzen, Jonathan: *Strong Motion*
Franzen, Jonathan: *The Corrections*
Gaiman, Neil: *American Gods*
Gardiner, Meg: *Crosscut*
Gardiner, Meg: *The Dirty Secrets Club*
Gay, William: *The Long Home*
Goddard, Robert: *Painting the Darkness*
Gruen, Sara: *Water for Elephants*
Hall, Steven: *The Raw Shark Texts*
Helprin, Mark: *A Soldier of the Great War*
Huston, Charlie: The Hank Thompson Trilogy
Johnson, Denis: *Tree of Smoke*
Keillor, Garrison (ed.): *Good Poems*
Kidd, Sue Monk: *The Secret Life of Bees*
Klosterman, Chuck: *Fargo Rock City*
Larsson, Stieg: *The Girl with the Dragon Tattoo*
Le Carré, John: *Absolute Friends*
Lehane, Dennis: *The Given Day*
Leonard, Elmore: *Up in Honey's Room*
Lethem, Jonathan: *The Fortress of Solitude*
Lippman, Laura: *What the Dead Know*
Little, Bentley: *Dispatch*
Malamud, Bernard: *The Fixer*
Martel, Yann: *Life of Pi*

On Writing

McCarthy, Cormac: *No Country for Old Men*
McEwan, Ian: *Atonement*
Meek, James: *The People's Act of Love*
Niffenegger, Audrey: *Her Fearful Symmetry*
O'Brian, Patrick: The Aubrey/Maturin Novels
O'Nan, Stewart: *The Good Wife*
Oates, Joyce Carol: *We Were the Mulvaneys*
Pelecanos, George: *Hard Revolution*
Pelecanos, George: *The Turnaround*
Perrotta, Tom: *The Abstinence Teacher*
Picoult, Jodi: *Nineteen Minutes*
Pierre, DBC: *Vernon God Little*
Proulx, Annie: *Fine Just the Way It Is*
Robotham, Michael: *Shatter*
Roth, Philip: *American Pastoral*
Roth, Philip: *The Plot Against America*
Rushdie, Salman: *Midnight's Children*
Russo, Richard: *Bridge of Sighs*
Russo, Richard: *Empire Falls*
Simmons, Dan: *Drood*
Simmons, Dan: *The Terror*
Sittenfeld, Curtis: *American Wife*
Smith, Tom Rob: *Child 44*
Snyder, Scott: *Voodoo Heart*
Stephenson, Neal: *Quicksilver*
Tartt, Donna: *The Little Friend*
Tolstoy, Leo: *War and Peace*
Wambaugh, Joseph: *Hollywood Station*
Warren, Robert Penn: *All the King's Men*
Waters, Sarah: *The Little Stranger*
Winegardner, Mark: *Crooked River Burning*
Winegardner, Mark: *The Godfather Returns*
Wroblewski, David: *The Story of Edgar Sawtelle*
Yates, Richard: *Revolutionary Road*

Even Further to Furthermore, Part IV

At a playoff game a couple of years ago at Fenway, a sports-caster cozied up next to me and asked if I *always* brought a book with me to the stadium. He seemed to think it was the funniest thing he'd heard of since the FOX News "Fair and Balanced" slogan. Books at baseball games!

I take a book with me almost everywhere. Books are the perfect entertainment: no commercials, no batteries, hours lost in other worlds. Why, I wonder, doesn't *everybody* carry a book around? These are the books I read between 2010 and 2019:

Atkinson, Kate: *One Good Turn*
Atkinson, Kate: *Started Early, Took My Dog*
Atwood, Margaret: *The Year of the Flood*
Barclay, Linwood: *Never Look Away*
Bardugo, Leigh: *Ninth House*
Bazell, Josh: *Beat the Reaper*
Bellow, Saul: *The Adventures of Augie March*
Benioff, David: *City of Thieves*
Berlinski, Mischa: *Fieldwork*
Blake, Sarah: *The Guest Book*
Boyd, William: *Ordinary Thunderstorms*

Braffet, Kelly: *Save Yourself*
Caputo, Philip: *Crossers*
Cronin, Justin: *The Passage Trilogy*
Cummins, Jeanine: *American Dirt*
De Haven, Tom: *Derby Dugan's Depression Funnies*
Donoghue, Emma: *Room*
Egan, Jennifer: *Manhattan Beach*
Ellroy, James: *Blood's a Rover*
Ellroy, James: *The Cold Six Thousand*
Faulkner, William: *Absalom, Absalom!*
Feibleman, Peter: *Charlie Boy*
Ferris, Joshua: *Then We Came to the End*
Fossum, Karin: *Broken*
Franklin, Tom: *Crooked Letter, Crooked Letter*
Frank, Scott: *Shaker*
Gay, William: *Twilight*
Gillham, David R.: *City of Women*
Harris, Robert: *The Ghost*
Huston, Charlie: *The Shotgun Rule*
James, Aaron: *Assholes: A Theory*
Jensen, Liz: *The Uninvited*
Johnson, Adam: *Fortune Smiles*
Johnson, Adam: *The Orphan Master's Son*
Joyce, Graham: *The Silent Land*
Kestin, Hesh: *The Iron Will of Shoeshine Cats*
Koch, Herman: *The Dinner*
Kushner, Rachel: *The Flamethrowers*
Larson, Erik: *Dead Wake*
Le Carré, John: *A Delicate Truth*
Lethem, Jonathan: *Chronic City*
Lippman, Laura: *I'd Know You Anywhere*
MacDonald, John D.: *April Evil*
Mantel, Hilary: *Bring Up the Bodies*
Mantel, Hilary: *Wolf Hall*

On Writing

Maugham, Somerset: *The Razor's Edge*
Mitchell, David: *The Thousand Autumns of Jacob de Zoet*
Nguyen, Viet Thanh: *The Sympathizer*
O'Connor, Flannery: *A Good Man Is Hard to Find*
O'Nan, Stewart: *The Odds*
Patchett, Ann: *The Dutch House*
Pavone, Chris: *The Paris Diversion*
Percy, Benjamin: *Red Moon*
Perrotta, Tom: *The Leftovers*
Phillips, Gin: *Fierce Kingdom*
Porter, Katherine Anne: *Ship of Fools*
Powell, Anthony: *A Dance to the Music of Time*
Proulx, Annie: *Barkskins*
Robotham, Michael: *The Wreckage*
Rowling, J. K.: *Harry Potter and the Deathly Hallows*
Rowling, J. K.: *The Casual Vacancy*
Sandford, John: *Escape Clause*
Sandford, John: *Rough Country*
Spiotta, Dana: *Stone Arabia*
Stevens, Chevy: *Still Missing*
Swofford, Anthony: *Jarhead*
Tallent, Gabriel: *My Absolute Darling*
Tartt, Donna: *The Goldfinch*
Tolstoy, Leo: *War and Peace*
Various Hands: *King James Bible*
Wallace, David Foster: *Infinite Jest*
Wambaugh, Joseph: *Hollywood Moon*
Waters, Sarah: *Fingersmith*
Waters, Sarah: *The Night Watch*
Winegardner, Mark: *The Godfather's Revenge*
Winslow, Don: *Savages*
Wolitzer, Meg: *The Interestings*
Zola, Émile: *The Beast Within*
Zola, Émile: *Thérèse Raquin*

Owen King: Recording Audiobooks for My Dad, Stephen King

This essay appeared in the *New Yorker* on June 16, 2018.

My father gave me my first job, reading audiobooks on cassette tape. He had caught on to the medium early, but, as he explained later, "There were lots of choices as long as you only wanted to hear *The Thorn Birds*." So, one day, in 1987, he presented me with a handheld cassette recorder, a block of blank tapes, and a hardcover copy of *Watchers*, by Dean Koontz, offering nine dollars per finished sixty-minute tape of narration.

This was an optimistic plan on my father's part. Not only was I just ten years old, but when it came to reading aloud I had an infamous track record. My parents and I still read books together each night, and I had recently begun demanding an equal turn as narrator. Along our tour through Robert Louis Stevenson's *Kidnapped*, I had tested their love with reckless attempts at a Scottish accent for the revolutionary Alan Breck Stewart, whom the novel's protagonist, David

Balfour, befriends. Even as they pleaded for me to stop, I made knee-deep haggis of passages like the following:

"Do ye see my sword? It has slashed the heads off mair Whigamores than you have toes upon your feet. Call up your vermin to your back, sir, and fall on! The sooner the clash begins, the sooner ye'll taste this steel throughout your vitals."

Despite this, my father enlisted me to narrate *Watchers*. (If Stephen King wants to listen to a Dean Koontz novel, he will listen to a Dean Koontz novel.) And for those nine dollars— an outrageous wage—I did, in fact, complete the task. Or I read *Watchers* as well as any ten-year-old could, seated at my bedroom desk beneath a poster of Roger Clemens in mid-delivery, stuttering my way through the hard words and letting the tape fill with room tone while I paused to contemplate the longer sentences.

The plot of *Watchers* follows a super-intelligent dog that communicates with his human master, an ex–Delta Force commando, via Scrabble tiles. Wikipedia tells me that the main threat in the story is a genetically altered baboon, which does sound frightening, but the Scrabble part is what I recall. One of the shortcuts that bad critics use to signal their dislike of a genre novel is to list all the wild elements— i.e., "[*Novel Title*] features a battleship in 1943, Siamese twins in 2017, a subplot involving a serial killer named Ducky, and a corpse that vomits locusts"—without putting them into any sort of context. I suspect that part of the reason Dad still loves to kid me about *Watchers* is that he's justifiably sensitive to this kind of dismissal. For the record, I would never reject out of hand a novel about a magic dog, an ex–Delta Force commando, and a genetically altered baboon. I'm certain that I didn't actually say I hated the book. It just bothered me, the convenience of this singular dog being found by an ex–Delta Force commando. That was awfully lucky, wasn't it?

I'd read plenty of books, but I hadn't thought much about them; I'd just consumed them. Paperbacks from the Three Investigators series lay in drifts around my bed, enjoyed and discarded. But when I closed my bedroom door, sat down, pressed the red button on the tape machine, and began to narrate aloud from *Watchers*, my experience of reading shifted. As always, the story made the world fall away, but now a part of me stayed present. It's much harder to neglect words when they are coming out of your mouth.

Watchers was just the beginning. Through my teenage years there followed at least two dozen more book recordings. My father hired my brother and sister, too. He claimed that he wasn't trying to broaden our literary horizons; he just wanted to hear the books. Nonetheless, they broadened mine. An incomplete list of my own assignments includes mainstream fiction (*A Separate Peace*), fantasy (*The Fellowship of the Ring*), crime fiction (*The Grifters, You Play the Black and the Red Comes Up*), science fiction (*Dune, Ring Around the Sun*), and various anthologies.

Left to my own devices, I'm sure I would have found *The Fellowship of the Ring* and *Dune*, but I doubt that I would have picked up a novel like Jim Thompson's *The Grifters*, the title of which meant nothing to me, and the cover of which bore an illustration of a simian-faced man, a morose woman smoking a cigarette, and a pair of large dice, perched atop a worrisome blurb from the *Boston Globe* that cautioned, "Strong meat." I must have been thirteen or fourteen when I read the book, and the harsh, mendacious world it described startled me. The insane contrast between it and *The Fellowship of the Ring* was a pleasure in itself; to go from one to another was a form of teleportation.

The job was also excellent practice for writing. Closing my door and sitting at my desk echoed what my parents did each day, when they shut themselves in their respective offices and sat alone for hours on end. (Dad sometimes returned to work after dinner and kept on into the night. If, lying in bed on the other side of the house, I discerned the sinister bass line of one of the AC/DC LPs that he liked to listen to at jet-engine volume, I knew he was revising.)

I was alarmed by the amount of time that my parents spent alone. I couldn't understand how they could bear it. I thought being a writer must be not only the worst job in the world but the scariest. I remember loitering on the carpeted step outside Dad's office, with Marlowe, our corgi, sprawled in front of his door. Marlowe was among the most gregarious of creatures, but if Dad shut the door he'd collapse into a bleak pile on the spot. His tragedy was my best opportunity to pet him, so I'd plunk down, too. In the background, the plastic tumult of Dad's keystrokes came from inside the office. It occurred to me once, as I petted Marlowe and the rattle of keys went on and on, to wonder if my father was actually typing anything specific, or just making as much noise as he could to keep bad things away.

To my knowledge, no tapes of *Watchers* survive, though I do have my reading of *Dune*. It's a lamentable document; I narrate, rhinal and breathless, like a telemarketer fighting to keep someone on the line. But I still record the odd book for my father as a gift. A few years ago, I undertook *War and Peace* as a Christmas present. It ended up being delivered a couple of Christmases late, and I committed crimes against Russian nomenclature that only God can forgive, but I believe it represents a major improvement in technique. I might have been a bad Alan Breck Stewart, but I had the right idea: when you read to someone else, it's easier for them to absorb the language if you put a little character into the characters. You're not calling from Resort Rewards Center. You're reading about a pissed-off man with a sword.

Dad's a much better reader than I am, though. He's recorded a number of books for me over the years: novels by Louise Welsh, Jon Hassler, Graham Greene. He doesn't do many accents, but he's terrific at shading certain voices, dampening the speech of a drunk, adding a touch of a sneer to an abrasive character. What he's especially good at is the pacing—no surprise if you've read his novels. Those tapes and CDs are very special to me, warm and living. It's a comfort to have a familiar voice there in the car, telling a story. I get why you'd be willing to pay for that.

Joe Hill: A Conversation with My Dad

The conversation between Stephen King and Joe Hill was hosted by Porter Square Books at the Somerville Theatre in Somerville, Massachusetts, on October 20, 2019.

Joe Hill: Hey, guys. Thanks so much for coming out tonight. I want to thank the Somerville Theatre and Porter Square Books for having us. I've never done this with Dad before. It's really cool.

Stephen King: It's a great thing for me, too.

Joe Hill: I guess the first thing I'm wondering is, how much do you need to know, and what do you need to know, before you start writing a novel? How much of it do you have to have already in your head? Because I know you don't work by outline, that you don't plan ahead. What gave you the confidence to start *The Institute*, and what told you it was time? How much of the story did you have?

Stephen King: I really didn't have any of the story. I had an idea from a long time ago about a school somewhere, a little country school that just started to move by itself. It would cut through homes, and streets, and trees, and the kids would be trapped inside, and it would go faster and faster. And somehow, this developed into *The Institute*. To start a novel, I have to have a couple of different things connect, and one of the things that I was thinking about was this job that one of the characters gets. He becomes a night knocker, which is an old-fashioned job where you go around through a small town, check on the businesses, and knock on doors to make sure that the doors are locked. It's a beat cop's job. One guy describes it as an analog job in a digital world. So I had that. And then I started to think about the kid and *The Institute*, and I really wanted to write a kind of *Tom Brown's School Days* in hell.

Joe Hill: The book has a fascinating structure. It begins with this guy who's getting ready to fly to New York, and the plane is too crowded and, almost on impulse, he decides to take the check they're offering to anyone willing to wait for tomorrow's flight. And then instead of flying to New York the next day, Tim begins to hitchhike north, and stumbles almost by accident into the night knocker's job. It's like one of those Steinbeck stories about a working-class guy hitting the road. So he gets the night knocker job and he has adventures on the night knocker job. And then suddenly he vanishes from the story for three hundred pages. Did you really write that section first?

Stephen King: No, I didn't. The first part of *The Institute* is called "The Night Knocker," and the second part is called "The

Smart Kid." I started with "The Smart Kid" and I changed the order around later on. I thought, well, I'm going to start with Tim, the night knocker, and if my story's good enough, you'll forget all about him until he returns to the story four hundred pages later and you'll think, "Oh my God, there he is, my old friend Tim."

Joe Hill: That reminds me a little bit of *The Day of the Jackal*. In the very first sentence you find that the Jackal failed. But the book is so great you forget that. He becomes this unstoppable terminator.

Stephen King: Well, people always ask me if I read reviews, and yes, I usually do. And I feel like if all the critics are saying the same thing, you screwed up. But if they're all saying different things, you're okay. A lot of the reviews of this book say that there is a very odd structure to it. And all I can say is that it seemed like a good idea at the time. Listen, let me ask you something about *Full Throttle*. I collaborated with you on a couple of the stories. The others in the collection had this feeling of Ray Bradbury and Jack Finney and some of the classics, like C. S. Lewis. So my question is, who influenced you in the fantasy field?

Joe Hill: To be honest, it's very hard to get around your work and Mom's work. The fantasy and horror novels that shaped me were *The Talisman*, *It*, and *The Dead Zone*, which were sort of the foundational books that I read when I was thirteen or fourteen and that shaped my idea about what a good story could be.

Stephen King: Wow, that's great. Thank you.

Joe Hill: And of course Jack Finney and Ray Bradbury are influences. *I Love Galesburg in the Springtime* by Jack Finney. And I think everyone who writes fantasy goes through a big Bradbury phase. I dearly love the fiction of Ray Bradbury. A lot of the short stories you can read in as little as ten minutes and then you can never ever forget them, stories like "The Fog Horn," where this giant prehistoric creature falls in love with a lighthouse. . . .

So you're pretty well known as a prolific writer. *The Institute* is actually your 203rd novel in the last two years. But I also know that sometimes books stall, and that's happened even to you. So for example, you had eighty pages of *Under the Dome* and then had to set it aside for what, twenty years?

Stephen King: Longer, actually.

Joe Hill: When did you take your first whack at it?

Stephen King: '72, and I did a whole bunch of work on it then, but there was too much research involved and it just kind of daunted me. So I put it aside and wrote a book about vampires called *'Salem's Lot.*

Joe Hill: And then *Under the Dome* steeped. I mean it *steeped* for thirty, forty years?

Stephen King: Yeah.

Joe Hill: And then you were ready. I think people probably think you must not have any self-doubts. But when you do get stuck, how do you get unstuck?

Stephen King: Oh man, I have a lot of self-doubts. I think the best thing to do, when I really run into trouble, is remember the saying "Hard writing makes for easy reading."

Joe Hill: Yeah, that might be Elmore Leonard.

Stephen King: Yeah. It could have been Elmore Leonard. But the important thing is to push through, to not become depressed. I try to remember that we're all amateurs at this, and every time I sit down it's like the first time. I battle doubts all the time about whether or not this thing is working or that thing's working, whether or not the idea is good. The one thing that I never really doubted is the language, the ability to put the words together. I had the devil's own time with *The Institute* because by the last quarter of the book, I felt like there were all these different balls that were up in the air, and I'm trying to make everything fit and at the same time to make the transitions, and to not make it look like it's strange.

Joe Hill: Yeah, hard work.

Stephen King: Yeah.

Joe Hill: You got stuck in *Carrie*.

Stephen King: I did. I got stuck in *Carrie* and threw it away, and Tabby fished it out of the wastebasket and said that she thought it was pretty good. My wife, Joe's mom, has this special smile sometimes. It's almost like a Picasso smile. It tilts her mouth one way, but not both. It's a very endearing smile, but I always know what it means. And when she read *Carrie* and she smoothed it out, and it was covered with cigarette ashes and all this stuff, she had that smile on her face and she said, "This is pretty good, you ought to go on with it."

And I thought of something that Samuel Johnson said about dancing dogs. "It's not that you expect to see it done well, you're surprised to see it done at all." And I said, "Well, I don't know anything about girls' locker rooms and they're all throwing tampons at Carrie. I don't know whether you get them from a coin-operated dispenser or whatever." And she said, "I will help you." And she did.

Joe Hill: Okay. So I have a few books that I use as points on the creative compass. *The Dead Zone* is one, *True Grit* is another, *The Friends of Eddie Coyle* is the third. What about you?

Stephen King: Oh man. I read an awful lot of books by a guy who's not read enough these days, Don Robertson. He wrote a wonderful book called *Paradise Falls*. For a long time Richard Matheson was a big deal for me. One of the stories Joe and I wrote together, "Throttle," is a riff on Richard Matheson's famous story "Duel." Richard Matheson was a formative figure in my life. "Nightmare at 20,000 Feet," *I Am Legend*, *The Shrinking Man*, all those stories. Robert Bloch and Ray Bradbury were also a big deal for me, particularly the stories. There's one called "The Small Assassin," about a baby that's a killer. And my favorite one as a kid was called "The Visitor."

Joe Hill: I have to tell a quick story about "Throttle," that story we wrote together. "Throttle" is about an outlaw motorcycle gang on the run from a faceless trucker. When we wrote it, I didn't have my motorcycle license. I didn't know much about bikes and meanwhile my dad has been riding bikes for forty years. I thought, all right, we're writing this story, and my dad will keep me shiny side up. He'll get the motorcycle stuff right and I won't sound like a fake. But I did get my motorcycle license not long after we wrote the story together. And a couple of years later in the summer, we went for a ride together. He's always been a Harley guy. So he went out on his Harley and I went out on my little Triumph Bonneville on this beautiful afternoon. We got to ride together for like thirty miles and a perfect summer day. And we got back and parked the bikes. He took a look over at my bike and he said, "That's a pretty nice ride, even if the engine does sound like a sewing machine."

Listen, we've only got so much time and we've got questions from the audience, but I want to do a speed round first, so let's hit that real quick.

Stephen King: Oh shit, I hate this.

Joe Hill: No, come on. Just go with me. It's going to be great. Okay?

Stephen King: Oh yeah, that's it. I've heard that all my life. "Come on, Dad, it's going to be great."

Joe Hill: If you could have one superpower, what would it be?

Stephen King: Man, if I could get—

Joe Hill: I've wanted to ask him this question since I was four.

Stephen King: I guess I'd fly.

Joe Hill: What movie have you seen the most?

Stephen King: *Sorcerer*, William Friedkin. It was the follow-up to *The Exorcist*. Go ahead.

Joe Hill: What's the best LP in the history of rock?

Stephen King: AC/DC, *Back in Black*.

Joe Hill: Cool. What's the best single?

Stephen King: The best single is "Sweet Soul Music" by Arthur Conley.

Joe Hill: Book you most wish you had written and didn't?

Stephen King: Man, there's thousands of them. I guess the book I was most jealous of was *Lord of the Rings*. I read that and I said, "This guy is so far beyond what I can do."

Joe Hill: How many games will the Sox win next year?

Stephen King: The Sox next year are going to win eighty-eight games. That's four more than this year, guys.

Joe Hill: Beatles or Stones?

On Writing

Stephen King: Stones.

Joe Hill: Wrong. Spielberg or Kubrick?

Stephen King: Spielberg.

Joe Hill: I thought so. Who's scarier, Chucky or Chuck E. Cheese?

Stephen King: Chuck E. Cheese.

Let's do the questions from the audience. Here's one. What would you say is your favorite horror movie of all time?

Joe Hill: *It: Chapter One.*

Stephen King: That's kind of nice.

Joe Hill: One for you: "Stephen, in *The Dark Tower*, you include excerpts from Stephen King's diary. Were any of these based on your actual diary?"

Stephen King: I had a bunch of old diaries, but I didn't have any from the year in question, so they were totally made-up.

Okay. "Joe, what is the most messed-up thing your dad did to you as a child?"

Joe Hill: I know. It's hard to decide. The thing is, I've thought about this a lot because there's this old Jay Leno joke, right? And it goes, Stephen King asked the kids, do you want to hear a bedtime story? The kids go, "No!" But the thing is, it was never really like that, you know? I mean, we always loved bedtime stories. It was the best part of the day. And I sometimes think that it's a basic misunderstanding of my dad's work that he sells fear. Politicians sell fear. I've always thought that my dad's stories sold bravery, that they essentially were making an argument that, yeah, things might get really bad. But if you have some faith and a sense of humor, and if you're loyal to your loved ones, sometimes you can kick the darkness until it bleeds daylight.

Stephen King: Sure enough.

Joe Hill: Another question from the audience: "When collaborating, who gets the last word?"

You have a lot of experience with collaboration. You did the two big novels with Peter Straub, the two stories we wrote together in *Full Throttle*, and a brilliant apocalyptic novel with my brother, Owen, called *Sleeping Beauties*.

Stephen King: Well, I think that with you and me, and with Owen and me, we rewrote each other's stuff and we worked together so seamlessly, that in the end you couldn't tell who wrote what. There's a movie based on our story "In the Tall Grass," and I read the story again to get ready for it. I couldn't tell who wrote what. And now we can't even remember who had the original idea.

Joe Hill: Yeah. I genuinely have no idea who came up with the concept. Although I remember where we came up with the concept.

Stephen King: Yeah. Tell them the story about where that was.

Joe Hill: I came down to Florida to visit you and Mom, and it was a late flight and we were driving from the airport. I said I was hungry, so we pulled into the Colonial House of Pancakes.

Stephen King: It was IHOP.

Joe Hill: International House of Pancakes, and—

Stephen King: IHOP. Right.

Joe Hill: And I got a couple of plates of flapjacks and—

Stephen King: IHOP flapjacks.

Joe Hill: Yeah. And it turned out that you had just finished working on something, and as it happened I had just finished working on something. And you said, "Well, we should write something this week."

Stephen King: No, *you* said, "We should write something this week." You said it.

Joe Hill: Well—

Stephen King: One of us said it.

Joe Hill: One of us said it, and it wasn't like we had any ideas. We just spitballed for about ten minutes and came up with something.

Stephen King: Yeah. It turned into that story and it was easy. And really, I mean, here's the thing, you and I have a family resemblance. We look a little bit alike, we think a little bit alike, and when we write together, it's almost like an Everly Brothers harmony, because the voices aren't the same, but they mix rather well. It was that way with Owen, too.

Joe Hill: I got a good one for you here. "Have you ever been censored by a publisher?"

Stephen King: I have been censored by my wife, your mother. I wrote a book called *Dreamcatcher*. I wanted to call it *Cancer*, and she said, "You can't call it that. You cannot call it that." There are other times when she said stuff like, "Oh, you can't call this book *It*, the critics will call it shit." And she said, "You can't call this book *Misery* because the critics will call it misery." I overruled her in those cases, but she was really stern about *Cancer*. And with my publishers, Scribner, I had a book that I wanted to call *Unnatural Acts of Social Intercourse*, and they said, "Absolutely not." And over dinner one night, I said, "Well then, if you're really firm about it, we'll call it *Full Dark, No Stars*," which we did.

Joe Hill: "Would you rather fight one horse-sized duck, or one hundred duck-sized horses?" Dude, I just read them. I just read them. I mean, I didn't come up with this shit.

Stephen King: Are you ever going to let me ask you a question?

Joe Hill: Yeah, go ahead.

Stephen King: Because we're almost—

Joe Hill: Go ahead. Yeah, yeah. We got to be almost done. Is there another one in there?

Stephen King: Well, yeah. This one says, "Do you have to pay your father to be able to reference his characters and places in your works?"

Joe Hill: Do you want the money now?

Stephen King: Thanks. "If you were trapped on a deserted island, which book, movie, and food would you bring?" Let's start with book.

Joe Hill: I'd bring *How to Escape from a Desert Island in 10 Easy Lessons*.

Stephen King: Yeah.

Joe Hill: And food? What food would I bring?

Stephen King: I'd get takeout pizza then go back with the guy. See, thinking all the time, man. That's the imagination at work. Where do you get those crazy ideas?

Joe Hill: Here's a good one. It says, "Songs and movies get remade all the time. Why isn't this the case with novels?" This question was obviously asked by someone who hasn't read *The Fireman*, and doesn't know I was just remaking *The Stand*.

Stephen King: No, that's not true at all.

Joe Hill: I've got a question for you. You've got a book that was just a number-one *New York Times* bestseller, a hit movie, and enough ongoing TV shows to populate your own channel. You also only have twenty-four hours in a day. How do you keep yourself from being creatively spread too thin?

Stephen King: Well, that's actually a really good question and it hooks up with a really serious question. And the question is, when do you get to the end and when do you stop, and come to a point where hopefully you and Owen, and Tab, my ka-tet so to speak, will come to me and say, "You know, Dad, it's good that you're continuing to write but it might be time to keep it to yourself."

But it's been a fantastic time for me, because usually when you get to be sixty, sixty-five years old, you kind of move from center stage to the character parts or something. And I've had a fantastic run the last four or five years, and so have you. This is an amazing time for people who are creative. It's great and it's crazy, and it's a lot of fun. But I think, that right now at my age, I've done a lot of work and every day is a new day and you just try to continue. I think you're probably the same way, aren't you?

Joe Hill: Yeah. I mean, if it's still fun and people still enjoy it, then I want to keep doing it.

Stephen King: That's right. And that's probably a good place to stop.